HOW NOT TO RUN 100 MARATHONS

AND OTHER STORIES

Nicholas Turner

Copyright © 2018 Nicholas Turner

All rights reserved, including the right to reproduce this book, or portions thereof in any form. No part of this text may be reproduced, transmitted, downloaded, decompiled, reverse engineered, or stored, in any form or introduced into any information storage and retrieval system, in any form or by any means, whether electronic or mechanical without the express written permission of the author.

The views expressed in this work are solely those of the author and do not necessarily reflect the views of the publisher, and the publisher hereby disclaims any responsibility for them.

ISBN: 978-0-244-41207-4

PublishNation
www.publishnation.co.uk

INTRODUCTION

It is said that every journey starts with a single step. For this unremarkable man (a Google search of my name reveals hundreds of others with the same name who have achieved various grades of infamy and greatness which seem set to allude me), the single step was in the form of a decision to sign up for the 2006 Nottingham Marathon. In a generation lucky enough to be unlikely to ever experience the sort of mass conflict lived through by our forefathers, we must all find our own way to justify our existence. It appears that a strand of this for me is running long distances, something which the Nottingham Marathon unleashed (albeit on an initially very slow burning fuse).

What follows is a summary of some of the highlights of a hobby which became something of an obsession and eventually a pursuit of completing 100 marathons (which was never part of the initial plan) – the stories cover over 20 countries, across four continents, and a spectrum of life's highs and lows, from glorious victories (five in total), spectacular settings and befriending natives to ignominious withdrawals, hospitalisations, and encounters with the local constabulary in three different jurisdictions.

The running was periodically intended to provide a distraction from a perpetually disappointing and stressful job as a commercial lawyer (primarily in a large international law firm, with a brief stint in Australia) and occasionally self-destructive drinking but, as a number of the tales will show, far from tempering the boozing, these two incompatible pastimes tended to follow the same irresistible incline. The coming years will reveal the damage this has caused to my body but, as a still relatively young (if your scale is large enough) and healthy man, I have enjoyed living as a non-celebrity James Hunt of long distance running (at least in my own mind).

There are a number of excellent modern books, written by highly dedicated and hugely impressive individuals who have achieved magnificent feats of human endurance and achievement. This is not that. This is far removed from that. In fact, this is almost the polar opposite of those books and nothing described in here should be emulated. Unless you want to. In which case, *bon chance* dear friend…

1

NOTTINGHAM 2006

Having never previously run further than a half marathon, and as a non-subscriber to prescribed programs, training for my first ever marathon - the Nottingham marathon - was somewhat ad hoc. In fact, the most gruelling preparation undertaken was The Three Peaks Challenge in the summer. With our team of four all hailing from different parts of the kingdom, we met at Glasgow Airport for the northbound drive to the foot of mountain number one – Ben Nevis. For various reasons, we had not arrived until nearly 9pm, were devoid of lighting equipment and all dressed in attire for a pleasant summer's day, not a night march up Scotland's highest mountain. Since there was little which we could be done about these issues, we scampered optimistically across the primarily flat grassy field which led to the foot of the mountain. We soon encountered walkers coming the other way, most of whom – after dubiously scanning our skimpy outfits – advised that we were idiots to be setting off on the climb so late in the day. But we were not to be deterred. Yet. Sadly, the boisterous optimism which accompanied our early strides evaporated almost immediately on reaching the steep steps which marked the beginning of our ascent. My quads were burning after maybe 20 strides, which had barely made an indent on the mighty mountain. Compounding issues was the fact that, in an attempt to travel light, we had taken very few provisions, to the extent that I was soon reduced to lapping water from a small stream which crossed the path as the relentless climbing took its toll. Although we had made excellent time - the light of a long summer's day was just fading by the time we reached the summit, the exact spot of which (a small pile of stones as it turned out) we had some trouble finding.

The small pockets of snow confirmed that our outfits had been ambitious and when one of our foursome began to complain of dizziness we decided that a swift descent was in order. We ignored the zig zagging track we had climbed to the top of the UK's highest mountain and instead took a straight line towards the base. Undertaken at pace in fading light, this was a fairly precarious exercise and it was only a few notches shy of a miracle that we all reached the car intact in almost pitch darkness. Very little time was wasted before the car was pointed southbound for the drive to the Lake District. We were treated to a few stags crossing the road – very 'Visit Scotland.com' – but otherwise the drive to the Lakes was uneventful but rapid. In fact the drive had been so rapid that we had to sit in the already filling car park – presumably other lunatics on the Three Peak Challenge – awaiting first light before we could set off up England's highest mountain, Scarfell Pike.

For three of our number, extracting our aching bodies from the car was a challenge in itself, but our fourth member – Thomas Waldman – was an ex-marine reserve and showed no ill signs, despite having been the driver from Fort William. We left Thomas to burn his own path up the relatively short (in comparison to Ben Nevis) but very steep ascent of Scarfell Pike. By the halfway point I was starting to regret the whole affair, primarily because we were effectively marching up a second mountain and making no effort to take in any of the beautiful surrounds of the Lake District. A brief pause at the summit – Thomas having long since passed us on his descent – revealed that it was not quite unspoilt beauty. The sprawl of Sellafield Power Station in the distance provided a significant blot on the picturesque landscape. Our slower trio – me and two Collard brothers, Ben and Joe – eventually reached the bottom of the mountain to find Thomas cooling his legs in a shallow stream, chomping at the bit to press on to the final challenge – Snowdon.

By the time we reached Snowdon, after winding our way through the single track stone wall lined roads of the Lake District, fatigue was showing in the entire team. However, we barely paused before setting off on the initially gentle ascent of the highest mountain in Wales. As with the two previous climbs, enthusiasm soon faded when the going got tougher, although we made fairly light work of the mountain and were soon belting down just about as quickly as was safe. We had completed an event for which 24 hours is a benchmark target in less than 18 hours, but had evidently wiped ourselves out in the process. This was best evidenced by the fact that we were all required to slap driver Ben's bald head on the short drive to our Bed & Breakfast, in order to keep him from falling asleep at the wheel. Sadly, by the time we reached the B&B (where we were subjected to England football team's two yearly penalty defeat in a major tournament), we had all succumbed to sleep with the result being that the much abused Mondeo hire car was gently driven into the wall of our accommodation. Thankfully, due to our very low speed at the time of the impact, no visual damage was done to the car, although the stench of rotting men which filled the vehicle and the 2,000 miles we had put on the clock would no doubt delight the car rental office on the vehicle's return. Still, the event had hopefully served the purpose of preparing me for a marathon debut towards the back end of the summer…

The day of the Nottingham Marathon 2006 did not go entirely according to plan, which itself did not exist. As well as running my debut marathon, I had agreed to act as the first leg runner for one of my law firm's half marathon relay teams. This had two undesirable consequences. The first problem was that it meant that I had to wear a thick purple t-shirt over my running shirt, in order to identify me as a relay runner. The second issue was that it obliged me to run faster than I should have done, in light of the long distance ahead. It was a pleasant September morning and the dual t-shirt approach soon caused me to over heat. It was therefore a huge relief to toss away the purple t-shirt when I located the firm's second leg runner, just over three miles into the run. By the halfway point a pleasant day had turned into a scorcher and I was 'blowing out of my arse', to coin a delightful phrase. I looked on with extreme envy as the lucky majority – the half marathon runners - peeled away to the left (the biblical goats) to finish their race whilst we marathon runners were condemned to go right (the sheep) for another 13.1 miles of purgatory…

Making matters worse was that, whilst the first half of the course took in some of Nottingham's more pleasant sights and areas and was generously lined with spectators, the second half of the run was largely devoid of both, save for a trot around the grounds of the nicely appointed Holme Pierrepoint Hall. Aside from that brief boost, the majority of the second thirteen miles was spent running through quiet residential streets, before a depressing loop of the huge man made water of the national watersports centre. Whichever way we ran, there seemed to be a steady head wind, which was the last thing my aching body needed at this point. It was in that context that I was for once pleased to see a partner from the office, who pedalled alongside me, like a support car for a failing Tour de France rider as I battled to continue. He stuck with me for around two miles offering sufficient encouragement to keep me moving when my inclination was to stop and as soon as he cycled off on his merry way I stopped for a walk and to promise myself that this would be **the last time I would ever put myself through such agony, especially as I managed to break my four hour target by a full five seconds**...

2

LONDON 2007

Determined that my second marathon would be my last, I adopted a far more serious approach to the London marathon. This was aided by a partner at my firm also signing up and making a competition of the run – dubbed *"The Tortoise and the Hare"* within the firm...

This time I stopped drinking from 1 January 2007 until the marathon, downloaded a variety of training plans and sought to eat well for the three and a half months leading up to the marathon. Sadly, as John Lennon said, *"life is what happens when you're making [training] plans"* and a busy few months at work, combined with some wintry weather meant that I had not quite managed to stick to the hoped for regime. I had managed to maintain my abstinence from alcohol however, so was at least generally healthier and wealthier, if not wiser, when the event came around.

I felt cautiously optimistic on the Sunday morning of the run, although this confidence began to ebb rapidly when the scourge of thousands over the years – London's transport system – failed me. The overland train I needed to get to the start in Greenwich was cancelled, which meant a scrambled change of plans. The outcome was that I started the race late, right at the back of the field, behind various costumed lunatics. I was frustrated, and this frustration built further when I found myself full of energy but with nowhere to go as I was surrounded on all sides by people treading water. After a few miles I decided that I should just forget my target time and soak up what was a carnival atmosphere on the streets of South London. This was a fairly effective method of suppressing the pain and discomfort, which was increasing at a similar rate to the temperature, which was by the midway point of the race uncomfortably hot. Against recommendations I had read in most publications and on running websites, I was taking on liquid at every drinks station but by the 18 mile point even this was not enough and I was reduced to a sorry, periodically wobbly, walk. I was not the only 'runner' struggling and the sight of more than one runner collapsed and another being loaded into an ambulance was enough to persuade me to respond to my body's feedback. What finally persuaded me to override the whisper of my brain which suggested that we call it a bad day and give up was the thought of the bald head of my 'tortoise' opponent passing me. My vanity could not stand the idea and I managed to dig deep and extract just enough from my ailing body to break four hours and keep the tortoise somewhere behind me. I hoped. Now was not the time to dwell on the disappointment of a time (**3 hours 55 minutes**) which was scarcely better than that achieved in my first ever marathon, a time which had resulted in my being here in the first place, nor the fact that I had lost to a large number of novelty costumed runners and pensioners. No. It was time to be grateful that another marathon was behind me and to go and get a bloody beer, which I did soon enough.

Sadly, even as I revelled in the delight of my first beer for over 100 days, I could not quite shake the seed of disappointment which had been planted as a result of my performance despite the sacrifices I had made. I feared I would be back on the start line of a marathon before too long. By the end of the week following the marathon I had more immediate concerns. I had indeed beaten the tortoise (by around 20 minutes) but the combination of relief and lack of drinking "match fitness" resulted in a very poor drinking display at a black tie work dinner on the Thursday evening. I suspected (knew) all was not well when I woke up in an enclosed car park on the Friday morning, still wearing my penguin suit, at nearly 10am. My attempt to scuttle into work below the radar failed and within minutes I was summoned into the office of the partner who had acted as my cheerleader back in the Nottingham marathon. There was little encouragement this time. He asked about my recollections of the dinner. I was feeling like death and my scrambled brain was in no condition for an interrogation so I opted for non-committal responses, or small lies (depending on your point of view), and said it was generally pretty good. When the response from him was *"Really?!"*, I knew I was in the crap. It transpired that I had heckled the guest speaker – David Gold (then Birmingham City Football Club Chairman) – and potentially various other guests before refusing to provide my address to my questioner when he tried to send me home in a taxi. Oops. The only thing which seemed to be saving me from potential disciplinary consequences was an acknowledgment that it was my first outing in a long time which meant that some clemency would be applied. I therefore escaped with a warning and would have maybe acknowledged that the law is not always an ass, were my brain capable of doing anything more than praying for the sweet kiss of death…

3

BARCELONA 2009

2008 represented a sabbatical from work and running as I sought to find the meaning of life with a nine month trip around the world. Whilst I discovered many things on the trip – including that one can never escape one's self – the meaning of life was not one of them...

Having not discovered the meaning of life, nor an epiphany about a more enriching career, in October I returned to the same job (and the same desk) I had left in January. By Christmas, I was thoroughly miserable so a friend's suggestion of a marathon in Barcelona in March was a welcome chance of a break from the monotony of the law and the UK.

My best intentions of a sensible approach to the marathon were scuppered when I learnt that two of our group of six who had made the trip to Barcelona were Geordies who would not be participating in the marathon. So it was that when we ended up in an Irish Bar just off the famous Las Ramblas I decided to join them in a few pints as we watched the Six Nations' rugby. A few pints turned into a few more which meant that by the time that Ben (of Three Peaks' fame), his brother and Richard (the three other marathon participants on the trip) returned to the bar to collect us for dinner I was in sight of ten beers and decided it would be rude not to end proceedings on an even number. The only thing which saved me from what I think would have been total catastrophe was a bag of crisps and bucketful of water before a patchy night's sleep. This meant that I felt bad, but not deathly, when I was summoned from bed to get ready for the run the following morning. Dehydration was my primary problem and seemingly no amount of water could satisfy my thirst. The other three runners were on good form and suggested a light jog to the start line, which was a few hundred metres from our apartment. This gentle exercise gave me hope that all would be OK, although there was a nagging thought in my mind that an inevitable collapse was on the cards at some point...

I started the race alongside Ben, having lost his brother and Boy Wonder, each of us by now wearing black *"Salvar Tibet"* headbands we had blindly accepted from activists to show support for an unknown plight of people in a faraway land. Ben proceeded to set off at a pace which was slightly beyond that at which I normally run. Despite the mild discomfort, I was determined to stick with Ben and aided by the fact that my drinking exploits meant that I would never need to stop for a pee, whilst Ben had to dash behind a wheelie bin early on in the race to relieve himself, which gave me some relief from the relentless pace Ben was setting. We got through the first half of the run – which included a run past Barcelona FC's Nou Camp and Goudi's famous unfinished cathedral – in under one hour 40 minutes, which was my second fastest ever half marathon. Gulp. This was not going to end well. However, it was the first time I had run a significant distance with company and Ben and I were managing to continue to chat, a factor which I credited with distracting me from what should have been more severe pain at this point. By the second half of the run, the sights of the city had dried up and we were primarily running up and down dual carriageways, lined with unattractive residential buildings. Shortly after running past an almost identikit version of London's Gherkin building, the chat suddenly stopped, as if a tap had been turned off. After a couple of kilometres of silence I tentatively enquired about my companion's condition, my own being sub-optimal. He confirmed that he was struggling badly and that every minor turn in the road was agony. I took some solace from our shared misery and we reverted to silent contemplation. A short while later and I asked Ben if he would mind very much if I trotted off without him. By now we had slowed to the pace of an elderly sloth and my preference was instead to instigate a sprint-walk-sprint-walk strategy. Our separation coincided with a return to an attractive part of town and large crowds which indicated the end was nigh. Gracias God! During the walk phases of my two speed approach I was regularly implored to *"Vamos!"* by Spanish spectators, which was enough to bring a smile to my salty face.

The sight of the inflated arch marking the finish was welcome indeed and I managed a final burst of acceleration with energy, possibly summoned from the calories offered by beer number 10, although we will never know for sure. Sadly, the inflatable which I thought marked the end was several hundred metres shy of the actual end, meaning another brief walk before a final scamper to the line. Miraculously, the combination of 10 pints, my sprint-walk strategy and inability to pee had resulted in me smashing my previous marathon PB by over 30 minutes, finishing in **3 hours 23 minutes**. In seriousness, the main reason for my improved performance had been the company I enjoyed for over three quarters of the run, which had helped distract me from the usual agony of a marathon. I was pleased and gagging for the remaining three to finish so we could hit the bar…

Ben finished within a few minutes of me and Boy Wonder was home and hosed within 15 minutes. We were therefore just awaiting Joe, whose preparation had sounded to be the best of the four of us. Alas, an hour later and we were still waiting and Ben was starting to feel the pangs of older brotherly concern. Joe eventually materialised at around the five hour mark with a remarkable tale of having spent a fair amount of time being massaged in a café after severe cramp set in. We were all just pleased he had made it so we could freshen up and have a beer or two.

Sunday night was a decent affair as I caught up with work colleagues before a night out with my five flying companions. The highlight of the night was when we abandoned the Geordie postman and discovered the next day that he had spent a chilling half hour in a low grade Barcelona brothel, where the door to his private room was fastened with masking tape by his 'date'. True to stereotypes the Geordies continued boozing throughout the flight until the bitter end of the trip, whilst we who had run were reduced to walking backwards down any stairs we had to face during the morning before sleeping through the majority of the flight back to the UK…

4

ROME 2010

New Year's Day 2010 had dawned in the familiar, although uniquely adapted, shame of a hangover. The twist my distorted mind had put on this year's instalment was that I was on the sofa at my then girlfriend's brother and sister-in-law, having apparently peaked hours before Auld Lang Syne, dishing out unwarranted abuse to various senior members of the family. At this point I was sent to bed, before being resurrected for the transition between the two years. Any optimism this should have brought evaporated on the sofa as my behaviour from the previous night was relayed to me and I vowed there and then to live an improved life during 2010. The details would need to be ironed out but I decided that I would run five marathons during the year, in the hope that the challenge would necessitate an improvement in my spiralling lifestyle...

A week after the warm up that was the world's first ever kilomathon (a 26.2 kilometre race from Nottingham to Derby), I found myself seemingly a million miles away from the industrial estates of the East Midlands, as I stood beneath the awe inspiring shadow of the Coliseum, ready for the start of the sixteenth Rome marathon...

I use "ready" in the previous sentence in an extremely loose fashion - 33 consecutive days at the office, comprising three 75 hour plus weeks in a row had pretty much put an end to any hope I had of training and being in any sort of suitable condition for a marathon. This had been compounded by my selecting a hostel in Rome on price alone, meaning that I found myself on the fifth floor of a building with no lift in the insalubrious surrounds of the Sandy

Hostel. The hostel can best be described as "basic" although that would be incredibly unfair to any "basic" accommodation that did not smell like bottom and did not have the "world's worst mattresses" installed in the "world's wobbliest bunk beds". To quote from Gladiator (loosely), "*Marcus Aurelius had a dream that was Rome, [Sandy Hostel] was not it...*"

I managed a decent sleep in preparation on the Saturday afternoon but was not so lucky the night before the marathon as the American in the bunk above me (who I thought at any point may be joining me on the lower deck as his mattress baulked at his weight) snored incessantly and threw in some incomprehensible but loud sleep talking for good measure.

I was not entirely disappointed when my alarm sounded at 7.15 am and I took the short walk down Via Cavour to line up for a run I was now starting to actively fear. Arrival at the majesty of the Coliseum briefly quells this trepidation however and the associated adrenaline rush gives me the (foolish) feeling that everything might be OK after all...

A succinct summary of my Rome Marathon observations is as follows:

- 9:05am - the race officially starts and I set upon a strategy of running as quickly as I can for as long as I can in the hope of limiting my time on the road...(the "**Strategy**").

- 9:08am - first toilet break; first crack in the Strategy.

- 9:20am - realise that the ancient Romans may have built a beautiful city but that the uneven cobbles and road surfaces are not entirely conducive to running a marathon.

- 10:47am - reach half marathon point in a reckless 1 hour 42 minutes; realise that the Strategy was foolish, that my legs have nothing else to offer and that I'm just about to embark on a miserable two hours plus of walking, shuffling and tripping around the Eternal City.

- 11:05am (approx) - pace maker with the light blue balloons indicating 3 hours 30 minutes passes me, as does a very old man in a Hawaiian shirt and a cowboy hat; I feel like I am going backwards.

- 12:49 - reach the Colosseum, which has never looked more beautiful as it did then, offering me the promise of stopping running. I am walking, red faced, sweating, bleeding heavily from various un-vaselined parts of my body and just want a hug from my mother. I only have 500 metres to go but can run no more - I am broken. Just at this moment, I spot the orange balloons of 3 hours 45 minutes approaching from behind. From somewhere I find the strength to put in a sprint finish, which I immediately regret as I collapse over the line in a shattered heap of useless flesh that had been a human being less than four hours previous...

- Final (official result) - **3 hours 44 minutes 1 second.**

As I clamber through the strewn, tangled bodies of my fellow competitors in a scene that probably resembles those of the battle fields of Europe as the Roman Empire was being built, my mind flicks to the short-term dread of clambering the five flights of stairs to my hostel and, with greater fear, to the long-term terror of realising that today only represents completion of one fifth of my current 2010 challenge...

My post-marathon "down time" in Rome did not quite pan out as the site absorbing, relaxing, healthy eating dream I had envisaged. On Monday morning I got the call that I had been dreading - I needed to go to my law firm's Rome office to do a bit of urgent work on something I had been flat out on right up until my flight to Italy's capital. With only ten lawyers, the Rome office was a relative oasis compared to working life back in the UK although, after three Italian espressos (which had the consistency of glue and were as black as coal), I had to be pulled down from the ceiling as my heart rate pounded faster than it had done at any point during the run the day before.

My second day of "holiday" of 2010 turned into around an eight hour working day as I travelled directly from East Midlands Airport to the office arriving to the orange flash of an incoming phone call and, on reflection, that may well have been the highlight of the day and I was suddenly craving a return to the relative sanctuary of a marathon...

5

BELFAST 2010

For reasons beyond my control, the preparation for the Belfast Marathon, being held on Bank Holiday Monday, were towards the calamitous. On the Sunday morning, the day before the run, on a football pitch in the outskirts of Nottingham I arrived to find only seven team-mates had deigned to join me. We nobly decided to go ahead with the match and the problems were exacerbated when our lone striker in the enforced 4-2-1 formation had to head for hospital with a suspected fractured shoulder in the fifteenth minute. This meant that we were down to seven players with 75 minutes to play on a fairly warm day, which was not an entirely edifying prospect. At this point, I thought that a lively challenge from a robust young skin head had finished my morning's work and marathon hopes. I hobbled on for the rest of the game, conscious that my withdrawal would lead to us forfeiting the game (which we miraculously only lost 1-0 despite the four man disadvantage!), and then peeled away my sock with trepidation at the final whistle to final a purple and black mangled mess that had previously been a right foot. There was no time to dwell on this as immediately following the full time whistle I had to drive to the airport for a flight departing in less than an hour…

Thanks to some "bold" driving, I arrived flustered at the airport, just in time to hear the final call for my flight to Belfast, where I arrived in a torrential downpour with one hour remaining to find registration for the following day's marathon. The 12 pound a night youth hostel offered everything one might expect when paying top dollar for accommodation, including a room smaller than the average bathroom to be shared with five other men, no towels and a 'wet room' featuring mould detailing on the walls and ceiling. The inevitable conclusion was that a few pints of the black stuff at Fergus McNasty's nearby bar nearby was the only way to assure a decent night's sleep pre-marathon...

With the Guinness having done its stuff, I slept well enough but awoke an hour and a half before the marathon barely able to get out of bed because of the strains and bruises of Sunday's football. I duly hobbled to the start point, outside City Hall in the centre of Belfast, in glorious sunshine, which had replaced the previous day's rain.

My pre-race routine was governed largely by the pain in various parts of my body and included four co-codamol tablets, four ibuprofen tablets and a can of freeze spray, which I applied liberally to my legs. This approach seemed to have worked for the first 16 miles or so as I numbly trotted round the undulating course. I even found myself seriously discussing the possibility of signing up for a few more marathons during 2010 with a co-runner as we ran up the worst part of the course - a two-ish mile, albeit gentle, ascent up Antrum Road, which took us just beyond the half way point in the race. After that stretch, there was the relative bliss of over two miles of downhill and I was feeling pretty good about life. It was as the course hit the seafront that my world fell apart. As a little bald elderly chap (probably over 70), who was hunched over almost double came shuffling past me, I took it as a sign that I should stop for a long overdue toilet break and from here (about 18 miles in) to the end I adopted a - not unprecedented – approach of walk-jog-run-stop. By now the painkillers had well and truly worn off and my groin was in agony (as an aside chaps - be very careful when applying freeze spray to your groin) and spent a few minutes pleading with a St John's Ambulance woman for pain relief/ illegal drugs to ease my pain - all to no avail.

I hit my lowest ebb at around the 20 mile point and it was then that fate intervened, sending me an angel in a lavender coat. I was a finished man, talk of more marathons the distant hallucinations of a lunatic and getting through the current misery my only thought. "*Do you want a Mars Bar?*" came the soft, sweet Irish voice, "*you've only six miles to go so you have...*" Yes - I wanted a Mars Bar, like I've never wanted anything in my life. I will happily marry you, or your daughter, or in fact your son my lavender clad angel. Bless your sweet soul. With the sugar of the Mars Bar and words of encouragement ringing in my ears, I managed a decent unbroken struggle of about two miles before my next brief pause to contemplate life but by this point kind folk with jelly babies/fruit pastilles/various other sugar delights seemed to be everywhere and it seemed rude to walk despite the agony.

Into the last mile I passed the elderly bald chap who had unknowingly unravelled me mentally - ha, in your face, more than double my age fellow competitor! Redemption was mine and I summoned the strength for my customary vanity sprint finish to finish in a respectable **3 hours 34 minutes and 58 seconds** - an advert for shambolic preparation and legal drugs.

6

EDINBURGH 2010

It did not necessarily augur well for the Edinburgh Marathon when a civilised end of season football dinner predictably descended into a heavy night ending at 3.30 am, which equally predictably resulted in a missed alarm and a missed train. Having overcome this slight hiccup (by boarding a later train), I arrived to find Edinburgh bathed in Mediterranean-esque sunshine. How dreadfully un-Scottish of it. Not good, especially for a man still physically shaking from the exploits of the night before.

At least I had the pleasure of adult, non-hostel accommodation to drag my preparations to date back from the ridiculous. Rachel – who's flat had been volunteered by a friend at work - turned out to be the perfect hostess on which to impose a semi-broken lunatic as I arrived to find that she had managed to fall on her face on a whisky-fuelled Friday night in the Highlands. My kind of girl.

After a carbo-loading session at the local Italian I passed out in front of a DVD and managed to tweak my calf sleeping for two hours in a strange position on the sofa. However, after a perfect - maybe too good - night's sleep, and the promise of showers rather than a heatwave, I felt OK to go. For these purposes "OK" meaning horrifically under prepared. I was however pleased to see overcast skies framing the stunning capital of Scotland as I surveyed the morning scene. Three bananas later and I was ready for action in plenty of time. I thought this was the case anyway, but hadn't realised that there were two alternative start points and, naturally, found that I opted for the wrong one. No problem - it would be quite nice to be starting at the back and heading the right way through the pack for once.

The sun - with a deliciously cruel sense of timing - burnt through the cloud cover at approximately 9.59am, with the race starting at 10am, and did not vanish again until approximately one minute after I'd finished - but more of that later. Edinburgh Marathon is reputed to be the UK's fastest marathon and I had been assured that the first six miles were downhill. **B*ll*x!** It certainly didn't feel that way anyway, as the course headed out of the city - never to return - and out onto the coast. Whilst the sea front sections did offer some breeze but, as a slightly overweight man, I was struggling dreadfully with the heat and losing around one stone per mile in sweat.

I had never felt so bad quite so soon into a run and after eight miles thought it might be the day I would have to walk off the course. A few minutes of reciting various motivational mantras ("*Pain is weakness leaving the body*"; "*Pain is temporary, quitting's forever*", etc.) helped a bit, but one cannot kid a failing body. I clung on until the halfway point and it was then a walking/shuffling disaster for the second half, which offered precious little by way of shade as the course weaved down coastal roads and through farmer's fields. I had inadvertently thrown a t-shirt reading "Madness" (nothing to do with the quirky London band) into my very lightly packed weekend bag and this suddenly seemed incredibly apt as I embarked on a several hour voyage of self-discovery through heavily gritted teeth.

As I finished at Musselborough Racecourse (in **3 hours 42 minutes 43 seconds**) I actually shed a couple of tears, which felt like acid trickling down my bright red torched face. "*Freedom!*" William Wallace may have shrieked and at this point I know how he felt (clearly not, but it seemed fitting).

7

ISLE OF MAN 2010

Between the Edinburgh and Isle of Man Marathons, I experienced something of a meltdown, triggered by my attaining the ripe old age of 30.

A couple of key high (low?) lights included:

- "Giving away" my newly acquired flat in exchange for someone paying for my entrance fee to a student night club (made worse by the fact that this happened the night before my new furniture was delivered, meaning that had to spend a few days under plastic sheets in the communal car park).

- A week long golf holiday in Scotland which culminated with a stag do in Saint Andrews on the Friday evening and a grey man leaning over the side of a boat vomiting for all he was worth into the North Sea on Saturday afternoon.

With the worst of the meltdown seemingly negotiated, it was time to focus on the fourth marathon of 2010, in The Isle of Man...

This adventure possibly started to go wrong with the acceptance of an invite to the pub with my department on Friday evening. The plan had been a quiet night, involving some pasta, lots of hydration and an early night. Instead, judging by the sight of my suit, when I woke up three hours *after* my train had left Nottingham for Liverpool on Saturday morning, it had involved a lot of beer and a curry or possibly a kebab...

Missing the train was annoying, but not catastrophic, and there was still plenty of time to get to Liverpool for the 19:30 ferry crossing to

Douglas, Isle of Man. With a hangover still inhibiting all key operational parts of my brain, I decided to head for Liverpool immediately late on Saturday morning. On leaving Lime Street Station, I found myself in the midst of the Pride (gay, lesbian and transsexual) march, which was a somewhat unexpected explosion of colour for my damaged senses. I decided to mull over my confusion in a nearby bar, the Rat and Parrot, and by the time I embarked the ferry at Princes Dock about six hours later, I had enjoyed further pints (and a few shots) at a number of establishments including the Cavern (pub), Yate's, Ha Ha! The Liverpool, the Cavern (club) and an Irish bar. Despite the seven pints or so consumed, I felt sober enough (to stand, not drive) and decided that a few more were in order on the shortish crossing. There was a certain rationale for this, as I had failed to book any accommodation on the Isle of Man and therefore suspected I may well be sleeping al fresco and therefore needed a few relaxants to help me sleep.

Arriving on the Isle of Man in a tracksuit nearly saved me as I was turned away from two hostelries before being admitted into Jak's Pub on the promenade. It was now 11pm, and the pint count was at 10, and I was starting to consider that I may have erred in my marathon prep. This was confirmed seven hours later when I awoke, bewildered and lost, outside on the promenade. A quick scan of the surrounding area confirmed that I had lost my bag, but I was luckily wearing my running kit and near the bus pick up point. The driver laughed as I approached and tried to have a conversation with him, despite still being quite clearly over the legal marathon limited. *"You're not thinking of running are you?"* he laughed. *"Cours-he I am"* I slurred. The 50 minute transfer from Douglas to Ramsey, in the north of the Isle, provided some much needed additional sleep and I thought there was an outside chance of making it after I had sunk a cup of tea with a few sugars in it.

The hilly course, through the Isle of Man countryside was picturesque but demanding and I was relatively pleased to complete the first 13 mile lap in around one hour 45 minutes (near enough my usual performance). However, all was not well. I was feeling increasingly green as the hangover gradually took hold. The steady incline of the first few miles after the start were enough to reverse my steady gait to a staccato walk…shuffle…stop…regret certain decisions taken the previous day…and repeat. With eight miles to go, I was in real trouble, feeling like my quads had turned into lead and being passed by seemingly every man, woman and his/her dad and grandad. It was a true mental battle, especially when I knew that I was not going to break four hours for the first time in seven marathons. In fact, I think that a little bit of me died in the pleasant green surrounds of the IoM. In the end, it was primarily a feeling of disappointment which prevailed as I crossed the finish line in **4 hours 09 minutes 56 seconds**. It had been a poor effort and my behaviour on the Saturday had been borderline ridiculous. A pleasant buffet, featuring quiche, sausage roll and Battenberg cake in the clubhouse at the finish line did help raise my spirits from the trough there were in, but the other consequence of having finished the run was trying to figure out how to get home with no possessions, except a debit card and passport.

It was about this time that I think my guardian angel arrived and I experienced a series of unplanned lucky/generous events. Firstly I stumbled across the only bus departing for Douglas (and therefore my ferry) which would get me to the port in time for my return crossing, just as the bus was leaving the terminal. I had only £1.30 on me, £1.40 short of the minimum fare, but the kindly driver saw my broken look and decided to let me off. My return to Jak's was less successful and confirmed my worst fears that I had actively lost my bag and belongings, rather than just having left them in the bar.

I had lost my ferry confirmation, but still having my passport meant that I had sufficient evidence to board the ferry heading back to Liverpool. Next up, I arrived at Liverpool Lime Street station at 18:58, the exact time the last train was departing for Nottingham. I still had the problem of having lost my return ticket but managed to persuade the kindly ticket inspector to turn a blind eye (I probably looked like I would have cried if she had made me pay, which I might well have done)...

The final obstacle was returning to Nottingham sans flat keys. After the experience cited below, I had had additional copies cut but foolishly failed to put the copies anywhere else in the city. Not fancying a second night on the streets (especially as a couple of weird insect bites had appeared the previous evening) I headed for the Premier Inn, causing quite a bit of amusement when I gave them my postcode - very close to their own - and pointed out you could see my building from their main door, I just couldn't get in...

From there, the news continued to get better, with calls from the Isle of Man Police Control Room (who had apparently been frantically trying to track me down the morning following the marathon, having been inundated with tales of a perished marathon runner) and the Admiral Hotel (which I don't even remember seeing, let alone visiting) confirming that my bag had been located and would be couriered back to me later in the week. The overall message from The Isle of Man Marathon was that there are many decent people who will go to great lengths to help out those experiencing difficulties. I am not one of them. I am instead one who needs the kind oversight of such people...

8

NOTTINGHAM 2010

After the travails of the Isle of Man, I decided on a (wholly) more sensible approach to my "home" marathon in Nottingham.

The slight caveat to this was that, after a hellish 70 plus hour working week, I decided that I needed a relaxing glass of red wine on Friday evening. A glass turned into a bottle and disaster then struck when a tipsy Turner found two thirds of a cheap bottle of red in a cupboard in the kitchen. I'm not entirely sure when said bottle had been opened but it was certainly at least two months previously, and it had the bouquet and taste of vintage port (just none of the quality). In my defence, any 30 year old man who finds himself in a flat alone on a Friday night watching Two Weeks Notice needs at least a couple of bottles of wine, or preferably something stronger (maybe taken intravenously) to survive.

Except for a slight twinge in my left knee, everything felt ship-shape on the Sunday morning of the marathon as I devoured the remains of a pan of pasta prepared the following evening before timing my arrival at the start line almost to the second of the start of the 30th Robin Hood Marathon. Conditions were good, maybe slightly warmer than ideal, but I found the first half of the run a relative breeze and as I passed the halfway point in just over 1 hour 40 minutes, I still felt like there was plenty in the tank. This feeling soon passed and I started the usual steady descent into Dante's hell after around sixteen miles, stopping at each of the drinks stations to load up on water, Lucozade and Lucozade gel (pure sugar in a treacle type consistency which allegedly helps top athletes go 30% longer – sadly it seems to have almost no effect on very mediocre athletes...). After 20 miles I was at the stage of promising (lying) to my body that if it just got me to the finish line I would never inflict such misery on it again. I was also fantasising about eating a huge amount of food immediately following the race.

As the crowds increased again in the last couple of miles, I found new reserves of energy and managed to sprint the final few hundred metres (the "change" left in the distance after 26 miles) which saw me get home in a 2010 best of **3 hours 33 minutes 56 seconds**. To put this in context, this saw me finish the marathon in 261st place (out of around 1,600 finishers) so is respectable, if not spectacular. More pleasing than this was the fact that, for the first time in five marathons, I did not feeling like curling up and waiting for the sweet kiss of the reaper and was actually looking forward to the Berlin marathon in two weeks' time.

Lessons learnt - if I do have to drink before a marathon (which it appears I do), a day and a bit before is better than a few hours before and eating loads of carbs the day before is a good thing. I suspect I am not breaking new ground here, or providing revolutionary thinking to the marathon community but at least I am showing that I can (eventually) learn…

9

BERLIN (GERMANY) 2010

It was the worst of times,

it was the wurst of times...

After feeling pleased with how my body had reacted to the fifth marathon of 2010, my physical condition deteriorated rapidly, in some sort of reverse evolutionary fashion:

- By Monday I had the shuffling feet and bent back of an infirm OAP...
- ...by Tuesday, I had the pained, wide legged gait of a Brokebacked cowboy and...
- ...by Wednesday, like a cow, I could not go downstairs (at least without yelps of pain accompanying every step – as an aside, awkward when one finds out this physical quirk of a cow for the first time)...
- Finally, by Thursday, there was light at the end of the tunnel and my body had recovered sufficiently to destroy it in a much more enjoyable fashion - by making the most of the free bar on the Nottingham Princess for the annual work do as we cruised the crystal clear water of the River Trent for three hours during the evening. As a result of the merriment, Friday was actually probably the most painful day of the week, albeit for entirely non-athletic reasons.

Once the working day (which felt like a year) had finally been seen off, I set about enjoying a civilised sensible weekend, acknowledging that the Berlin marathon was just a week away (already).

Sadly things took a turn for the worse on Sunday...It all started well enough as my Sunday League football team - Alumni - took a two-goal lead away in a Cup game at Bilborough. My sublime flag technique as linesman were playing no small part in the attractive football the boys were exhibiting as they dominated against a previously unbeaten team. With 20-odd minutes to go I took my bow and played a small part in the third goal which underlined a comfortable victory. Unfortunately, it appears that the third goal was too much to bear for their stocky, skin headed goalkeeper, who saw an innocuous through ball from our winger which had bounced past both me and him as an opportunity to smash me in the face with his huge fist. Recollections from here are pretty sketchy - there was a lot of blood; I vaguely remember seeing him slap one of our other players as he was sent off the pitch by the referee (being their second sending off of the day, following a head butt, which was quite feeble and crap unlike the punch). I was babbling and making slightly less sense than usual but would have gone on had our resident team doctor - Marcus - not suggested hospital was probably a better idea given the amount of blood and the deep gash in my chin. Three and a half hours, and six stitches, later I made my way home, feeling pretty sorry for myself...

Luckily the working week brought no face to face interaction with clients as my lips were inflated with bruising (think Will Smith in Hitch), there was a blob of clotted blood on my chin, interwoven with stitches and stubble, on my chin and I generally looked like a sorry state (even more so than usual). There was also a slightly unnerving rattling in my jaw, which I initially thought may be broken but it turned out that the punch had knocked out a wisdom tooth, saving me a trip to the dentist and several hundred pounds. Every cloud...

After a mildly traumatising week, marathon preparation hit an all time low at the weekend as I headed to Berlin for marathon number six. After a particularly heavy week at work, culminating in a hugely frantic Friday, I dashed out of the office at 4:45pm for a prepaid taxi to East Midlands Airport relieved that it looked like I was going to make my flight without issue. Within about 20 minutes of getting in the taxi the wheels began to come off (not of the taxi thankfully) as I received a text from a colleague asking if I would be needing my wallet for the weekend, as I had left it on my desk. The financial implications of this were bad enough, but I had also put the contact number for Ben (see *Nottingham* and *Barcelona*), who I was meeting at the apartment we had rented for the weekend, on a post it note in my wallet as I did not have it in my blackberry. As a man who faces personal disaster caused by his own incompetence on a weekly basis, I didn't panic. I had 20 pounds sterling in my pocket and could text someone else for Ben's number - everything would be OK. I duly sent a text to another friend asking for Ben's number and settled down for an uneventful Ryanair flight to Berlin. I slept like a nodding dog baby from take-off until a bumpy landing rudely jolted me back to reality.

After turning on my blackberry at Schönefeld Airport, I thought I had the text I wanted, except that it turned out my friend's pretentious i-Phone had sent me some sort of picture message, which I could not open, instead of a good old fashioned number. I texted him back and set about changing my 20 pounds into Euros. My calm demeanour was tested when I found the exchange counter closed, only the card machines were available, meaning that I now had no usable money, no contact number and no target address. I have never been as stronger proponent of the single currency than I was at this point. It was 9:45pm local time and I decided to set off walking in the direction of central Berlin (11 miles away as the crow flies). At this point, despite only having a rail map of Berlin - which was of absolutely no use in terms of general direction - my spirits were quite high. I had spent plenty of time faced with similar catastrophes on my travels and the days of alone time during those eight months had forced me to become creative in terms of self entertainment. So it was that I spent the next few hours doing a variety of monologues and skits, including resurrecting my fictional travel companion, Rolf von Schmitz - an exiled Prussian Prince who wanders the globe in search of new lands to re-establish the Prussian Empire (you had to be there).

The merriment was starting to wear off by midnight, at which point I was in some dark, odd streets in the outskirts of Berlin. I did at least now have Ben's number so gave him a call to explain my predicament and advise that he didn't wait up. He gave me the address and suggested I get a taxi and then call him on arrival so he could come down and pay. This was a very good idea in theory, but I had not seen a taxi since the airport and would not for another couple of hours, at which point I decided it was too late to risk jumping in a taxi and hoping Ben woke up when I arrived. I did not think my German GCSE C-grade German would be adequate to explain what had happened to a taxi driver - sure, I could ask him where the nearest sausage stand was and chat about my pets, but in-depth conversation might be difficult...

By 4am my spirits were pretty low and I was incredibly thirsty. Like an oasis in the desert, a discarded McDonald's cup at a bus stop offered hope of a sugary drinks hit, but alas it was empty. Instead - and I'm not proud of this - I settled for drinking some water from a half empty bottle of water I found on a road somewhere. Judging by the tangy taste, the water had clearly been there for some time but at this point I didn't care. Based on the underground stations I was passing, I was at least getting closer to my target by now and, mercifully, had managed to avoid stumbling into any dodgy areas, although I did have to scamper for a while when I was walking by the unlit banks of the river for a while and a large group of youths was approaching.

By now, I had not stopped walking once in seven hours and my legs were starting to fall to pieces. I had searing pain in my right foot, left knee and calf and not even banter with Rolf could lift my breaking spirits. Finally at 5:35 am, I located the underground station which was next on the line from my target, Bundesplatz. I could have wept with joy. Unfortunately, I manged to get my guess as to the direction of Bundesplatz was wrong and what should have been a few hundred yard stroll turned into another 30 minutes of misery. At 6:05am (after eight hours unbroken walking), shining in front of me was the most beautiful "U" I have ever seen - Bundesplatz underground station. I called Ben and, on the third attempt (I was starting to panic after the second ring remained unanswered), he picked up his phone. When he appeared minutes later - looking full of sleep - it was like an evangelical presence had come into my world. I could have laughed, cried or just collapsed with relief. The leopard skin covered settee offered an even more welcome sight, bringing with it the promise of some desperately needed shut eye...

The four hours sleep I managed before Ben, his two brothers and Rich came into the living room to wake me up, had done wonders for my overall tiredness but sadly the horizontal time had done nothing to repair the damage to my legs and I was less than optimistic about my chances of completing the marathon, which started in less than 24 hours' time.

I managed to shuffle along with them to the Marathon Exhibition and registration, which was at a huge old airfield just outside the centre of Berlin. By now, I was walking like Kevin Spacey's character in the Usual Suspects and can only assume that everyone else there assumed I was part of the support team as opposed to a competing "athlete". Having signed in, I left the boys to it and decided that sleep was the only tonic which gave me any chance of lining up for the run. When I woke up on Saturday evening, the pain had eased slightly and the usual pre-race bath full of pasta and couple of beers at least raised my spirits ahead of Sunday.

In truth, my legs did not feel as bad as expected when I woke up at 7am on the Sunday morning of the marathon, and I decided it was definitely worth giving the marathon a go, albeit I was fully expecting my legs to disintegrate at some point. I loaded up on bananas, ibuprofen, paracetamol and freeze spray (not unfamiliar prep) and we headed for the start, which was just in front of the impressive Reichstag. A mis-timed portaloo visit meant I was separated from the other four boys and when the race started I was stuck, with tens of others, in a bottle neck in some adjacent woodland, making it one of the most anti-climatic starts to a marathon I have experienced. When I finally managed to climb the metal fence to get to the start area, it turned out I was now going to be part of the second start, which was ten minutes after the main race had left - nicht gud. This may have turned out to be a blessing as it meant I was surrounded by people targeting a slower time and, with 40,000 people crammed into the streets, I could only run as quickly as those immediately in front of me. This probably spared my fragile legs from early collapse although I did appear to have some sort of pain imp with me throughout. After six kilometres he was working his mischief in my right foot, and from there he moved to my left calf, then right hamstring before really getting stuck into my left knee. Despite this, I was generally feeling very comfortable even after 30 km and going along at steady five minute kilometre pace. After 35 kilometres, I made the near fatal mistake of stopping to take on some energy gel and this is when my left knee very nearly gave up the ghost. I dragged it along for the next couple of kilometres and my body seemed to reluctantly accept my brain's instructions that we weren't stopping so it was going to have to live with the pain. It had been a misty, drizzly day - perfect conditions for a marathon in many ways but not great weather in which to see the best of the city. The last two kilometres did suddenly take us into a more pleasant part of the city and by the time I saw the impressive Brandenburg Gate, which was just a few hundred metres before the end, I felt uplifted and even managed a flat out sprint, taking me past a few hundred fellow sado-masochists and to the finish in a time of **3 hours 34 minutes and 18 seconds**. When one of the boys I had travelled with told another runner about the trials and tribulations of Nicholas Turner at the Berlin Marathon 2010, he commented, "*Men like that are not born, they are made...*" I'm not entirely sure what this means, but like it and assume the implication is that one catch brain damage and the desire to continually self-destruct...

10

JERSEY 2010

As I headed off on Saturday morning for marathon number seven in Jersey, despite the not unfamiliar trace of a hangover, I felt full of optimism. My body had seemingly recovered remarkably quickly from the trials and tribulations of Berlin, sufficiently even to allow me to play in a five a side football match on Wednesday evening, followed by a top notch curry and Michael Buble sighting in Nottingham. Strange times.

I had not intended to drink on Friday, but one should never turn one's nose up to the offer of free beers on work and so it was that I had a few relaxing ales - *"The fault dear Nickos lies not in the stars but in yourself..."*

Anyway, aside from my perennial weakness, the Jersey experience promised to be one of military precision in comparison to the six preceding disasters. One of my colleagues, Ann, had put me in touch with friends - David, with whom she had lived with previously in Jersey and Yvonne - who had kindly agreed to take the spectacular risk of welcoming Nicholas into their lives. Saturday was every bit as smooth as hoped - David collected me from the airport and took me to their house in St Helier. The damp weather made the prospect of an island tour not particularly appealing so the afternoon was spent relaxing before a huge meal, and very restrained wine intake, at a nearby restaurant in the evening. So far, so good...

The miserable weather continued throughout Saturday night and the prospect of a marathon in the rain on Sunday was not hugely appealing. However, I was feeling good and much prefer running in colder conditions due to a propensity to overheat in anything approaching mild temperatures. I had briefly reviewed the course map and most of the pain appeared to be front loaded (in a hilly first half) so I decided that if I could get to halfway in a good time, a PB may well be achievable. This was further aided by the fact that there were only around 400 competitors (approximately 100 times less than the Berlin field) meaning that shortly after the initial scrum, I could dictate my own pace. I fairly flew around the initial miles - reaching three miles in less than 20 minutes and eight miles in under an hour. It had been a hilly but attractive route and I still felt like I had plenty of running in the tank. It was just as I began to think about a great time that disaster struck. I felt a sudden pang of pain in the back of my left knee and within a few hundred metres could barely put any weight on my left leg. This fortunately coincided with a St John's Ambulance stop where I asked whether my knee could be strapped up. This caused quite a bit of consternation, as apparently there were various forms to complete, but my look of concern eventually swayed them. The doctor who was manning the vehicle did also suggest that I should stop and, if I were his son, he would insist on me doing so. He was unfortunately providing sensible advice to a thick, brick wall.

The bandage seemed to do a job and held my knee together for a mile or so before the monsoon type conditions blasted it off in a swathe of rain and wind. I was now in a mess. I had not yet reached halfway and was alternating between shuffling walking and a sort of hop/ drag movement. In addition, although the least of my worries, there were rivers of blood streaming down either side of my white adidas t-shirt as my un-vaselined nipples chaffed against the material. I somehow limped to the halfway point in about 1 hour 40 minutes, and promised myself that the second half must be downhill and that my body would therefore get respite at some point. I could no longer complete anything beyond a limped barely above walking pace gait for more than a few hundred yards and waves of people - including many post-middle aged folk - had passed by me.

At 16 miles, the thought of ten to go was almost too much. I had a plane to catch at 3pm and, having started the marathon at 9am, I could not guarantee that at my current snail's pace I would make the flight. It all suddenly became too much and I was crying like a baby as I wandered round another bend and people cheering on the runners (of whom I was no longer one). I staggered to another St John's tent, and might possibly have given up at this point, had it not been unmanned. I had been turning the air blue for some time now and let loose another barrage of expletives, aimed at my leg and the situation in general before continuing my stumbling hobble towards the finish line, which was still a depressingly long distance away. I was getting a huge amount of encouragement from spectators and fellow runners alike and all this was serving to fuel my pathetic tears as the pain continued unrelentingly. An unfortunate side effect of my enforced hopping was that my right foot was now starting to throb with pain as well and it was all threatening to get too much. At 18 miles, I again saw the good doctor from mile 18 who laughed and said "*Oh, you poor man*" as I hobbled past him, grimacing with pain.

Part of what kept me going through what was probably the most prolonged experience of pain in my life was the abuse at which I had privately levelled at Paula Radcliffe following her two famous race withdrawals at the Athens Olympics. I believe you should "*never, ever give up*" (unless you literally collapse) and so gritted my teeth and plodded on. I reached 22 miles at 12:30, meaning that provided I could drag my carcass for a further 4 miles I should make my plane and this gave me enough comfort to lose the tears and shuffle on to the end, almost man like. A well known local resident, who had suffered a severe stroke earlier in the year had been completing the marathon in instalments throughout the week and was due to finish around 1pm. As I came into the home straight - where I would normally sprint - I realised that I had just wobbled past him. I was praying that I would not cause confusion for the crowd as to who was supposed to be the hero overcoming adversity. I was just a weak limbed fool. The chance for confusion may not have been aided for a sudden attack of cramp in my right calf yards from the finish line, which nearly meant that I was forced to crawl over the line, instead I settled for a weird hop/ bounce. My finish time of **4 hours 21 minutes 26 seconds** meant that I had taken an hour longer to complete the second half than the first. I was emotionally destroyed, and burning with pain. I felt pathetic. I managed to make the airport just in time for my return flight and suffered the indignity of having to ask an octogenarian man to prop me up whilst I tried to put my trousers on. Despite all this, and the fact that it was easily the worst time I have ever done, on reflection it's probably the proudest I had ever felt to complete a marathon...

11

RUTLAND WATER 2010

If, as it is said, pain is just weakness leaving the body, then I'm starting to wonder how weak one man can be.

Weather conditions for marathon number eight, at Rutland Water in Leicestershire, were perfect, unfortunately the same could not be said of the physical and mental state of competitor 634 – Nicholas Turner. After a three week holiday to the United States, my weight had increased significantly and the thought of another marathon was pretty abhorrent. My mood was not improved when the AA route planner decided to show me and my support how to get out of Nottingham but refused to provide any further directions (just details of lots of nice B&B's in the vicinity of Rutland Water). After a panicked stop at a petrol station in Melton Mowbray - famous home of the pork pie – I was back on track and arrived 15 minutes before race time. This would have been perfect were it not for the fact that (a) I needed an urgent "sit down" visit to the toilet (where the queue was huge) and (b) the start line was at least 15 minutes away from the car park. Fortunately, this was the inaugural running of a marathon at Rutland Water so there were many others in the same boat as me resulting in the start being delayed by 15 minutes to 9:15am.

It was bitterly cold at this point but I was soon warm, and even sweating, after negotiating the fist couple of flat miles, in what I assumed would be an almost completely flat race (on the basis that it takes a route around the lake). I think it was the first hill, after about 7 miles, which mentally broke my spirit, especially as it heralded the start of a small two lap section of the course. The ten miles or so which made up these two mini laps were undulating and any sort of rhythm was interrupted by cattle grids every few hundred yards. I will use these as my excuse as to why I started walking on and off after about 10 miles. The secondary reason was the thought of the Nice marathon the coming Sunday and the fear of doing any permanent damage before that event. However, it was probably primarily a sign of mental weakness and the fact that my brain and body were by now at war, with my body, and legs particularly, deciding that running was no longer enjoyable and demanding that my brain stops sending them signals to operate.

I was at a pretty low ebb as I neared the end of the second loop, and the 18 mile point, and this was partially driven by not really wanting to spend at least another one hour 20 minutes in my own company in the Leicestershire countryside (which, as an aside, was beautiful in the winter sun). The gloom was momentarily lifted when a pack of about 20 escaped sheep got out of a field in front of me and acted as pace makers for the next half a mile or so (rumour has it they ultimately beat me to the finish). The involvement of animals in a marathon was a first for me and the amusement took my mind off my pain and hunger for at least 20 minutes. When it eventually wore off and I realised I was incredibly hungry and craving sugar. My prayers were almost immediately answered when I spied an orange jelly baby on the floor in front of me which must have been dropped by a fellow runner. This incident highlights the detached, almost trance-like, mental state one visits during a run, as - despite being relatively undiscerning when it comes to food - I would not normally eat discarded sweets from a gravel path, but at this moment it looked like the most delicious food morsel I had ever seen. I stooped to pick it up, dusted off the gravel and dirt and was not disappointed as I benefited from an almost immediate sugar high. The orange (not normally my favourite flavour) sweet was - at that moment - without doubt the most amazing treat I had ever eaten. The sugar spurred me on until the next series of hills again destroyed me, this time with around four miles to go. For anyone who has not done a marathon, it may sound pathetic that one does not have the mental strength to spur oneself on when so close to the finish but I'm ashamed to say, the hills defeated me and I walked up them before trying to make up some lost time by bombing down the other sides. It had been steady inclines from around 21 to 23 miles, despite an old woman - who I now assume to have been a witch - assuring me that I was very close to a section which would be downhill all the way to the finish. When this promised land of descent did not materialise I was tempted to return and give her a very weak kick or piece of my by now flaky mind but decided that I just wanted to finish as quickly as possible and maybe eat some more confectionary products from off the floor. When the downhill did eventually come, it was bliss. I knew the time was not good, but I also knew there would be only two more marathons to go once I finished and with that I managed to kick on and deliver a decent paced last mile in **3 hours 54 minutes and 20 seconds**...

12

NICE (FRANCE) 2010

I dedicated my usual level of military planning to the Nice marathon. My flight from London to Nice arrived 35 minutes before the registration for the marathon closed. There was no choice to take a cab and I got my first lesson in the expense of this part of Southern France when a 15 minute cab ride cost me 35 Euros. Ouch!

My non-existent linguistic skills were at their best at the registration village and I left with my race number but no idea where the race started or the time I needed to be there. It was after this that my luck undeservedly turned. By sheer miracle, my hostel - Villa Saint Exupery - was just a two minute walk from registration. I had booked it exclusively on price (26 pounds for two nights) but it had come up trumps. More good news followed as the chef's special was just 6 Euros 50 Cents and a bottle of red wine 5 Euros 50 Cents. Sold and sold. Before feeding and watering myself, I decided to check out my 12 bed dorm. It was nice and clean and only one of my fellow dormers was home. I couldn't see him but could hear strange noises coming from the bathroom and was quite surprised when a 60 something year old man emerged from the large, mouldy smelling bathroom looking pleased with himself. I selected my bunk (managing to secure a much sought after bottom bunk) and tried to not make any further eye contact with him...

Dinner was excellent - a mignon of pork in red wine sauce (slightly superior to the usual hostel fare) - and washed down with an equally pleasant, if strong (13%), bottle of red wine. I realise this was a slightly risky strategy but nine months of world travel had been enough to teach me that sleeping in a room with several people coming in at various times in varying states of sobriety was almost impossible without a little assistance. It proved to be a smart move as

I had typically parked myself on the bunk below snore king (he probably reported the same about the man below him) who made some incredible noises. Despite his best efforts, I slept soundly enough, and got up at 6.30 am, in plenty of time to enjoy the complimentary breakfast. I was really warming to the hostel, especially as my breakfast of coffee with toast and honey was enjoyed against a backdrop of classical music. Magnifique...

I had decided that the race would not start before 8am and that it must be near where registration had been and my assumptions both turned out to be accurate as I wandered out into a grey, but dry, mildish morning and found some other runners heading towards the sea front and race start. There was no need for portaloos for the gents as we had the vast and beautiful turquoise Mediterranean Sea to relieve ourselves in (although I'm not proud of this). As usual, I felt sorry for the ladies who did not really have the same option (although a couple of them did not let this stop them). France being France, the race did not start at the scheduled time, instead inexplicably starting 15 minutes after 8am. I didn't mind though as there was some uplifting Euro-trance to get me in the mood and some fascinating Euro dancing as everyone got into the spirit...

The course hugged the stunning coastline (I think "Nice" could be a little bit more confident and call itself "Very Nice") for the first 14 of so kilometres and I was finding the going fine in the perfect running conditions of an overcast sky. Conditions aside I suspect this had more to do with my liberal application of bandages, freeze spray (most of a can had been emptied onto my aching legs) and consumption of maybe 8 pain killing tablets. The trouble with reliance on external pain suppressants is that when they wear off, you know about it and this happened with a vengeance after around 19 kilometres. Luckily I had pocketed a pack of paracetamol and ibuprofen but I knew that the next 23 km's would be challenging. It was now that the usual argument in my mind commenced. Half of my brain was sending the message that everything was fine and that we should press on, whilst the other (which had formed an alliance with my limbs) was suggesting that stopping for a bit of a stroll would be a great idea. In the end, a pseudo-Treaty of Versailles was reached and the competing halves agreed that I should try and get through the halfway point in a good time and then just try and cling on for the remaining 21 kilometres which would left at that point. It was an uneasy peace and, like the 1919 Treaty, created problems which would surface later in the day.

My other problem at this point was that I was over heating quite badly. Bizarrely, after wearing just a t-shirt in the freezing climes of Rutland Water the previous Sunday, I had decided that the South of France warranted two tops (one long sleeved). So it was after 21 km (reached in a respectable 1 hour 42 minutes) that a perfectly good Nike-Fit top was jettisoned. This also gave the good ladies of the Cote d'Azur a chance to marvel at the pasty, untoned midriff of an Englishman (grounds for leaving the EU in itself?). Oh, how they recoiled and turned their olive faces away...

As expected, the second half was becoming a stop-start affair, not helped by the fact that a few hills had suddenly cropped up. I was not prepared for this and decided to adopt the cowardly approach of walking up them and trying to make up some of the lost time by running (what felt like, but probably wasn't) quickly down them. My legs seemed to have inherited some of the attributes of the host nation and were pretty much on strike by the time I reached the outskirts of Cannes, still with 5 kilometres to go. As a general comment though I did find the race being measured in kilometres as opposed to miles a lot better for the soul, as even when one is struggling the distance markers never take too long to appear and at least one always feels that progress is being made...

The final kilometre, where the streets of Cannes were thickly lined with spectators, spurred me on to a fast finish and I had staved off the 3 hour 45 minute pace maker (the 3 hour 30 pacemaker paced me after about 28 km - always a bit dis-spiriting) to finish in an acceptable **3 hours 41 minutes and about 20 seconds**. It is amazing to see how one revises down targets as a marathon progresses and the pain increases. After 10 km I had aspirations of breaking 3:30. After 21 km, I had decided that breaking 3:40 would a good effort. After 30km, I thought cracking 3:45 would represent a good day at the office. After 35km, I couldn't care less what the clock would say, I just wanted the pain to stop and would have paid handsomely if anyone had the power to effect that.

All in all, a beautiful course and enjoyable day, but if anyone is thinking of visiting Nice and Cannes - both of which I would recommend from my fleeting visit thus far - I would suggest that the train (which puts ours to shame) is a better bet than running between the two. Just a thought...

THE MARATHON THAT NEVER WAS...

PISA (ITALY) 2010

The tenth and final marathon of 2010 was due to take place in Pisa in mid-December 2010.

The Friday before the marathon the Sunday was relatively exciting, predominantly due to my relaxed approach to travel. It kicked off with a National Express coach from Coventry to Stansted at 1.45am. Having not pre-booked this represented something of a wing and a prayer approach and I got one of the last two free seats on the coach, arriving at Stansted at 4am. Airports in the middle of the night are more akin to refugee camps than civilised venues and everywhere I looked, there were people trying to steal a little sleep before heading off. I had not managed to print my boarding pass, owing to computer error rather than a cavalier attitude, so had to face the wonder of the airport's internet system. For one pound I had ten minutes to check-in and print my pass. This was all down in countdown mode and the system was unnecessarily over complicated. A German lady who was stranded, with most airports in Germany having been closed due to the freezing weather gripping Europe, saw my increasing sweat as the clock ticked towards zero and explained that the completely indecipherable system had already claimed over ten pounds from her in exchange for a single printed sheet. When one clicked print, a code came up, which you had to remember and then run to another computer and type in and pay for your printing. This doesn't sound difficult, but the second computer refused to recognise the codes, and then required a number of other steps before the sheet was finally delivered for the bargain price of one pound. Five pounds later and I had my pass and a new German friend.

Next up was check-in and the requirement to buy a plastic bag to house my toiletries. A young chap had been turned bag because his bag was "not sealable" but I was a bit baffled by this as I wouldn't have thought that a seal would stop a determined martyr, if that is the idea. Anyway, the bags could only be purchased from a machine dispensing four at a time so I made myself a small scale hero by distributing the spare three to other frustrated travellers.

The flight was fine, although I foolishly took a seat next to a child who turned out to be Rainman in the making. Every waking moment on the flight was spent listening to how he would distribute the monies he and his mum were going to win on the in-flight scratch card (they didn't) and asking dumbfounded eastern European flight stewardesses for the exact euro/pound exchange rate.

Shortly before arrival we received the news that we could not land in Pisa, owing to snow (I had never checked) and instead would land in Bologna. About 30 minutes later there was a further update and we were instead heading for Parma (of ham, and violets, fame). I assumed this was quite close to Pisa but a four hour bus ride through snowy, spectacular mountains revealed otherwise. Neither the snow nor ice deterred our driver, Fredericco Kruger, from driving insanely fast, speaking on his mobile and trying to eye up one of the girls on the front row of seats. The elderly English lady sat next to me refused to open her eyes throughout the trip.

We were eventually deposited at Pisa Airport, from which trains were not running. Fortunately, the airport is very close to the city and I guessed right in terms of direction and soon found the beacon of "HOSTEL" shining out above the buildings. At 10 euros a night "Hostel Pisa" offered a decent enough bed (sadly I had to take a top bunk) and in my room were three unwise men, from Scotland, America and Germany respectively, whose asses lowed throughout the night (nice Christmas reference).

On the basis of the icy streets of Pisa, Saturday was spent assuming the marathon was off, but - having never had it confirmed - I moderated my behaviour accordingly. Much of the afternoon was spent sleeping off a heavy lunch which followed a private walking tour of Pisa. It is actually quite difficult being the sole participant on a walking tour, as there is a lot of pressure to feign interest in the most banal facts about a city which is famous for only one thing, an architectural mistake (like Chesterfield, with its twisted spire)...

I received the news at 9pm on Saturday night, from a fellow athlete, that due to the snow and ice the Pisa marathon was cancelled. Within ten minutes of this news I had signed up for a bar crawl, which was led by a young Italian lady who drove us to the club in a Fiat Punto which was completely frozen and had a sheet of frost on its windscreen, rendering it useless. She did not drive slowly. The "club" was full of Italian gentlemen wearing shiny "bin liner" jackets and me and my fellow hostel crew, consisting of three Aussies blokes and an Argentinean man, merely added to the sausage fest. Despite this, I had a lot of fun and managed to leave my jacket, containing my boarding pass and several credit cards, in da club...

On reflection, there was a lot of disappointment in the fat that – ultimately through no fault of my own - I was unable to complete the tenth and final marathon of my 2010 challenge. In an attempt to make it right in my own mind I did run at least a marathon in the last week of 2010 week, albeit the fact that it has been stretched over five days rather than under four hours does somewhat detract from the achievement. Despite the running efforts, I actually seemed to have gained weight during the year. This contradictory state of affairs was a result of the fact that I did not manage to give up the party lifestyle despite the challenge (which was one of the primary personal drivers for starting it in the first place). In fact, I fear that the extremes of my behaviour became more pronounced and 2010 was probably a record year for sightings of Rick, my evil, drunk alter ego. I blame my birth sign, Gemini, for giving me such erratic bi-polar behavioural tendencies.

On reflection, the unfinished business of 2010 were potentially key to my decision (deliberate or otherwise) to keep on running. Eventually...

COAST-TO-COAST 2011

The nine marathon ordeal of 2010 had clearly been enough to put me off marathons for a while and so it was that by late summer 2011 no further marathons had been added to my tally and I was beginning to feel restless.

It was against this backdrop that I set upon completing the Coast to Coast challenge – to travel on foot from St Bees in Cumbria to Robin Hood's Bay on the Yorkshire Coast. A distance of 192 miles...

In Rocky IV terms, I adopted the Stallone (rather than Lundgren) approach to C2C, opting for Trailblazer's 'Coast to Coast Path' book and bin bags over GPS and any sort of NASA designed waterproof sleeping bag technology. The night before my departure, I was visited by two angels of mercy in the form of friends Robin and Melissa...Such was their ethereal glow, I could barely see the gifts they carried, but when my mortal eyes finally adjusted, the sight was truly heavenly to behold. For in their cherubic hands were a "survival bag", an emergency shelter, whisky, ready to eat Chilli Con Carne and Spotted Dick & Custard (all in a form one can imagine being stashed on a space shuttle) and Kendal mint cake. In summary, life support of the most precious and welcome sort.

The six hour train journey from Nottingham to St. Bee's on Friday afternoon (via changes at Manchester Oxford Road and Barrow-in-Furness) was probably the last element of my coast to coast adventure which went smoothly. I loaded up on final provisions at Hartley's Tea Rooms, which sit on the edge of the Irish Coast, and then went to their gents to change into my shorts, except that I hadn't packed my shorts. Perfect. That meant I would be starting the walk in thick, "house pants" (basically tracky bottoms). The Trailblazer's 'Coast to Coast Path' book, which I hoped would act as my bible for the next few days, splits the 191 mile route into 13 stages, which were designed to be completed on a one per day basis with a couple which could be combined for the brave. Each stage description included hand drawn small scale maps of the route and it was at precisely 7pm on Friday that I dipped my trainered toes into the Irish Sea and set off on the 14 miles of stage 1 which would take me to Ennerdale Bridge. In the words of Julius Caesar, *"alea iacta est"* (*"the die is cast"*) – it was now time to cross the Rubicon and not look back...

Stage One – St. Bees to Ennerdale Bridge

Conditions were perfect, and I was full of optimism, as I jogged/walked along the coastal path in pleasant sunshine. By around 8:15pm I'd chalked off about six miles and was already starting to think that I'd crack the challenge in no time. It was probably distraction and forward thinking which led to a misreading of the directions, and by 9:15pm I'd still done six miles, having spent an hour – and maybe four wasted miles – trekking through farm fields in the wrong direction. It was frustrating but I was keen to not lose my optimism so instead told myself that it should be a first and last mistake. An hour later and I was retracing my steps down a country lane, again having lost track of the directions in the book, and this time I was slightly more annoyed, particularly as I had sought to learn the lesson from the first mistake but could just not follow the book. As darkness fell, my next problem became apparent – I hadn't brought a torch. So it was that at about 11:30pm on Friday night I was trying to navigate my way up and down the steep, slippery slopes of Dent Hill, using my blackberry screen for light. For anyone unlucky enough to find themselves in a similar situation, I would recommend *"Compose MMS/SMS"* as the best source of light. Suffice to say, I ended up on my backside, and laughing at the ridiculousness of the situation, at least five times. Despite another couple of minor wrong turns (resulting primarily from the darkness), I reached the end of Stage One, Ennerdale Bridge, at 12:15am, but having no accommodation booked I decided to press on another mile or so to the banks of Ennerdale Water, where I found a nice smooth patch of grass, put on my hat and lay down inside my survival bag for a spot of sleep.

Stage Two – Ennerdale Bridge to Borrowdale

I woke up at the crack of dawn (who seemed surprised) to a sensational view. The calm waters of the huge lake were starting to be lit by the breaking sun and I could easily have been the only human on the planet, given the peace and solitude. Although the survival bag had been perfectly adequate, the hat had not worked so well, picking up a spot of morning dew, which made my face feel pretty uncomfortable. By 4:30am I was on my way again – Stage 2, to Borrowdale, was 14 and a half miles – and I initially made steady progress, firstly around the rocky lake path and then through pleasant, if dull, forest tracks. I stopped for a cup of tea at the incredibly remote Black Sails Youth Hostel at around 7am before facing the first significant climb of the walk to date, up Loft Beck. I was still pretty fresh at this point and the views at the top were simply incredible – with lakes in view on two sides of the panorama. What goes up must come down, and I jogged most of the way from here to Seatoller before reaching Borrowdale at around 9:30am. So far so good.

Stage Three – Borrowdale to Grasmere

There wasn't a great deal to stop for in Borrowdale, so I ploughed straight on into Stage 3, a short leg at 9 and a half miles, although it started with a fairly arduous climb up Greenup Gill. The weather was pretty perfect, dry and cool, although large patches of ground on top were boggy. Most of the boggy areas were only about six inches or so in depth and this encouraged me to try and increase my pace. This quickly proved to be a mistake, when I skipped into a small boggy patch only to sink in as far as my thigh, spraining my left ankle in the process. Although this slowed me down briefly, I soon managed to walk/jog through the discomfort and walked to Thorney How Youth Hostel, on the cusp of the end of the stage at around 12:30pm. A proper lunch was hugely welcome, although the 20 minutes inactivity did slightly worsen matters with my ankle. In addition, my legs and feet were now drenched and it was starting to rain persistently. Fortunately, Grasmere – the official end of the stage – was well stocked with walker's shops and I purchased a couple of pairs of walking socks and a torch before leaving the pleasant village, described by Wainwright (the pioneer of the coast to coast walk) as *"the fairest place on earth"* (don't think he ever visited Milton Keynes though).

Stage 4 – Grasmere to Patterdale

Stage 4 was another shorty – at 10 miles – so I pressed directly on. Like the previous stage, it started with a brutal ascent, this time up Great Tongue. The persistent but light rain soon became incessant and incredibly heavy and I was drenched to my very bones by the time I reached the summit. It was at this point that I realised that my rucksack was not waterproof. As a result, my blackberry – sole point of contact with the world – had been drowned and would turn on but not unlock and was therefore of no use. All of my spare clothes changes (including new socks) were soaked through and the bag (including its contents) weighed about half a stone more than it had done at the start of the climb. From the top, I opted for the easier descent down the valley and from there it was an easy enough plod through to Patterdale, which I reached at 4:30pm. Although I was soaked to the bone, covered in mud from the bog, and generally sore, I was pleased enough with progress and decided to treat myself to a pint in the White Lion pub. It would have been incredibly easier to stay in there drying out and enjoying a few pints, but I dragged myself up after 30 minutes and set off out of Patterdale. This nearly turned out to be a fatally flawed decision.

Stage 5 – Patterdale to Shap

Stage 5 started with a testing climb up Patterdale Common and, about half way up, I turned fully over on my already sprained left ankle. I didn't even need to remove the socks to see the swelling – it looked like a balloon had been inflated. I initially took to going up the hillside sideways, leading with my right side but suspected that this could not go on for another 145 miles to Robin Hood's Bay, so instead strapped the ankle with duct tape, gritted my teeth and got on with it. I managed to develop a steady, if ungainly rhythm, and reached the top feeling OK. It was here that me and the book had the first fall out of the day. I stand by the fact that most people would have followed the path I did, but after over an hour of descending and then skirting the edge of the hill, I was slightly worried that I had not found Angle Tarn – the lake I was heading for. I was fortunate enough to stumble across a man who knew what he was doing (evident from the ski poles, waterproofs, covered map and compass he was carrying him). Luckily he had just come from Angle Tarn but, not so luckily, it was way back over the other side of the hill I had just climbed. I grimaced, and suddenly the pain in my ankle felt more pronounced, as I retraced my steps from whence I had just come. Even with my fellow walker's help, the correct path took some finding and I was finally looking at Angle Tarn about 3 hours after I should have been. My ankle was in agony, the night and the weather were closing in and I was near one of the highest points on the route – Kidsty Pike. There was little point in dwelling on this miserable set of circumstances, so I got my head down and tried to get off the hills before the darkness descended. Sadly, this did not work out perfectly and as the rain started to fall, I was on a high ridge, although there was the small mercy of a wall for some shelter. It was about 10:30pm, I had walked over 50 (probably nearer 60 given the problems I had experienced) miles during the previous 27 hours and I was in pain. I pulled out my survival bag, together with the foil of the emergency shelter, wrapped myself in both, made my peace with the world, and prayed for some sleep.

What followed was maybe four hours of broken sleep, uncontrolled shivering and what I think was a descent towards hypothermia as I was having a multi-party semi-conscious conversation about whether international sanction was needed (from Russia and Scotland oddly) to allow me to sleep there. By what I guess was around 3:30am (I had no means of telling the time by now as the blackberry was now totally dead), I was cold to the bone and thought I just needed to be lower down to be warmer and safer. Unfortunately, the sleep deprivation of the previous two nights had probably affected my directional sense and I made the very poor decision to head down towards a reservoir I could see and which I thought may be Haweswater, which was the next point I needed to reach on this stage. On the plus side, the grassy hill down to the water was so steep that all I could do was slide down and this proved to be comfortably the most fun I had during the day (unfortunate to peak before 4am).

When I got down I realised this lake was Ha*y*eswater not Ha*w*eswater, although to be fair the name and the water element turned out to be the only similarity – Haweswater is maybe 20 times bigger – and I think it was hope I was so close to the right route, rather than rational evaluation that drove my decision. Either way, the net result was that I haul my way back up the near vertical slope before again trying to find the correct path. It was now that the weather turned against me again, as thick mist engulfed the hills. I couldn't see more than 20 yards ahead and certainly couldn't see anything meaningful to direct me, including in my book which was very sketchy at this point. In fact, hopeless. By now I had already decided to write to its author, Henry Stedman, to point out that certain of his maps/directions could have been clearer and maybe to vent some frustration – which was rapidly building. I best guessed where I was going, first scrambling down a steep, scree covered slope towards a lake I saw when the mist occasionally lifted and then scrambling up a steep, scree covered slope out of the same valley when I realised I was wrong. Out of the valley, another brief break in the mist showed another large expanse of water in the distance. I thought I had found my target and the optimism and a downhill grassy pathway helped speed me along. My only nagging doubt was how far away the lake was, as Haweswater should have been relatively close so I decided to confirm I was on track with a passing fell runner. *"That's not Haweswater mate, that's Windermere. Haweswater is way over that way..."* he said, pointing back towards the hills I had just scrambled over. Brilliant. Maybe two hours later, I was back in the scree sloped valley described above and starting to feel a bit dis-spirited.

There is not really any time for self-pity on a challenge like C2C, so I worked out where I thought I was – deciding it was Blea Water, which flowed into Haweswater – and carried on. About an hour later, I again had that sinking feeling I was going the wrong way and so when I saw a family returning to their house just off the track I was plodding down. I showed the man my map, pointed to where I thought I was and asked for his confirmation. *I'm afraid you're not on* **this** *map*" came the response, *"...but I think I have one in the house that you'll be on"*. He also said that I did not look well and suggested that I went into the family house. I tried to be polite and British and initially said no, only to accept immediately on the extended offer of hot tea and toast. The whole family (husband, wife and three little daughters were also there) also seemed fascinated by the wild eyed mountain man who had appeared into their Sunday morning. Such was my condition and appearance that they suggested I sleep at their house for the day, an offer I did decline. Instead I did gratefully accept the offer of being returned back to the last point at which I had gone wrong. Climbing into a Land Rover is no mean feat when all of your joints are screaming with pain and it took me several attempts to climb on board. We found my guide book on a wall on the way back (I had not realised I had left it, and had mixed feelings about getting the thing back). Twenty odd minutes later, I was at the same reservoir for the third time that day, but I did at least now know which direction I needed to go from it although this meant climbing a horrible looking hill to a distant shelter at the summit. Still, the family's kindness had lifted my spirits and their toast and tea had given me the energy to continue. Approximately two hours later, I was finally on the shores of Haweswater, which is simply huge, having been created by the flooding of a previously inhabited valley. It had taken me the best part of 20 hours to reach there from Patterdale (despite it only technically being 10 "Coast to Coast miles") and I felt pretty broken. I had long since run out of water and had taken to filling up and drinking stream water despite the book warning that it probably contained cow or sheep faeces or pesticides, any of which would make you very ill. Faced with Hobson's choice of dehydration or the risk of sickness, I opted for the latter. My gait was now somewhere between Mr Bean and a 90 year old man and no less than four cars stopped to offer me a lift during the three miles or so skirting the road around the giant reservoir.

Before reaching the end of the stage, there was still time for me to get horribly lost once more and, after about 30 minutes looking around a field for a building which I'm sure did not exist, I gave up and followed the longer route of a B road to Shap. It was a long miserable plod to Shap but once there I decided to treat myself to fish and chips and accommodation in a B&B. Life is about context and given how bad I felt, I can safely say, they were the best fish and chips I have ever had, followed by the best bath of all time and the most comfortable bed I had ever enjoyed. The eight hours or so sleep must have done me the world of good but it still took a lengthy pep talk to get my by now crumbling body to start moving the next morning.

Stage 6 – Shap to Kirkby Stephen

I had now left the Lake District but had very little confidence that I could finish the walk and certainly not in the next few days. Stage 6 started with the crossing of the M6 and the 21 mile route was relatively plain sailing, mostly across gently undulating farm fields and moorlands. My feet were very sore and I had already decided that the trainers in which I had foolishly started the challenge would be ditched in favour of walking boots at the end of the stage in Kirkby Stephen. It was still my ankle giving me the most trouble and my pained limp caused quite a few walkers to advise I maybe seek medical attention in Kirkby Stephen. As it turned out, the stage took me a lot longer than I'd hoped (despite not getting lost for once) so when I arrived at 3:30pm, there was no time for anything other than purchasing a couple of pairs of new socks, some freeze spray, painkillers and a pair of walking boots. I also sent a couple of quick emails to the world to confirm that I was still alive.

Stage 7 – Kirkby Stephen to Keld

Stage 7 was mercifully short and the walking boots appeared initially to be a miracle cure to some of my walking problems. My feet immediately felt better, my overall posture and speed improved and I suddenly felt hopeful that I could finish the walk by the end of Wednesday (even if that would mean completing another 100 ish miles in two days). Having left Kirkby Stephen at 4:30pm, I arrived in Keld at 7:45pm and paused only for a banana and drink before continuing directly onto Stage 8, also short.

Stage 8 – Keld to Reeth

Stage 8 was also noteworthy only in so much as I managed to again complete it without incident. I kept myself amused with some of the nearby place names on the map – Muckel, Rash and Crackpot. I finally pitched up at Reeth – very Last of the Summer Wine – at 11:30pm on Monday night. I desperately wanted a bed but the whole town appeared to be asleep. It was then that I saw light coming from the window of the King's Arms Hotel. I could see the publican, but he was at the back of the bar area and seemed oblivious to my tapping at the window, so I took to flashing the torch through the window. I could have kissed the big man when he finally saw the light (as it were), let me in and allotted me a bedroom with a bath. He charged me 40 pounds, but I would happily have paid 400 pounds for a bed at that point (luckily he was unaware of that). After a long, blissful soak, I hit the sack.

Stage 9 – Reeth to Richmond

Tuesday morning was the toughest yet. Each part of the leg had become a personality by this point and it was time for a tailored Churchillian-esque motivational speech to each foot, my left ankle, left knee and right knee. With the speech delivered at 5:30am, Maximus style, it was time for the pain relief routine – duct tape on both feet, left ankle and both knees, a liberal amount of freeze spray on the same and a couple of paracetamol and ibuprofen to start the day in a liver pickling way. The ten mile walk across farmlands and woodland to Richmond in bright sunshine was pleasant, as was Richmond itself and I would have liked to have stay longer. As it was, I had an agenda to stick to so, after stocking up on essentials, off I went on the next stage, 23 miles to Ingleby Cross.

Stage 10 – Richmond to Ingleby Cross

The going on Stage 10 was fairly flat, which was just as well, as it was the hottest day of the four so far by quite a way and I was struggling to stay hydrated. Fortunately, the savvy local farmers had identified the opportunity offered by the coast to coast walk and there were cooler boxes filled with drinks, together with honesty boxes for payment, in most of the fields on the route. I was still shuffling along but made OK time, reaching the Blue Bell Inn in Ingleby Cross at 5:30pm. I enjoyed my last pint (my third on the trip in total) before heading out of Ingleby Cross to start Stage 11 – I now had 52 miles to go and, for the first time since Saturday afternoon, actually thought I might finish.

Stage 11 – Ingleby Cross to Clay Bank Top

I stumbled up through Arncliffe Wood in pleasant weather, but aware – through other walkers – that the upcoming forecast was terrible. I therefore decided to try and go as far as possible whilst it remained dry. I made good progress until darkness fell, by which time I was on top of the North Yorkshire Moors, looking left to the bright, twinkling, lights of industrial Teeside. It was a beautifully clear but mild evening and I carried on using torchlight for as long as I could, but at around midnight decided to lie down for a couple of hours sleep in a clearing in a small tree plantation. Maybe two hours later I was up and walking again, and the going was quite tough as the path climbed up and down uneven stone steps. One of these sets of steps turned out to be a nesting ground for some game birds. It was like a computer game, as every time I inched forward a couple of startled birds shot up from their perch. The first time scared the life out of me and I very nearly fell head first down the steep steps. The rain started to set in towards the end of the stage as I trudged for what seemed like hours along a disused railway track before finally reaching the incredibly remote Red Lion Inn at Blakey Ridge for a much needed coffee. I called home to my worried mother to make arrangements for my evening pick up from Robin Hood's Bay before heading back out into the now horizontal wind and rain.

Stage 12 - Clay Bank Top to Grosmont

Stage 12 started steadily, with only the weather making life difficult as I crossed the moorland towards Glaisdale. About three quarters of the way through the stage, I was passed by two middle aged guys from Birmingham who had said that they had been behind me for a few miles and had commented that I was either a man with a very odd walking style or a cripple. Their advice was that I catch the train from Glaisdale to Robin Hood's Bay to save any further injury. I think they soon realised from my reaction and the look in my eye that I was not going have walked 170 odd painful miles, only to give up with one stage left, but it was nice of them to try. From the pleasant Glaisdale, it was another three miles, via the pretty Egton Bridge, to the penultimate village – Grosmont. The village was busy with life as they was some sort of steam train display going on and I managed to terrify several families when completing my final pre-stage pain relief routine. I had not taken my boots off for 34 hours at this point, during which time I had walked about 68 miles, and the sight was not for the faint hearted. My right foot was like giant bubble wrap – covered in about five huge blisters, including one under a toe nail, which was barely clinging on for life. All toes on both feet were gashed and bleeding and the smell and swelling was feral (almost the sickly sweet smell of death). Dwelling on this was not going to help so I dealt with things as quickly as possible so I could crack on...

Stage 13 (Final Stage) – Grosmont to Robin Hood's Bay

The final stage cruelly started with a near vertical climb out of Grosmont, at the summit of which the North Sea became visible. Sweet Hallelujah – the end in sight. Typically- after two stages where relations between me and the book had improved – the directions were poor and I got lost twice. The first time stumbling back onto the right route by sheer fluke without too much damage done but the second time, very close to the end, was more severe. Eventually I just headed free style towards the sea and again, by sheer luck, quickly found the path I was supposed to be on. There was also a phone box but my 60 pence minimum payment (seriously?!) was swallowed by mum's voicemail so I wouldn't be able to let her know I was about three miles away and should be with her by around 10:15pm. In my excitement to finish, I stupidly chose to freestyle, assuming that I could get to Robin Hood's Bay by following the coastal path around. After about an hour, with no sight of the Bay or an orange glow to even suggest it was near, I realised something was wrong and referred to the book, only to find that I should have left the path a while ago and headed for a road. It was now pitch black and I was sure I could cut across to the right and shorten the pain of the correction. To make matters worse, I was by now hallucinating quite badly, presumably a combo of sleep deprivation, pain and sheer exhaustion. In a small village, I had approached what turned out to be a statue in a garden for directions and I now staggered towards a campsite where I could see people as I wanted someone to call my mum with an update (i.e. I had messed up again). When I got to the campsite, it had been a mirage and all that was before me was an empty field. Odd. I was also struggling not to collapse, not helped by the strong winds. Anyway, I eventually re-found the road I had crossed at about 9pm and decided this time to stick to that. I cut a sad figure, although that did not tell the story of elation and relief on the inside as I hobbled down the steep hill in Robin Hood's Bay to see my very worried looking mother heading the other way, relieved to see me. I struggled down to the beach and finally dipped my toe in the North Sea at 11:15pm - 5 days, four hours and 15 minutes after setting off from the Irish Sea. The primary emotion was relief – that I didn't have to walk again (ever?), could take my shoes off and could sleep, sleep, sleep...

Epilogue

I managed patchy sleep on the three and a half hour drive home with mother, but before I went to bed we decided a trip to accident and emergency may be sensible. I had washed my feet but the smell still gave an indication of the problems which lay within and I was quick to apologise to the young doctor who looked at them with disgust and poked tentatively at them with a surgical gloved hand. *"I have never seen anything like this"* was the slightly worrying first impression, but a second opinion from a more senior colleague who suggested I had very nasty blisters (clearly), a sprained ankle, severe, possibly infected cuts and trench foot (always nice to pick up a World War One condition in modern times – glad to hear I didn't also have scurvy). The prescription was antibiotics, pain killers and rest. I was wheeled out of hospital, being told I wouldn't be able to walk for a while, feeling quite a fool at having managed to inflict such problems on myself in such a short space of time.

I think in time, when the blisters and cuts have healed and the skin infection has cleared up, I will hopefully reflect happily that I didn't give up, but suspect that would have been the prudent course of action (probably on Sunday evening)...

13

ROUND ROTHERHAM ULTRA 2011

Physical recovery from the trauma of the Coast-to-Coast was remarkably swift, although it did involve 10 days of "shirking from home", during which time I was reduced to peeing in a bucket whilst my rotten, plastic covered feet convalesced. The mental damage may well never heal and who knows what subconscious time bombs the ordeal planted?

I was keen to get back in the proverbial saddle and so accepted the invite from recurring enabler Benjamin Collard (see *Three Peaks, Barcelona, Berlin*) to join him and his then current squeeze for a 50 mile run in Rotherham. I was fairly sure that I was going to struggle with the event and this ended up manifesting itself – not for the first time – as a drinking binge. There was at least an event of sorts to which the booze fest attached itself. At the start of 2011 – in an attempt to foster some team bonding – I had initiated *"Corp Dine With Me"* within my work team (an hilarious play on the fact that we were the corporate law team and would each go round to each others' houses and cook for each other). The Thursday night was the final dinner and I had therefore (naturally) determined that it would be rude therefore to not get double drunk. My last recollection of the evening was some sort of dance game on the Wi in a Colleague's living room. I woke up in the spare room of my flat (good start), found my front door wide open and work phone in my fridge. The latter two facts pointed towards potentially too much fun having been had. The clincher was a note on my living room table which read along the lines of:

Dear Nick

We saved your life last night. We found you lying on the road and so brought you home. You should be ashamed of yourself Mr Lawyerman.

Take it easy.

Your neighbours

Lucy and Michelle

Ah. It was therefore with some trepidation that I headed to the office – not quite (at all) on time – although I found my fellow diners with similarly sketchy recollections and smudged appearances. It was non-ideal preparation for my first foray into the world of ultra marathons and the hangover was so severe that my hands were still quaking when I was picked up from Rotherham Train Station by Ben that evening. Having witnessed Barcelona, together with countless other disgraceful displays, Ben was not surprised by my condition and suggested that the going would no doubt be very slow so all should be well. I was not entirely convinced…

By the time we arrived at the sports hall which marked the start and finish of the run early on Saturday morning, I was in much improved condition, although there was a degree of trepidation at being ready to embark on a distance of nearly double the longest I had ever previously attempted. We set off in the dull dusk light and were treated to a mixture of encouragement and abuse by some South Yorkshire revellers who were still making their way home from no doubt a much better Friday night than we runners had experienced.

We stuck together as a trio, taking the generally flat sealed roads at a steady pace before we were taken for the first off road section of the course, where the gradient became slightly more acute. With a long, long way to go we decided it was best to walk the uphill sections to conserve energy. Soon enough we reached the first aid station, which was something of a revelation. There was the usual marathon-type fare of water and energy drinks, but alongside that was fruit, sandwiches and cakes. Sweet praises. I would get my 30 pounds entry fee back in food and drink! Feeling suitably sated, we pressed on at a similar pace until the halfway stage, where the provisioning stakes were raised further and we sat and enjoyed soup followed by sweets. This was clearly not conducive to completing the event in a good time, but the event was already about survival only. We had remained together as a trio until this point, but had left Ben's girlfriend behind by the time we reached the last aid station. There is little room for sentiment in the cold world of ultra-marathons. It was there we stocked up and realised that there was an outside chance of breaking ten hours if we could manage to grit our teeth and put together a few quicker miles. We managed this for approximately 500 yards across a flat field before both calling a halt to such energetic movement. By now Ben and I were shuffling wrecks, although the next uphill section revealed I was in slightly better condition than my friend as he declared he was giving up and calling a taxi, despite being within five miles of the end. For a short while I implored him to press on and spouted as many clichés as I could about the permanence of giving up compared with the transience of pain, together with telling him that he would not be fit to raise children if he quit on this field here and now. It was to no avail and I eventually decided to lose him, lest the appeal of quitting rub off on me.

It was not a pretty last few miles, although I somehow found reserves of energy to finish the last mile in reasonable style and at a decent pace. The overall time of **10 hours 40 minutes** was not impressive, but completely academic to me as I sat broken in the sports hall waiting for my two companions to hopefully finish. As it was, Ben's girlfriend arrived before him and happily confirmed that Ben was still out there and moving, as she had seen him a couple of miles from the finish. We waited and waited and eventually a husk of the athlete formerly know as Benjamin Collard trudged into the sports hall looking utterly fed up with life, although at least he had finished. It transpired that he had been talked out of calling a cab by one of the oldest competitors in the field – a 60-something year old lady who had at some point held the world record for the furthest distance covered in a 24 hour period. Her bowed legs and arched back suggested that her achievement had come at a price which may not be worth paying. Anyway, I was pleased we had all finished although, as with my first ever marathon, as I sat in excruciating pain in the sports hall in Rotherham, I vowed that I had just completed my first and last ultra-marathon…Time was to make a lie out of this utterance…

14

APELDOORN, NETHERLANDS (MIDWINTER MARATHON) 2012

Yet another marathon which fits nicely into the title of this book.

In my defence, I was labouring under the assumption that the marathon would be cancelled. This was on the basis that I arrived in Amsterdam at 6:30am on Sunday morning to find the city covered thickly in snow and temperatures well below freezing. I checked the Midwinter Marathon website which had no updates but was still in two minds as to whether to travel across town to catch a train for the hour or so journey to the location of the marathon as I thought there was no way it could be on.

The thick white covering of snow did not let up as we headed east bound out of Amsterdam through the Dutch countryside towards Apeldoorn and the weather was causing the train to fall behind schedule, further convincing me that I was embarking on a fruitless journey. It was only when we were forced to change trains about 20 minutes from the target destination and I saw a few other loonies in trainers, carrying kit bags, that I thought there was a chance the run would take place. It was also at this unplanned stop that we were all given coffee to make up for the delay to our train (which was only 20 minutes) - are you listening UK train providers?!

Once we disembarked at the larger than expected town of Apeldoorn, there was no question that the marathon was on as runners were everywhere and there was a free shuttle bus for the mile or so journey from the train station to the start of the marathon. It was at registration that I realised my decision to wear shorts for the race was possibly a foolish one as I was literally the only runner out of thousands not wearing lycra leggings. Compounding my poor kit choice was the fact that I had also left my hat and gloves behind reception at the hotel back in Amsterdam which I had left in a cold, tired haze...

On the basis that I have stood on start lines of many marathons in worse shape (in particular the Isle of Man marathon), I shrugged off the incredible cold and trusted that I would soon warm up once off and running. The quizzical look on other competitors faces when they saw my bare legs suggested they may know better...

Things started well as the marathon tracked through a few streets in the town before heading out down narrow woodland tracks. I had soon warmed up and was going along at a decent enough pace, enjoying the beautiful snow covered surrounds. It was a very short time after the halfway point of the marathon (which I reached in a respectable, if not spectacular, 1 hour 39 minutes) that things started to go wrong. Such was the cold that my hair had frozen and my legs had turned to jelly. I also realised I was incredibly sleepy and would love to have laid down for a quick nap. I had never quite experienced a sensation like this during a marathon (despite various other manner of mini-disasters) and, when I decided to walk for a while at the next drink station to take on water, tea and bananas, I was not sure if my legs would ever get going again as they were full of cold and felt very wobbly. My mind was also shot, and none of this was looking good with still nearly 15 kilometres to go to the end. I was still with it enough to realise that standing still for any great period of time in a remote forest in the Netherlands in minus temperatures had no future...

For the remaining 15 kilometres, it was a huge battle, even with plenty of fellow runners (who were all passing me by this point) shouting encouragement to me (in Dutch - on account of my blonde hair and the low number of overseas' competitors it was their fair assumption that I was Dutch). I thought I may still have enough in the tank to put in a decent last couple of kilometres, hoping that the mercy offered by the finish line and promise of warmth would spur me on. It was not to be. This was even despite the presence of a

Dutch man who decided to ride alongside me for the last 1,000 metres, screaming at me in Dutch every time I looked like I was slowing down. I still stopped a couple of times in that short stretch and from the exasperation in his voice can only speculate how pathetic a specimen he thought I was. I didn't care. I was incredibly cold. My face and hair were completely frozen. I thought I may collapse at any point. I just wanted warmth and food and he could go Flem himself for all I cared...

As I crossed the finish line (in about **3 hours 50 mins** I think – I didn't care less by this point), I staggered sideways and had to cling onto the barrier for a few minutes to avoid collapsing on the spot. When I finally managed to wobble my way back to the registration centre I couldn't talk. I spent the remainder of the afternoon, including the train journey back to Amsterdam, shower and change at the hotel and dinner near the hotel, steadily recovering my basic human skills, like a man awakening from a period in a coma. Never again ('til next time)...

The Down Under Years

15

HUNTER VALLEY 2012

The start of 2012 saw me set out on an adventure to a brave new world. After a few months spent living in Thailand and travelling around South East Asia, it was time to start a new life in Australia. It turned out to be a move that would result in a significant upturn in my running, for reasons I have never fully understood, although perhaps the nearly guaranteed 300 plus days per year of sunshine were a factor...

The 2:30am alarm on Sunday morning after going to bed at 11:30pm on Saturday night at the rented apartment in Ultimo, Sydney, was about as welcome as a nasty itch downstairs and raised the question of whether it is better to have very little sleep or no sleep at all.

I somehow managed to raise myself from slumber, slam down a couple of coffees and head to the hire car – comparable in responsibility to being asked to look after someone else's child - to make the journey northbound. I thought briefly that I may have slipped through a wormhole back to the UK, as I found myself heading northbound towards Newcastle in driving rain, but this was not the case and I reached Cessnock - near the marathon start point - at 5:15 am. I decided that one final calorific hit was in order and so it was that at 5:30 am I was start in the car park at McDonalds' Drive Thru scoffing a Bacon McMuffin - the choice of Olympians. The wisdom of this was questionable and proved to be undeniably flawed when one hour later (30 minutes before the start of the run) I was sat in a portaloo having what can only be described as a *"McSplurry"*...Not good, but nothing to stop me running.

Conditions for the marathon were decidedly British, i.e. dreary and cold - good for marathon running but not typically good for a wedding, which must have created a contradiction for one young couple who it was announced would be stopping at the halfway point of the marathon for their nuptials.

As for the marathon, it started pleasantly enough, weaving through the grounds of the picturesque Hunter Valley Gardens and a number of vineyards before heading out on a fairly dull, undulating stretch of road at the end of which we were required to double back on ourselves. The only bonus this provided was that I ran past the soon to be bride and groom in the return section, and was amused to see a group of smartly clad wedding guests cycling along beside them. True dedication. The scenery throughout was stunning and I twice caught sight of groups of kangaroos - a first for me in marathons. Having seen their speed of bouncing I would also have liked to have tagged Skippy into the action to run a few kilometres on my behalf.

I had run a handful of times in the month following a minor Thai "motorbike" (scooter) accident of my own creation, but despite that my body held up quite well for the first half and I felt relatively optimistic about life. However, shortly into the second half (another loop of the first - always a little depressing), various parts began to cease up and the heavens opened as we reached the steepest section of the course. I decided that I would not lose much by walking this short but painful ascent and from then on adopted the approach of running the downhill sections and walking the uphill parts. This led to lots of leapfrogging of positions with those who determinedly insisted on trotting at a steady pace throughout. The end - as always - was a mighty relief although it was slightly tarnished when I realised that the people who had completed the 10km jog/walk also taking place were receiving exactly the same medal, t-shirt and goody bag as we fools who had run 42.2 km's. A bitter pill indeed. Having checked the result today it transpires that I finished in **3 hours 43 minutes and 40 seconds**, finishing 28th out of 131 marathon runners. Acceptable for the first lengthy run since February (a run which entailed a lengthy pursuit by several wild dogs in the Thai countryside, and potential world record pace during such pursuit)...

16

AUSTRALIAN OUTBACK MARATHON 2012

The Thursday night before the flight to Ayer's Rock featured a dinner party. The food and company were great and the wine flowed with Bacchanalian gusto, but was fortunately capped at five bottles between the four guests, meaning that I was not able to completely self-destruct...

Friday started with an event free journey to Sydney Airport. I had expected to be slightly later so had plenty of time to pass at the airport and – remembering I was a member of the Qantas Frequent Flyer program from my 2008 travelling days – decided to try and gain access to the Qantas Lounge where I assumed there would be free coffee. Alas, I was told that Bronze members were not welcome – loyalty point grading is 21st century Apartheid – and was forced to hang with my own caste over a Hungry Jack's coffee.

As some of you may be aware, Australia is big, so big in fact that the first of the two flights I would need to reach Ayer's Rock was long enough to watch The Hunger Games and an episode of An Idiot Abroad. Big. That flight got me as far as Alice Springs, at which point I had to change planes for the final 45 minute leg of the journey. Everything had run smoothly and there was time for me to check-in to the Outback Pioneer Hotel – average – before wandering across the resort to the central square where the welcome to the third ever Outback Marathon would take place.

The supposed highlight of this welcome ceremony was a traditional dance by the indigenous Aborigines. This consisted of a group of mainly elderly Aborigines with wooden instruments sitting on the floor facing a semicircular stage of red earth. As they started clacking together their instruments, including boomerangs, and singing in a haunting but not unpleasant fashion, the stage remained empty and all that could be heard was excited bird-like arguing behind a screen at the back. Eventually, a middle aged Aboriginal woman with large exposed breasts dangling down to her waist shuffled out to the back of the stage and began fidgeting from foot to foot, looking thoroughly unconvinced about what she was up to. There followed a similar display by three women, one of whom looked incredibly old, and another by another solo female performer. The best was saved until last when an elderly white bearded chap – the Aboriginal Father Christmas maybe? – took to the stage and put on an altogether more convincing display, helped by two branches which he swung around as if gently swatting flies whilst strutting through his number. In summary, if Danny Boyle found himself at a loose end post the London Olympics then I'm sure his creative input could be used here.

After the opening ceremony, we runners all headed for a carbo loading dinner at the nearby Sails Restaurant in the Desert Hotel. The food was actually very good, albeit it is always depressing to reflect that it probably takes around 45 minutes of hard running to burn off the calories contained in one slice of chocolate cake (and I had three). All of the runners had very conscientiously retired to bed by 8pm so I took the half a kilometre or so walk back to my accommodation, only to find that life was altogether livelier at my end of the resort. There was a full bar and live music so I decided a couple of medicinal pints would ensure an unbroken night's sleep ahead of the marathon. Remarkably, I did manage to stick to the two pints rule and woke up at 5:30am feeling ready to go, especially after taking in an enormous fried breakfast and an hour of the London Olympics opening ceremony for inspiration...

It was unbelievably cold at the start area, which had the pastel orange of Ayer's Rock providing a beautiful back drop to proceedings, and I was happy to get running at 7:45am to warm up. The track was pretty sandy at the start – not ideal if one has the after effects of a previous marathon still burning in the thighs – but I was sure most of the run would be on sealed roads so was not too worried. This turned out to be entirely wrong and whenever there was any elevation in the course the sand became even deeper and it was like running on sand dunes. I had also compounded my problems by front loading my iPod playlist with trance music, which meant that I ran far too fast for around 10 kilometres before having to grit my teeth and hang on in there for the next 32 as Snow Patrol and other more chilled musical accompaniment took over. The scenery was incredible – like being on another planet or in some sort of post-apocalyptic landscape, especially where controlled burning of the foliage had taken place leaving the ground charred black next to the deep rustic colour of the sand. There was also a helicopter circling to take photographs of the runners in the first few kilometres, making me feel like OJ Simpson. Anyway, I somehow managed to hold things together – even though the sand started to feel like quicksand in the second half as my legs became heavier and heavier. It was all in all a once in a lifetime experience, with the only disappointment being that the course did not get closer to Ayer's Rock than the distance at which the race had started, due to National Park access restrictions...

I spent a short time watching other runners come in before heading back to base for a few well-earned beers. The combination of exhaustion and beer was not an invigorating one and I fell asleep in the reading room. I decided to head back to the room for a few hours of proper sleep before heading back to the bar in the evening to toast the day with the other runners.

The benefit of the soft ground, which had made running a nightmare at times, was that my legs felt far less battered than normal after road marathons and I was able to walk closer to an evolved humanoid rather than the usual post-marathon Neanderthal man. Again, the night was all rather civilised and the beers and music stopped at 11:30pm, ending off a memorable day safe in the knowledge that the following day would not be too painful...

17

BRISBANE 2012

The 3:30am alarm on Sunday morning capped off a truly hideous couple of days of build up to the Brisbane Marathon. The breakfast of Aldi ham and cheese muffins, a Snickers and a couple of ibuprofen to ease the pain in my Micra shortened leg muscles did little to lift my spirits...

I did however quite enjoy walking through the dark streets of Brisbane, which were deserted save for the familiar fallout of a Saturday night – including panda eyed young girls sitting on the pavement puking whilst friends comforted them and young men propping themselves up on bus stands by their heads, whilst sending texts they would no doubt regret in the harsh light of sobriety. I have stumbled in all of your alcohol sodden shoes and will do again you marvellous escapists. It is only from the gutter one may fully appreciate the stars. Drink on...

Anyway, I walked beneath the historic Story Bridge, like a mini Brooklyn Bridge, attractively lit with countless lightbulbs, and from there descended to walk around the boardwalk which sits a short way above the broad Brisbane River. I located the marathon congregation point – the Botanical Gardens – at around 4:45am, clearly way too early for everyone there and still pretty cold and was soon registered and laying back down trying to steal a last few minutes rest before the run. There was a short walk back through the Gardens to Alice Street for the start of the run, which started just after daylight and which soon had us all climbing onto Story Bridge, which looked less attractive when approached uphill with a pounding heart, strongly resenting such hard graft at an unfeasibly early hour. Things improved once we swung back down onto the banks of the Bris River, which the course then hugged for most of first half, only deviating for the odd up and down section. I had spent the bulk of the first half being "motivated" by the 1 hour 40 minute half marathon pace marker, only losing him towards the 12 mile mark. By now my legs were screaming with lactic acid and it was clear that I had paced my race very badly – one could argue that this was race imitating life; a fast start, uncertain and painful middle and limping, pathetic finish. Fortunately those chapters of life remain to be written, but they were written in respect of the marathon. I managed to plod along until around 27 kilometres – at which point the pacer for a 3 hour 30 minute marathon passed me, her perky balloons in stark contrast to my deflated spirit – and from then on I stopped at each of the enthusiastically staffed drinks stations to take on as much fluid as possible. By 9am, the sun was firmly out and hotter than it has been at any time since I had arrived in Australia and I could understand why the race had started so horribly early.

Something finally clicked in my competitive spirit when a 70-something year old chap who was nearly bent double shuffled past me with about five kilometres left and I managed to hobble round him and keep going for the remainder of the marathon to finish in a time of **3 hours 37 minutes and 48 seconds**, putting me a moderate 115th out of 429 finishers. This did mean that somehow it was the fastest marathon of the three I completed in three pain filled weeks in Australia. The finish brought a number of treats to go with the sheer relief of the ordeal being over, including a Mizuno towel, water bottle and all sorts of sugary food. I wolfed them down gratefully before struggling the few kilometres back to Fortitude Valley, enjoying the view much less this time...

18

BRIBIE BEACH BASH 2012

Bribie Beach Bash 2012 stands alone as the most bizarre event in which I have participated. It took a huge effort to propel my body out of bed at the sounding of the 3:30am alarm on Sunday morning to start preparing for the 42km run. The key element of this is applying freeze gel to my legs, which has the dual effects of: (1) soothing the mild sunburn this foolish English rose has on his thighs after falling asleep in the blistering Queensland spring heat on Saturday afternoon with inadequate sun protection applied; and (2) hopefully numbing the pain that will be coursing through every sinew in about five hours time...

My journey to Bribie was either perfectly timed, or recklessly risky, depending on how relaxed one is about having time to get sorted pre-race. I had arrived at 5:25 am, twenty minutes before the start of the marathon, and quickly headed for the three lightweight gazebos which constituted the "Athlete's Village". I was slightly perplexed by the lack of fellow competitors, but this was explained by the fact that there were only **three** of us running the marathon (most sensible folk had opted for the half marathon or shorter). On the plus side, this meant I was certain of a podium finish, provided that I could shuffle along for 42 kilometres, but on the downside meant there was a distinct possibility of finishing last. I needn't have worried as I met my "opponents" at the start line to find that one was a veteran of seven marathons, but had yet to break five hours, and the other was a marathon debutant. I was the favourite!

It was an absolute stunning morning already as we trotted a short distance through some thick sand before reaching the hard sand of the north beach of Bribie Island, which the sun had just started to transform from the gentle pastel shades of a Monet to the vivid colours of a contemporary masterpiece. The race would consist of a 21 kilometre southbound run followed by a turn and the same 21 kilometres back – potentially a little monotonous but at least there was little chance of getting lost.

I set off at a steady trot which was enough to move me away from my fellow marathoners, who I would only see once again during the day. The sand below the feet was firm, which made life easier, but with enough cushioning to soften the usual impact on the joints. I did not see another human being for about the next hour, when I passed a dog walker and a few people starting to have fun on the beach in 4×4 vehicles. My company for the journey was therefore the wildlife – there were a couple of sea eagles circling hopefully above a small campsite, a kangaroo bouncing along the scrubland above the beach, and loads of the usual suspects (mainly seagulls) – and my iPod music, an eclectic mix of classic and modern greats, including Beethoven, Gaga, Kris Kros and Girls Aloud. A brief scan behind me at the 10 kilometre mark revealed that the other two runners had become tiny dots on the horizon, meaning that all I had to do to win was plod around and not pass out from heatstroke. The increasing heat and stiff head breeze were the main challenges during the first half, during which we headed towards a distant modern skyline, in stark contrast to the simplicity of the beach. My mind started to wander to all sorts of subjects, including the fact that I was a modern day explorer, heading towards the distant City of Oz, along the yellow sand road, lacking heart, brain and courage…

The halfway turn was hugely welcome for all sorts of reasons. It meant that I was 50% of the way through the endeavours of the morning; that the scenery would change slightly, in so much as the sea would go from being on my right hand side, to the left; and, most importantly, it also meant that the breeze would switch from being a hindrance to a help. Unfortunately, the flip side of this latter news was that I started to overheat rapidly. This was compounded by the fact that I had decided to wear all black, which may be slimming and stylish, but has all of the wrong properties on a hot morning. Making matters worse was that event organiser Geoff, in his wisdom, had neglected to put any drinks stations between the 21 kilometre and

31.5 kilometre markers, meaning that I was becoming dangerously dehydrated. I blame this for my decision to break from my steady jogging rhythm and to begin to alternate between walking and running, but this may actually be explained by my Tinman-esque lack of heart. Anyway, when the water station finally arrived I felt slightly rejuvenated and managed to slip back into a moderate stride, which was aided further when I was again able to mingle with other humans as I reached the stragglers in the fields of the half marathon and shorter event runners. The tide had by now started to come in though, meaning that the sand became a bit soggy and the going – particularly with heavy, sun burned legs – a bit tough.

My finish was utterly unspectacular as I struggled back uphill through the short thick, loose sand of the pathway which led the way to the finish line at which I was met with utter indifference by the small group of people there, who had no way of knowing what event I had run. It was about 9:30am by now, meaning that I had completed the marathon in just over **3 hours 46 minutes**. After sinking a few energy drinks to start the recovery process, I headed straight to the car to drive back and muse (over a delicious pie – excellent athlete fodder) on whether Bribie Beach Bash was an IAAF recognised event, the winning of which would give me automatic qualification for the 2016 Rio Olympics. I suspected not…

19

TOOWOOMBA 2012

Thanks to the cushioning impact of the Bribie Island sand, my body had recovered remarkably well from the marathon the previous Sunday, to the extent that I was even able to complete short training runs on Wednesday, Thursday and Friday. Sadly, my otherwise diligent preparation went somewhat out of the window on Friday evening when I decided a night of carbo-loading on beer, rather than the traditional pasta, was in order. The fog which engulfed my brain and body on Saturday confirmed that, like men, not all carbs are born equal and the mist had not really cleared by the time I had to drag my body out of bed at 2am on Sunday morning for the drive to Toowoomba.

Aside from a few problems finding my way out of Brisbane, the drive to Toowoomba, under a beautifully clear and starry sky went smoothly and I arrived at campus of the University of Southern Queensland at 4:30am, slightly shocked by the cold air when I left the warmth of the car to pick up my race number. I quickly retreated to the comfort of the car and managed to steal a few more minutes' precious sleep before taking my place on the start line at 5:30am with 39 other lunatics for the Toowoomba marathon. The marathon had been brought forward from the previous year's start time as unseasonably hot weather had apparently meant that three runners needed hospital treatment. This is exactly what one wants to be thinking about when standing on the start line feeling a little sketchy. Anyway, this time around the conditions were perfect – a beautiful clear morning and a pleasant cooling 9 degrees to start the run.

On the basis that I was generally feeling tired, and expected the efforts of the week before to impact on my body at some point, I decided on the primitive approach of running as fast as I could before the inevitable disintegration of my body. After five kilometres, this meant that I was right on the leader's heels, where I still found myself after 10km – having run that distance in less than 40 minutes, way faster than ever before in my life. The marathon was divided into four loops of the same circuit of just over 10 kilometres and it was during the second loop that my legs began to stiffen, although I did manage to hold on and complete the first half of the marathon in around 1 hour 30 minutes (again, comfortably a personal best).

Loop three was probably the worst of the event, and I began to go dramatically backwards through the field, with every minor incline feeling like Everest to my failing body. As I passed the finish line for the third time still with over 10 kilometres to go, the temptation to stop was almost irresistible but I persevered...

For some reason the final lap passed with relative ease, especially once I had struck upon a new strategy of running on the flat and downhill sections and walking on the uphill sections. This also gave me a chance to take in some of the impressive scenery offered by Toowoomba's elevated position (although one may describe this as clutching at the proverbial straws). I had stopped the rot somewhat and reached the end in a time of **3 hours 28 minutes** (on the official race clock), for a finishing position of 11th out of 40 (a way more realistic reflection of my abilities than the previous week's victory). Either way, not too shabby given the trials and tribulations of the day, which had seen plenty of blood (from a blister picked up the previous Sunday) and sweat, but no tears (which were to come further down the line)...

20

WASHPOOL ULTRA 2012

After the relative success of the marathons on the previous two weekends, it was time for the challenge to go ultra, which it ultimately did in every sense of the word...

Proceedings started smoothly enough when, after loading up an eskie with carbohydrate-rich food and energy drinks, I left Brisbane at around 11am on Saturday morning, bound for Washpool National Park. The drive down was pleasant, allowing me to take in plenty of impressive sights, including the Great Dividing Range, the Big Apple, Bluff Rock and the Standing Stones at Glen Innes (by which time I had crossed into a different time zone between Queensland and New South Wales, thanks to Daylight Saving Time).

There were a couple more treats in store on arrival into Gibraltar Range National Park as I took in Boundary Falls and the Raspberry Lookout, before making my way down about 10 kilometres of dusty dirt track to Mulligan's picnic point, from where Sunday's ultra marathon would commence. It was by now around 7pm and just thinking about going dark, so I set up my makeshift bed in the back of the Honda Jazz and settled in for the night. The dimensions of the Jazz were probably about 10 centimetres short of allowing me to stretch out fully, and so I spent a slightly uncomfortable night shifting between various iterations of the fetus position and waking up regularly, always to one of the most incredible starry skies I have even witnessed. First light arrived at about 6am and it was only when I stood up out of the car for the first time that I recognised the drawbacks of my accommodation, which had left me fairly stiff. My appearance from the car did cause quite a bit of amusement amongst the other runners, all of whom had spent the night in a variety of camping shelters. Little did they know it was the best night's sleep I had managed for any of my past three events...

By 7:20am I was down at Mulligan's Hut, ready for action, having carbo-loaded, sun-creamed and applied copious amounts of freeze spray to various parts of my body. The event organiser, Greg, was delivering a race briefing, which ran through the course twice and pointed out that it was possible to get lost (I briefly scanned my fellow runners to try and work out to which fools this unnecessary warning was being directed). My scan of the other 30 or so runners also revealed that I appeared to be the only runner without a backpack, but again my lack of provisions did not worry me as I was only planning to be out there for five and a half hours or so, and there were four drinks stations on the course. It took a few kilometres to iron out the tightness in my legs but I was soon trotting along at a decent pace, through some stunning countryside, and feeling generally positive about the event. By the first checkpoint (after about 12 kilometres) I was placed fourth, although the leading trio had long since disappeared from view, and I maintained this lofty position during a blissful descent through woodland tracks.

Unfortunately in these events, what goes down must come up and I was slowed dramatically by a long steady incline through the woods, although I was still in fourth place as we neared halfway. It was around this time that I jogged passed an innocuous sign off to the left to Grassy Creek. This didn't ring a bell so I merrily continued on my way, by now alternating between steady running on the flat and downhill sections and hard walking on the hills. I was slightly surprised to have not been passed after adopting these tactics and that, in fact, I had not seen another human being for at least a couple of hours. I was expecting the 35 kilometre checkpoint around each bend of the track but it refused to materialise and it was only when I stumbled on a locked gate blocking my path that I accepted something must have gone wrong. Initially I was so determined that this was not the case that I actually climbed the gate and continued for a short while, before accepting that I had gone the wrong way, and probably now had around 10 kilometres of retracing my steps to return to the Grassy Creek sign, which must have been the course route. I have to admit that as I trudged back through the woods I shouted several fairly choice (*"French"*?) screams into the wilderness. As if my current predicament wasn't bad enough, it was starting to get incredibly warm and I had not had anything to drink for over two hours, and faced the prospect of having nothing to drink for another two hours. It was at this point that a dingo stepped onto the path in front of me, which was not exactly what the doctor ordered but I think that his sixth sense kicked in and he saw from my deranged eyes that he was facing a man capable of anything at this point. I was beginning to lose hope, particularly as there was no way of sending a message to the organisers, or getting to a road/civilization, when another runner– Gary – appeared. I had to break the news to him that he was also on the wrong path, but he sounded like a man who had faced such travails before and turned out to be a decent companion on the walk back to the course. A short while after meeting Greg, we collected a third runner, Bridgette, who had made the same mistake. I have to say that it was a slight relief that Bridgette turned out to be Australian (as Gary was from Liverpool, meaning that it had appeared to be a Brits' only cock up until this point).

Once we reached the accursed Grassy Creek sign, I said my thank yous and goodbyes to Gary and Bridgette – who had also spared me a small amount of water – and set about finishing the run. It was a pretty unedifying thought that I would pretty much have been finished had I not gone wrong, but instead had nearly 25 kilometres of pain to go. After a promising second wind, I quickly began to run out of gas, which was not too surprising given that by now I had not eaten for over five hours and was also fairly dehydrated. The latter problem was dealt with to a point by me kneeling down every time I crossed a creek and lapping up the water like a dog. It was a bit of a life low point, and certain of the creeks looked more appealing than others (Tin Ore Creek was particularly dubious in name and colour), but I had a stark choice between dehydration and potential stomach cramps and opted for the latter. Thankfully, I suffered no side effects and my efforts had also been aided by some cloud cover, which meant a merciful drop in temperature. The course however was not so accommodating and this section proved to be its most brutal, with several steep climbs up uneven surfaces. I had lost count of the number of times I had stubbed my toes, which were numb, and the back of both heels were streaming with blood caused by logs kicking up against them as I struggled to lift my tired feet.

It is a close call as to who was most relieved when I reached the third checkpoint, at around the 37 kilometre mark. The event organiser had come out, having heard that entrant 530 had disappeared from fourth place to **M**issing **I**n **A**ction and seemed genuinely delighted to see me. He asked to be de-briefed on what had gone wrong. I explained that it was probably my fault, and that the other two MIAs were safely back on track somewhere behind and that all was good. He suggested that, as I had probably done 52 kilometres already, I could get in his car and be escorted to the finish line (I think this may partially have been driven by him wanting to go home). This was so very tempting, but his kind offer had something of the feel of Eve offering the apple to Adam in terms of the likelihood of me ever completing an event in future if I gave up now, so I thanked him, shoved down as many energy drinks and lollies as I could and shuffled on…

The first food I had consumed for six and a half hours had an immediate impact and I trotted on with renewed optimism – albeit with the gait of a drunkard – for the next few kilometres, which were primarily downhill. Another physical wall appeared soon enough and I was regretting my decision not to have accepted a lift within about 20 minutes of checkpoint three. There wasn't any part of my lower body which was not in a significant amount of pain by this point and I also felt mentally shot. I only recovered upon reaching a sign which told me that Mulligan's Hut was just 6.4 kilometres away, meaning this should all be over in around 40 minutes. There was still time to encounter a very small (hell, no one else was there, a GIGANTIC) snake in my path, before putting in the definition of a futile sprint finish as the organisers dismantled the finish area. It had taken me (pretty pathetically) just under **8 and a half hours** to complete what was probably around 70 kilometres. It transpired that Gary and Bridgette had accepted the offer of a lift, which meant I was the last finisher and I also had the prospect of a five and a half hour drive back to Brisbane on completely broken legs. I had at least learnt a couple of things during the prolonged misery – (1) my iPod Shuffle has better battery life than its owner (as it was still playing away merrily by the time I finished); and (2) having previously questioned the ethics of McDonalds sponsoring sport, the only thing which kept me going for the last hour or so was the thought of a Big Mac meal, so maybe there's something in it after all…

21

SOLAR ECLIPSE MARATHON (PORT DOUGLAS) 2012

I left the office just before midday on the Tuesday to start my northbound journey to Port Douglas. For once, everything ran like clockwork with each leg of the journey and I was sat in the shuttle bus from Cairns Airport to Port Douglas by 4:30pm, as we followed the attractive coastal road as it wound its way beside the turquoise ocean through lush countryside and tropical rain forests. I was quite relieved to be the last passenger to be dropped off in Port Douglas, as my fellow passengers (a young couple and a trio of South East Asian women) disembarked at the Ramada and Rendezvous Reef Resort respectively, whilst I was bound for the somewhat less salubrious surrounds of Dougie's Backpackers. That said, it was probably one of the nicest hostels I have stayed in, boasting a swimming pool, large bar area and clean spacious rooms. Less pleasing was the enormous Golden Orb spider perched above the door to my room. I was assured that this arachnid beast is harmless to humans, to which my question is *"why would something harmless be made to look so creepy?"*

More super sized nature was to follow as the skies were filled with tens and tens of huge fruit bats as I wandered into the town centre in the evening to load up on carbs. Between the bats and the spider, I felt like I was the main protagonist at the start of a Marvel Comics film, although it would probably have been most useful to be bitten by an ant or a cockroach and imbued with some of their superior characteristics given the challenge which lay ahead. Back at the hostel I was on the top bunk in a room of four, two of whom were intent on an early night to ensure they were up for the Eclipse. As a result the lights were out in our room at a scarcely believable

8:30pm, although this did not wash well with our fourth room mate who staggered in after a few beers, exclaimed that we were all boring ****s, before wobbling back out into the night, never to return. I saw a lot of myself in that young man and wish him well.

After a turbulent few hours of broken sleep, filled with nightmares of spiders, the 4:00am alarm was actually quite welcome and I set off on the few kilometre walk (Dougie's was not well placed in this respect) to the start of the Solar Eclipse Marathon, on Four Mile Beach. The beach was already littered with people jostling for the best position to watch this rare solar event, although the thickish cloud cover did not look promising. By 6:30am, the beach was almost full as far as the eye could see with people wearing dark glasses and staring hopefully towards the still cloud obscured sun. As the eclipse started, the clouds began to clear, to widespread cheering across the beach, only for clouds to drift back into the picture to universal booing (as a Brit I am familiar with just how shy the sun can be). This pattern of cheering and booing continued for the next couple of minutes and was probably the highlight of the spectacle, together with the eerie silence which accompanied the black out. Some cultures attribute solar eclipses to supernatural causes or regard them as bad omens, and I was hoping this was not the case for me as I took my place on the start line of the marathon amongst a diverse league of nations.

What was bad news for eclipse enthusiasts was good news for marathon runners as the cloud cover meant pleasantly cool conditions in which to commence the run. The main conversation amongst participants and locals about the run centred on the "Bump Track", an old mining track which ascends very steeply for around four kilometres into the rain forest (see below).

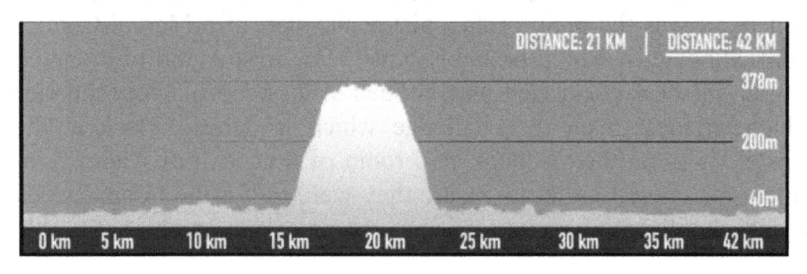

The Bump Track would be reached after 15 kilometres of undulating running primarily on sealed roads, which meant that my tactics were to run as quickly as possible until the Bump Track, which I would then walk up. Things started well enough and I was in second place after 10 kilometres (the leader long since having become a dot in the distance), when some conflicting course map arrows meant I had to stop and wait for the next few runners to confirm the route (I did not want a repeat of the nightmare in Washpool). By this point the cloud cover had all but disappeared and I was beginning to struggle slightly, meaning that this pack of runners soon passed me and vanished up the road. I suspect that more would have followed were it not for the fact that I now reached the infamous Bump Track, which was probably even more severe than I had feared or be warned. I could not imagine any human being running up this and myself settled for just trying to walk up it as fast as possible. It was still painful. Really painful. To make matters worse my trusty iPod, which had outlasted me in Washpool, chose this moment to make a crackly exit from this world, leaving me alone and up against it in the rain forest. By the time I reached the summit, the leader and about eight others had already looped round and passed me on their descent and it was a huge relief when I was able to do the same, particularly as I excel at running (and cycling) downhill (which is far from a claim to fame)…

A time check at the water station at the bottom of the Bump Track indicated that I had chalked off 23 kilometres in just under two hours, which was OK in the circumstances. Unfortunately, the reality was that I was pretty much out of gas, and it was getting hotter and hotter. The bulk of the second half of the run was through sugar cane fields. The incredibly vibrant green colour and beautiful scenery did not compensate for the fact that there was absolutely no shade, which I needed urgently. I battled on, walking up any hills and jogging on the flat and downhill, just waiting for the next swathe of people to pass me, but it never happened. It looked like being a respectable placing despite my travails. Then, at the 41 kilometre mark, I took a cursory look over my shoulder to see a few runners bearing down on me. Despite the fact that I was spent and the finishing position is irrelevant (unless you are the guy at the front), from somewhere I felt a surge of determination not to be overtaken and managed to accelerate down Macrossan Street – the main shopping and restaurant street in town – to the finish line in Rex Smeal Park, and in doing so held on to finish in 7th place (out of about 240) despite a disappointing time of **3 hours 55 minutes and 52 seconds**. There is always the nagging doubt at the end of a marathon as to whether you could have put in more effort but I think the fact that within an hour of finishing I was being violently sick in the toilet back at the hostel probably indicates on this occasion, I gave it all I had.

22

NERANG ULTRA 2013

Our morning boot camp instructor had rather ramped up the intensity of our twice weekly sessions and, whilst my legs can cope with the running drills, the upper body exercises have exposed the debilitating effects of a career lifting nothing heavier than the odd 100-page document and pen. Devolution?

By the time I went to bed on Sunday morning, at about 2am, I didn't actually know where the event was or what time it started (I guessed 7am). It turned out that the race was 80km south and starting at 6am, meaning I had just over two hours of sleep to charge the batteries...

At least by now I had a sat nav, but it transpired that sat navs are subject to human error and I had inputted the wrong street starting with "Ho" in Nerang, leading to a nerve racking scramble across the small town to arrive at Nerang velodrome for 5:50am, ten minutes before the race start, and still yet to register. Down at the damp start line were the usual array of either 30-somethings carrying less body fat than supermodels or slightly deranged looking 50-something's who dominate these events. All were laden with back packs, drink bottles and gels in some sort of budget batman style utility belt for gimps...

I took my place amongst this bizarre cast, and we were off, trotting into the trails of the national park for two 25 km laps, both of which would be under the welcome shade of thick forest. The soil track had been soaked with weeks of unseasonal rain and I slipped and slid around as we initially climbed up gently inclining paths. The going was OK and conditions great –cool and fresh – and I was actually quite enjoying the run, especially the descents. Things soon became somewhat more challenging though as slippery descents led to knee deep muddy creeks, followed by seemingly vertical climbs on the other side. The worst of these had been labeled 'Heartbreak Hill' with a handmade sign, and the race photographer had cruelly been positioned there, making for plenty of shots of muddy, depressed looking fools on their hands and knees.

The highlight of the first lap was a large kangaroo bouncing across my path and the drinks break at 12.5 kilometres – my first sustenance for the 1 hour 10 minutes it had taken me to get there. I still felt in pretty good shape by the end of the 25km first loop, 1 hour and 10 minutes later, although what had felt like a minor incline shortly after the start/finish line first time round now felt like a minor mountain. I opted for the usual strategy of walking uphill and running on the flats and down, although my definition of "uphill" by the end was basically anything other than a steep descent. This third quarter was probably the most miserable of the day as it began to get hotter and my approach of having brought no food or drink finally looked flawed. The consequence was that the sweets which I greedily scoffed down at the 37.5 kilometre checkpoint had the restorative powers of lembas cake to a Frodo, or EPO to a Lance…The final quarter was only more bearable than the one which had gone before because it brought with it the hope of finishing within 90 minutes or so. During this time, I was passed twice – deservedly so – by gentlemen who were actually trying to run regardless of topography, although there was a period of leapfrog with each of them as my special skill of running downhill swiftly carried me past then a couple of times, until their steady graft eventually took them out of sight. By the time the final descent to home began, I had lost count of the number of times my increasingly heavy and soaking wet feet had kicked the back of the opposite leg and, when I very nearly stacked it into the thick mud, I decided a slow trudge to the end was in order.

It had been a destructive ordeal, but I had held on for a respectable time of **5 hours 6 minutes**, and tenth place (out of about 50 competitors). All in all, a tiring but oddly satisfying experience…

23

YULEBA 2013

It would be fair to describe Saturday, 27 April 2013 as a busy day.

The alarm sounded at 12.30am, around three hours of patchy sleep after I'd climbed into bed. As a word of advice, I would suggest (particularly for chaps) taking a sleeping pill and settling on the sofa for kip whilst Priscilla Queen of the Desert is on TV is not to be recommended, as I awoke periodically to a couple of bizarre images which informed some equally disturbing dreams.

Having loaded up a flask of coffee, I hit the road – destination, the small outback 'town' of Yuleba (population 212). I had found the marathon on an Australian marathon calendar website, and very quickly assessed the distance using Google maps. Had I grasped the scale of the map I was looking at, I may not have signed up, as the sat nav informed me it was a journey of around 450 kilometres and would take around five hours. The first few hours of the drive were negotiated well enough, save for a scare when the no petrol light flashed on when I was a long way from any towns, which by now were decreasing to settlements of around 10 buildings, including a shop and a pub, and could not guarantee a petrol station. Fortunately, the small town of Oakey offered up a 24 hour Caltex, from inside of which was blasting out some fabulous bhangra music. I also took the opportunity to stock up on chocolate and energy drinks as by now I had drained the entire coffee flask and was feeling fairly alert, if a little sick, but this state gradually eroded, despite the introduction of the high sugared energy gloop. I resorted to every tactic I could to keep going – window open, radio blaring, chewing gum, slapping my face, singing, holding loud conversations in a variety of accents – but have to admit that there were a couple of brief black outs, mercifully on long straight stretches of the deserted roads. Silly boy. Progress had generally been good until the last 150 km or so, when there was the familiar UK frustration of unmanned roadworks requiring me to travel at half the speed limit despite the absence of any workers. Even worse was having to sit at a red light for what felt like hours at a temporary traffic light erected at some works, whilst nothing came the other way.

One way or another, at 5.40am I pulled into Yuleba Golf Club, which was already humming with life. There was a tempting breakfast sizzle in progress; the 25 or so participants in the marathon walk were receiving their race briefing and various folk were delivering goods for the day whilst engaging in good humoured banter. I wandered into the basic surrounds of the wooden golf clubhouse itself and was greeted with smiling faces of the ladies who had organised the event. They could not have been more welcoming, as they enquired about my journey, why I was in Oz and what I thought of it. Having heard about my travel arrangements they suggested that they would notify the first aiders on the course to look out for a collapsed man on the route, which was a nice vote of confidence.

It turned out that only five of us were running the marathon and we were all driven to the start by an old chap named Tony, in a borrowed SUV. He spent the 42 and a bit journey fluctuating between cursing "*f*#king modern cars*", as he struggled with gears and the wing mirrors, and bemoaning the encroachment into the area of large gas companies, who were apparently laying fibre optic cables under the many acres of agricultural land and paying zero compensation to land holders. The other four runners in the car were all local – or had arrived the night before – and so talked about some of the residents as we passed their farms and we also stopped to have a natter through the window to the local policeman – Charlie Brown (I kid you not). After what seemed like a lot further than 42km's we were deposited on a non-descript section of dirt track, with an orange line spray painted across its width. This, and the portaloo to the side of the road – which I subsequently filled will the coffee disturbed contents of my stomach – marked the start of the marathon. Happily, if slightly unnecessarily, the race was started with a hand gun being fired into the air. Given my disturbing lack of sleep, I decided to hit the road as hard as possible as I suspected there would be an inevitable crash once the effects of the gallons of caffeine still in my system wore off.

I was soon well clear of the four other runners, if travelling dangerously too fast, and passed the marathon walkers about 7km into their event before passing through 16 kilometres in around an hour. There were a couple of very minor inclines after this point and my pace markedly began to drop, although I was still going fairly well after 25km, but could now see the luminous yellow bib of Gary, one of the other marathon runners, slowly closing in whenever I turned round. The sad sight of several dead kangaroos and wallabies, which had been mowed down when trying to cross the road, was quite poignant as the outback heat climbed and I really began to struggle at around the 30km point, threatening to add my carcass to the roadkill toll. My resolve finally gave in at the 32km marker and I slowed to a walk as I took on some much needed water. History has taught me that it is almost impossible to regain momentum after stopping, and so it proved again. The luminescent vest of Gary soon came past and vanished into the distance as I struggled home on a familiar walk, run strategy as the sun relentlessly warmed up the day. As I turned back into Yuleba, the sight of the golf club, which I had seemingly arrived at a lifetime ago, gave me the final injection my legs needed and I managed a decent sprint over the last 500 metres to smash my PB by nearly ten minutes, finishing in a time of **3 hours 14 minutes and 57 seconds**.

It all got slightly embarrassing (for me) after this. In order to attract people to the event, the organisers had offered very generous prize money of $500 to the winner, $200 to second place and $100 to third place in every event on the day. This meant that I was summoned onto stage in front of a crowd of about 100 or so to collect my winnings. It transpired that Gary, who had comfortably won the marathon, was a complete legend and he was asked to tell his story to the crowd. He had been in a near fatal car accident in 2002 and told he would never walk again. Since then he has battled back and run several marathons and raised tens of thousands of dollars for charity in the process. Truly humbling stuff. I was asked to follow this with my tale of driving through the night and having to drive back, which all seemed completely trite in comparison to Gary's story, and the hugely worthwhile cause of the day – Help Kids Like Nick. I had long since decided to hand back my $200 prize, for what was in reality just finishing in the top half, as it turned out that one of the five runners had downgraded to the walk having found that his farming shoes were not built for the demands of a full marathon...

Anyway, I had a great time and felt truly welcomed by a small community welcoming in an influx of people and putting on what was a fantastically well organised inaugural event. The drive back was altogether more sensible and I took the time to take in a few of the sights of the countryside on the long, but altogether safer, journey after which I rewarded myself with a couple of beers on the sofa (the second of which ended up mostly on my leg after I passed out mid drink)...

24

GOLD COAST 100 – 2013

The best time to reflect on life adventures is probably when they're at their most fresh, or raw. I wrote my thoughts on the Gold Coast 100 whilst sat in the Burleigh Surf Life Saving Club, a couple of beers to the good (well, at least better), in what could only be described as exquisite agony. If one were to highlight the areas on my body which were screaming in pain, the result would be a red glowing radioactive man. To be fair, my ears did not hurt. Otherwise, the once white socks covering my battered feet were blood soaked; I had searing pain in my left shin, which started around the halfway mark; I had severe stomach cramps, although that may have been a product of only consuming heavily sugared items between 6am and 4:30pm; and every leg muscle was dangerously taut. I was also an emotional wreck – such was my fragility that the sight of an injured bird on the road during the third of the four laps of the event, which was surely conceived in hell, that I started crying, and didn't stop for about 10 minutes. This could have been awkward and damaged my ice man image, were in not for the fact that I was all alone at this point with the field either way, way ahead (majority) or a fairly long way behind and much of the course was on deserted streets.

In the preparation for the "Super Marathon", on Friday evening I got involved in the mandatory end of month drink action, resulting in feeling moderately sketchy on Saturday. This in itself would not have been a problem were it not for the fact that I had to go into the office to finish something if neglected in my eagerness to go play. I found remnants of the previous night's festivities in the communal fridge and helped myself to a splash of wine and cider, both of which had a positive effect on my legal drafting, I think. After that it was all systems go for the Queensland Reds vs British Lions' game.

Booze is as integral to watching rugby as the moon is to night so I saw off four pints of XXXX as I enjoyed a decent game before good sense fortunately prevailed post game and I headed straight home.

The net effect of the above was that I felt less than spritely, or human even, at the 4am alarm call. Somehow I got my game together and was on the road by 4:30am for the hour or so drive to Burleigh Heads. On arrival, I found myself in the company of the usual band of maniacs who participate in these sort of events and, having surveyed the 30 or so 'super marathon' runners, I decided that I would definitely beat at least five of them, which was the extent of my ambition.

The official start time was the slightly vague 'first light' (don't think that would do at the Olympics) and I settled in a group of five or so in the second pack, although we were only a small way behind a largish leading group. The pace was steady and I felt relatively comfortable, if ever so slightly hungover. My rhythm was rudely interrupted by a call of nature after around 10 km's, which moved me into the no mans land referred to above, where I spent most of the next eight hours. There were drinks stations every 2.5km, which was just as well, given my parched condition, and I think I had finally sweated out the booze and replaced it with water and energy drinks as I finished the first 25km loop in just under 2 hours. This was now clearly a solo mission and I decided to take in the sights on the second lap. The route started with a short ascent out of Burleigh Heads before dropping down into Palm Beach. The course then went through a fairly miserable residential stretch before hitting the sea front for the first time after six kilometres, as we again descended, this time down towards Elephant Rock. The next four or so kilometres on the beach front, already busy with surfers, was probably the nicest of the whole loop and I even found time to take a brief detour to pose for a picture with a raunchy sculpture. The lady who took the photo asked why I had a running number on and was surprised to hear that I was participating in a race, until I explained that I was only technically in a race, now being so far behind, so was going to try and enjoy the day out.

Towards the end of lap two, by which time we had completed just in excess of a marathon, the sharp pain in my stomach hit feeling initially like a muscle tear but I think being attributable to the huge amount of sugar I had consumed over the past four and a half hours. Competing with that was a mild pain in my left shin which was forcing me to adopt a lolloping style. As the leading group ran past on their third lap – one of whom was a chap who looked old enough to be my father's father – I was given a few sympathetic looks, as I noted that the field had thinned out slightly with a couple of withdrawals. I was concerned that I may have to add to that number if the competing stomach/leg pains got worse, but for now tried to push thoughts of quitting to the back of my mind as I set off on lap three.

For reasons unknown I had a sudden upsurge in optimism as my rapidly failing brain convinced me that my ailing body could make it 'just' another 50km. Most perturbing of all at this stage was that my iPod had long since offered up all the variety it could and I was now on something like the third rotation of various songs, including one Christmas song which I never, ever want to hear again. This optimism lasted for all of about two songs and it was at this point that I saw the injured bird, which confirmed a worrying mental collapse. It was the support of the volunteers manning the drinks stations which kept me going forward, together with the sugary drinks and lollies, which tasted like heaven.

By the end of this loop, the intervals of running vs walking had become shorter and my left shin was now a constant source of extreme pain, which I was just going to have to deal with. At least the stomach ache had now gone, although the flip side of this was that all my attention was now focused on my sore leg. Not helpful. The mildest incline now felt like a mountain and I was shuffling rather than running to try and limit the impact on my shin bone. It was neither pretty nor enjoyable. The only minor respite came at one of the drinks stations when a man holidaying with his family asked what the run was about. The volunteer told him it was a 100k run, of which I'd completed 95, at which he offered to run in front of me with his beer as a carrot to keep me going. Sadly this was not a serious offer, otherwise I would have leapt at it. A time check at the last drinks station told me that I had a remote chance if breaking ten hours, if I could somehow muster some energy and mental resolve from my shattered reserves. There was no way I could maintain a steady run for 5km as I was completely wrecked but did manage to alternate between 500 metres of reasonably paced running followed by 500 metres of walking for the duration before a decent sprint finish to break the psychologically important – but realistically irrelevant to anyone normal – 10 hour barrier at which point I immediately cramped up in both hamstrings. My final time was actually **9 hours 54 minutes and 30 seconds**, for a finishing place of 13th out of 22 finishers.

The post run beers were an almost spiritual experience, partially because they started to take the edge off my misery although it would have needed a much stronger, more illegal, stimulant to have any real benefit…

The epilogue to all this was a slow but certain deterioration in condition over the next couple of days. On Monday, I had to resort to rolling everywhere in order to get around the apartment, and slowly but surely my left leg took on an angry reddish hue as it steadily ballooned. By the end of a day back in the office on Tuesday it was unsightly and painful enough to persuade me to visit the Royal Brisbane Women's Hospital (for men!). After a nearly two hour wait amongst the usual colourful, and mostly hammered, characters that make up any hospital emergency room anywhere in the world it seems, I was finally being examined. After a second opinion, some blood and urine tests, it was determined that I had probably not done anything too severe, but would be out of action for a while. I took both of these opinions to be very good news!

25

GOLD COAST 2013

Being at the start line of a marathon with sore legs and the traces of a hangover is like being on a float at the start of Rio Carnival, with pasty white skin, uncomfortably small shorts and only a fairly safe, yet physically unsustainable, dance repertoire surrounded by tanned, toned men who know how to work it. One knows that it will not end well…

The sore legs were the result of three and a half weeks forced absence from running following the 'Super Marathon' (see above), which only ended three days before the marathon with two gentle 2.5 kilometre runs to and from work, both of which caused severely tight hamstrings and various other problems. As a general comment, it seems to me a great injustice that fitness which takes months to make can take just days to break. Maybe there is a life metaphor buried in this physical mystery. Maybe not. Anyway, the first gentle jog I undertook after 24 days away from running felt like I had spent the entire intervening period smoking crack through the exhaust pipe of life and living in a cramped cage, causing my muscles to turn from elastic bands into wire. It was truly horrific and nearly enough to warn me off exercise for good, for a more hedonistic life…

Sunday's residual hangover was a product of mild hedonism, in the form of a end of year financial party on the Friday, which ended with this man roaming the streets of Brisbane wearing a pirate hat (not well – Mr Depp can sleep easy), having put in some dancing which made a lie of the 'Máquina de Humo' ('Smoke Machine') – a nickname earned on a brief but eventful tour of Chile a few years previous (and probably contributing further to my injuries). Such were the exertions of Friday that I lay awake for over an hour in bed on Saturday morning agonising (generally, and specifically) over whether to bother making the two hour return trip to the Gold Coast Exhibition Centre to collect my race number. In the end it was the spirit of Yorkshire frugality which tilted the balance. Maybe it was just the old wooden panels or floorboards of the Queenslander property settling, but I could have sworn I heard the whisper of my grandfather's northern tones chastising me for considering kissing goodbye to my non-refundable $120 entry fee. So it was that an hour later that a shady, hungover 30-something year old was loitering, and sweating, suspiciously around the door to the national cheerleader competition (if only Phil Dunphy of *Modern Family* could have been there) before collecting the race pack from the room next door. For good measure a few steadier beers were thrown into the mix on Saturday night to toast the Lions' series victory and compound my problems.

There was another battle of wills when the 4:30am alarm sounded on Sunday morning, but I steeled myself and shuffled on out of the house, trying not to think too hard about what was ahead…

The sun was just raising its beautiful orange head over the still waters of Southport, scene of some shark defying sprint triathlon re-defining breast stroke from the author a few weeks earlier, as I dumped the Honda Jazz and headed towards the already large mass of competitors awaiting the start of the Gold Coast Marathon 2013. As much as I tried to distract myself, there was no escape from the fact that my legs were in bad shape and I was generally in no way marathon fit. As a result of this, I decided that reserve would be the better part of valour and I shuffled back from my sub-3 hour 30 pen to the next one back, hoping to just be able to plod along without inflicting too much damage.

The first half went pretty much according to this hastily concocted plan as I trundled along at pretty much five minute kilometer pace, enjoying the beautiful weather and large crowds who were lining the streets of Surfer's Paradise and beyond. There was also the odd musical interlude and it was the scale and spectacle of the event which proved to be the saving grace. The course was also predominantly flat. I reached halfway at the same steady trot (the leaders already nearly home by now), apparently in just over 1 hour

35 minutes, putting me 542nd out of the 4,828 who would finish apparently. It was at this point that the crap literally hit the plan, as a call of nature – involving a short sprint to a portaloo or "rent a dunny" as it is called in Australia – meant that I was forced to sit down for a short period, giving my legs the chance to cease up and my brain the chance to give up. From here on in it was a complete battle and the pain became far more pronounced with seemingly every step. There was fortunately the odd distraction, including some exotic dancers and a few more bands to help along the way (although I would not describe the guy who was murdering Peter Andre's 'Mysterious Girl' (which I thought not possible) as easing any pain), but it was not pleasant. Just when I thought I was hitting rock bottom, a guy with one leg came past the other way (the course was pretty much an out and back). He was on crutches (obviously), going at a decent pace, and far from last, and this was the inspiration I needed to push through the final 17km. It was far from a run all the way in, although when the crowds really thickened up in the last 2km or so I manage to summon up some sort of misplaced Narcissistic vanity (not easy for a man wearing a white bandage to his left knee, and with hair rusted by sweat and cheap hair dye) to carry me home at a decent pace.

The final result was **3 hours 33 minutes and 10 seconds** – nearly 20 minutes down on my previous marathon, but nevertheless much better than I expected. I had slid fairly spectacularly down the field since the mid-point though, finishing in 930th after barely breaking two hours for the second half…

26

BRISBANE 2013

Welcome to Groundhog Day. Taking you to the same destination via a slightly different journey.

A couple of post stressful work week drinks turned into a slightly bizarre Friday evening. I cut some shapes at Fridays Bar (for the benefit of people in the UK, this is a place where smug people in suits go to get drunk and congratulate themselves on being exceptional at the end of the working week; in England it's called "**London**"), flying solo of course, before heading home respectably early. Oddly, I decided to cut the taxi ride home short and ended up chatting to an indigenous chap on Brunswick Street, about a kilometre from home. We clicked and I decided it would be a nice gesture to buy him a couple of beers. I returned from the 'bottle shop' and delivered them – feeling suitably benevolent – before a middle aged lady carrying two bags of bread turned up, seemingly slightly angry. Her initial rage was aimed at my companion, who apparently she was helping but who had recently vanished from his lodgings. He came up with a fairly poor excuse. Her anger soon turned to me having irresponsibly put him in beer. Oops. Many a philanthropist takes a wrong turn before truly helping the world…

Anyway, feeling suitably chastised I scuttled home, where I awoke nine hours later in an incredibly warm flat, fully dressed, having managed to put frozen chips and a steak in the oven on 200 degrees before passing out. Good work.

Saturday was altogether more sedate – I spent a morning at the golf driving range followed by a Thai massage. The latter offered the opposite of a happy ending – 85 Australian dollars for a one hour massage. 40 times more expensive than Thailand. Ouch! Anyway, an afternoon of cheap beer at the local crown green bowls club (an Australian institution) was probably less conducive to a marathon, but I curtailed matters within acceptable boundaries and spent an evening relaxing in front of the TV.

Sunday's 4:30am alarm brought with it trepidation of an incoming hangover. However, it never came. It instead transpired that the most dangerous aspect of my trip to the marathon start line was picking through the wreckage of drunken young souls finishing their Saturday night social movements. Like a vulnerable animal in the wild, it pays not to make eye contact with those transcending an enhanced mental plane and liable to use one for their amusement. God bless you 20-something's. I was once in your beer stained shoes. Friday night in fact...

Things all became slightly more exciting than needed as I headed to the start line via the office and dallied sufficiently to only make it five minutes before race registration closed. Luckily it's not as if a marathon entrant has as much to gain as an illegal immigrant seeking residency by deceiving the officials, so they turned a blind eye to my lack of photographic ID slide and let me persist with 42 kilometres (and change) of misery. Merciful.

The event was kicked off by previous marathon world record holder Robert do Castillo – whose banter was excellent – and conditions were perfect. Cool and still. All was well with the world, except that I did need a number two rather urgently. Nothing interesting transpired for the next 22km, except for my being passed by one of the hairiest men (I think it was a man) I had ever seen.

The course of Brisbane Marathon is nice, primarily hugging Brisbane River, and all was good with my body except for still needing a dump. After 25km I had my chance – a toilet right by the route, and it is not pleasant. For a very surreal moment I noticed a discarded nappy in the toilet cubicle and considered it may be a good idea, as I clearly had some rear end problems that may not have been solved by a single visit.

Anyway, I trotted on, sans diaper. The sun shone (as it tends to in Brisbane). The expected pain in my legs never increased beyond mildly uncomfortable and I pushed on further. On a beautiful sunny morning which is registered at 20 something degrees, but feels more like 30, I also took the time to appreciate the beauty of Brisbane as one of the nicer marathons I have run. That said, the gas ran out with about 2km to go and it was a struggle home before a strong second wind allowed me a sprint finish and acclaim by the finish line announcer who seemed to know more about me than I did and speculates that at 33 I may have room to improve (despite my best ever marathon time of **3 hours 16 minutes and 37 seconds**). Here's hoping. On every level. A short time after this, the finish line deflated and the finish area descended into some sort of farce with a man wearing a cape briefly having to hold the finish line up to allow people under it. Which seemed to be a fitting ending…

27

LAMINGTON ECO CHALLENGE I – 2013

I don't think I will ever find a 5am alarm call acceptable, especially not on a Saturday, but at least there was no cloud of a hangover on the occasion of the Lamington Eco Challenge Marathon. I had restricted myself to a Napoleonic single bottle of red wine the night before – just a comment here for anyone in wine marketing; despite your best efforts, and no doubt millions of dollars in advertising spend, as per always it was the sub-five dollar wines which had sold out at First Choice Liquor. Probably more of a comment on the consumers to be fair, who are generally more interested in the destination than the journey when it comes to drinking (also applies to air travel – see Ryan Air, et al)…

On this particular Saturday, *Nicholas and the Honda Jazz* (potential name for a band?) were heading southbound for a two hour drive into Lamington National Park. It was a beautiful clear morning and I had managed to build some slack into the itinerary so was able to stop periodically to take snaps of nature. Travelling through the countryside early in the morning really gives one a sense of encroaching into nature's world and it makes for some encounters one would not otherwise have at busier times, including a close range kangaroo, with Joey in pouch, undeterred by the gentle purr of the perfectly tuned Honda Jazz engine. The scenery got even better as I moved further from civilisation and through lush green cow filled fields, with hilly backdrops which took me back to my beloved Peak District. My destination was O'Reilly's Rainforest Retreat, and the climb up to the resort snaked its way on mostly single lane roads worthy of the Pyrenees. Fortunately at this time there was little danger of anyone heading the other way so it was a slow but safe ascent. It had been a truly life affirming drive, topped off by a llama farm and some vivid red parrots on top of the mountain. Life was good.

The event which had brought me up the mountain was the inaugural Lamington Eco Challenge – unique in Australia, as far as I'm aware, in that it offered competitors the choice of running either a marathon or half marathon and on one day or two. I had opted for the double marathon option, but was trying not to contemplate what that meant for Sunday morning at this point. There were probably slightly more competitors than I had expected, but it was all very relaxed as we huddled onto a fenced off section of the resort road and set off towards the wilderness at 8am. The going was initially steady, following the resort road and then an undulating forest track followed by a brutal descent down a grassy paddock, which was thankfully dry. I had been leading the pack until we had to climb up the steep other side of the paddock and a very light looking chap positively floated past me. I was only passed by one other runner before we went through a gate back onto gently undulating forest tracks and I reclaimed second position on the road. From here until the 10km checkpoint the going was predominantly downhill and I decided to make the most of it – reaching 10km in a slightly reckless 45 minutes. The downward slope steepened further from here and I continued to blast along, not wanting to contemplate the return journey. The fun eventually ended as we left the shade of the forest and the landscape opened out into flat farmland.

In slight contrast to some of the big marathons I have done, the only spectators lining the course of this one were uddered, and they seemed to be slightly perturbed by the arrival of several colourfully dressed runners onto their patch and they began to charge around, seemingly aimlessly, but a bit close for comfort. It flashed through my mind that being trampled to death by livestock would be a pretty dreadful end, but thankfully they eventually made their way into a fenced off field. Disaster averted. The guy who had first passed me had been doing the half marathon so I was the on-course marathon leader at the 20km mark, although I had been passed by the time we reached the halfway point – still travelling at a dangerously *[Taylor]* Swift pace (around 1 hour 30 mins).

The second half of the marathon was always going to be tortuous as – in a reverse of Newton's Law – what had gone down must go up. The first few kilometres were none too painful, passing back through the flat road which bisected the farmland, which by now included a couple of camels amongst otherwise standard cattle. These exotic additions raised my spirits briefly.

However, as soon as the course swept left and back into the rainforest it was a crawl, literally at times. There were also a few enforced stops as 4×4 vehicles struggled their way up the track which was too narrow for a wobbly athlete and a vehicle, meaning the former needed to give way. The 30km checkpoint gave brief hope and revival in the form of electrolyte drinks and water but the road soon turned upwards again. I had been now passed by two more runners and the fifth placed runner was closing in. Frankly, my dear, I didn't give a damn by this point. I wanted to be sat in the sun with a cold beer, not clambering up a sheer ascent. Anyway, I ran when I could, walked when I had to, and crawled when I could neither run nor walk and was only brought to a complete standstill when confronted with the return up the paddock, which meant I was (only) 3 km from the end. This was not accurate. I was actually at least 4 km from the end and most of that was spent tripping and tangling myself through a rainforest. By now I felt faint and did collapse immediately after finishing, overwhelmed by the support of the five or so people who happened to be feeding the parrots as I ambled across the line. Finishing time = **4 hours 15 minutes**; Finishing position = **3rd** (slightly unfair since the rightful third place runner had got lost somewhere)

I took my approach to recovery and preparation for the repeat event the following day from that of a 1970's English First Division footballer, rather than a 2000's Tour de France rider, as I washed down a lamb rogan josh with five beers on Saturday night before passing out in front of the TV.

28

LAMINGTON ECO CHALLENGE II – 2013

The second marathon of the weekend started an hour earlier than the previous day, meaning that I had to deal with a 4am alarm call on Sunday morning. Nasty but not insurmountable. A slightly bigger problem presented itself at 5.30am after I had incorrectly made a call about whether a service station in Tamborine, a 'town' of about 3 people would be open. By now it had been around 30km since the orange warning light had flashed on, since when I had driven past three service stations, and I knew for a fact there were no more service stations before the resort, which was over 40km away. I had to decide whether to sit and wait for 35 minutes for the service station I was outside to open or head back to Beenleigh to fill up, thereby adding an unwelcome 50km detour to my drive. I opted for the latter and gave meaning to the phrase *"drive it like you stole it"* (which, ironically, is exactly what I would like to happen to the Jazz). As I arrived back into Tamborine, the station I had left was just opening up. I believe this is called "life"/"sod's law". Anyway, I blasted on – undeterred by thick fog which was had reduced visibility to tens of metres – and soon got a chance to conduct a quick test of the condition of the brake pads on the Jazz when from out of the fog emerged a motionless kangaroo. I slammed on the brakes and flung the steering wheel violently to the right, and somehow avoided killing anything. With time continuing to slip away and a couple of cow based road blockages, my ascent up the winding single road was completely terrifying. Somehow, I arrived at 7am and was still dressing and eating a banana as the Lamington Eco Challenge Marathon Take II commenced.

In all of the excitement, some rather important business had been left unattended and the portaloo at the 3km mark of the course bore testament to the fact that beer, curry and athletes are not compatible...The visit somewhat rejuvenated me physically however and I picked my way through the field, most of whom had passed me as I sat in the blue (somewhat tranquil) confines of the portaloo, and I was soon at the head of the field. I remained out in front until a short distance after the 10km marker, at which point we were told that, due to an accident halfway down the mountain, leg 2 of the marathon would entail two loops of the same 21.6 km course. I was fairly pleased by this news. Repetition aside, the first half represented a slightly more even balance between up and down, which I thought would be a little bit easier on the body. The only two runners to pass me during the second half of the first lap were two half marathon runners, which meant I was in the very exciting position of leading the marathon! I was well aware of my weakness in going uphill so sought to let everything go on the descents, although this somewhat exemplified the pain in my quads, which by now felt like steel bolts had been driven into them. Fortunately, despite the flawless prep, I had managed to sling a few painkillers into my shorts and decided that now was the time to imbibe them in the hope of numbing things enough to press onto the end. I was still in front as I reached the complete misery of the second climb up the almost vertical grass paddock and spent a large part of the way up on my hands and knees, prostrating myself at the feet of the gods of marathons. When I reached the top and scanned the horizon behind me the second placed runner was just coming into view and I knew I was all but home and hosed as the rainforest finish was almost impossible to run through. It felt like a hell of a long trot to the finish but it felt good to be the first one across the line! Finishing time = **4 hours 29 minutes**.

In the aftermath, including the presentation of a not unattractive duck sculpture as a trophy, I learnt that I had run in the company of some long distance legends. Second placed male Kelvin Marshall has run over 280 races of 42km or more, including running across France and Germany, whilst first lady Jodie Oborne runs 170 km per week. This added to the satisfaction and helped take away some of the pain of a truly arduous weekend, not to be repeated, or at least only to be half repeated in seven days time at the Sunshine Coast Marathon...

29

SUNSHINE COAST 2013

There are various theories on the amount of time it takes the human body to fully recover from a marathon. Nowhere in this spectrum of opinion have I found one recommending another marathon within a week, especially after two marathons in two days. There was no one to blame but myself for this state of affairs, although I was starting to get concerned when I was still in quite a bit of discomfort by Thursday, feeling as if there were nails in my quads. I was able to run into the office for the first time all week on Friday and everything felt OK, if not perfect. As a result, post a few Friday night beers I decided that a massage may hold the key to restoring my powers. I had assumed that massages in Australia would be more legit than those in Thailand so was taken slightly aback when the first question in chosen massage venue in China Town in Fortitude Valley was "*Why you no take your pants off mister? You shy?*" Erm, not shy, per se, just slightly nervous about what you're planning to do to me without my underwear that you can't do with it. In the event, there was nothing to worry about, although on a couple of occasions fingers got slightly closer to restricted territory than was comfortable.

Saturday was a beautiful day, slightly spoilt by having to spend a large part of it driving up the coast to collect my running number for Sunday's event. As annoying as this was at the time, it probably saved me from myself as it reduced the time I could spend at New Farm Bowls Club significantly and restricted my c-alcoholic intake to two jugs of beer, which is apparently exactly the same number as Mo Farah likes to consume the day before an event.

Sunday itself very nearly turned into a disaster. I woke up with the 4am alarm but procrastinated badly before finally hitting the road and then realised shortly afterwards that I needed petrol. This all meant that the schedule had become far tighter than planned and resulted in limited rest for my right foot on the 80 minute drive to Mooloolaba. On arrival, I parked up, scurried past runners of the later starting half marathon, made my peace/piece in the portaloo and was still tying my laces as the starting speeches were made and the race began.

The course was four loops of an approximately 10 km lap course, all undertaken in glorious sunshine. I was fairly certain that the exploits of the previous weekend would catch up with me sooner rather than later so decided to hammer myself for the first half and try to cling on thereafter. This plan initially went well as I reached the halfway point in just over 1 hour 30 minutes, still feeling passable. By 28 km the news was not so good and I decided that a short walk was in order, only for a Network Seven News' bike and cameraman to pull alongside me for an action shot. Vanity and sanity are uncomfortable bed fellows at the very of times and the thought of me being beamed across the State walking along was enough to prompt a near kilometre long sprint until the bike happily went on its way. By now my main physical concern was extremely chaffed nipples, which were starting to spill blood, but otherwise everything was painful but not intolerable. It is generally around this point when the mind is shouting to stop and has to be tricked by being asked whether the body can take the very next step. Just that. One more step. Best not to consider that this feat still needs to be strung together several thousand times in a row at this point.

The last loop was far from glorious but obstinence and painkillers kept me going, including for a decent 500 metre sprint finish for a closing time of **3 hours 17 minutes 33 seconds** and (for what it's worth) a finishing position of **29th out of 399**. The day was capped by a photo opportunity with two storm troopers at the race end, and the opportunity (during a beautifully scenic drive home) to reflect on three marathons in eight days, which I hoped never put myself through again...

30

NUNIMBAH TO POLLYS ULTRA MARATHON 2013

September 2013 served up a fairly unrelenting running schedule...

On 1 September it was Brisbane's largest participation running event – **Bridge to Brisbane** – which attracts around 40,000 runners and walkers. The most exciting thing about the day was the walk to Fortitude Valley train station at about 4.30am on a Sunday morning. To provide a meaningful frame of reference, Fortitude Valley is to Brisbane what the Big Market is to Newcastle – a den of under dressed, under aged girls, lashed up beefcakes out for a fight and various other night out characters/shenanigans. The revellers were stopped in their tracks as a number of scantily clad 'athletes' wandered through the carnage, which on this particular night featured two stabbings and numerous arrests. They seemed unsure whether to assault us or applaud us but the worst – and best – it got was a high five from a red eyed youth who had just prior to that been dancing to the rhythm of his own beat outside a dirty looking kebab shop.

The trains were so full of runners that we were unable to house any more runners after the first station and headed straight through about 10 stations before arriving at the start line. Work had arranged entries for me and several colleagues so we were all in the green pen, behind the 'elite' red and blue runners. As the run started with a steep climb over *"THE Bridge"*, which gives the run its title, I decided that I would be best served by moving to the front of my section and trying to clear as many of the masses as possible.

This worked well, although I was already gasping by the time I reached the start line after a few hundred metres of flat out sprinting.

I was happy enough to be slowed down ascending the bridge and from there on settled into a steady but unspectacular trot on the generally slightly uphill course. There was plenty of support en route but I was fairly pleased to enter the Royal Show grounds to finish. It had been hard work and I was relatively surprised to find out I had broken 40 minutes (**39 minutes 42 seconds**) and finished 166th out of over 24,500 in the 10km. The remainder of the day was spent slipping in and out of a coma in glorious sunshine at the local park...

In the following week, of particular note for being completely indistinguishable from nearly every other week at work, I maintained an average of about 10 kilometres per day. Of some note was my decision taking at the weekend, which involved a late moderately boozy Friday, followed by an 8.30am gym session on Saturday morning, which focused on my Achilles stomach and Achilles arms, and as a result all but finished me off. On Saturday evening I headed for an art gallery opening, which turned out to be excellent, generally entailing drinking red, white and sparkling wine – sometimes in a Chav style, rose mix.

I had slightly overlooked the fact that I needed to get up at 4am to drive two hours for **Toowoomba Half Marathon**. I suspect that I was slightly over the limit during the drive, a state which sadly didn't last during what turned out to be a pretty arduous run. It took five kilometres of running around beautiful blooming and cool Toowoomba to realise that I was dangerously dehydrated, and had been passed by a shoeless man and another man with his dog. Not everyday running sights. Anyway, the water stations helped, but I was over the safe blood alcohol limit for running and shamefully resorted to walking short stretches despite it only being a half marathon. In my defence, it was a fairly hilly course but one man (and his dog) managed to be one of eight runners ahead of me – despite them having to stop twice to deal with nature's call (thankfully the canine in both cases) – out of a field of about 70 as I finished in 1 hour 34 minutes.

I was thoroughly sober by the end of the event and spent the next few hours of a stunning day driving a thirsty Jazz around the countryside whilst blasting out classical music. I felt like Inspector Morse, were he ever to be part of public sector cutbacks forcing him to turn to Ocean Finance and trade the Jag for a Jazz.

On Sunday 15 September, my preparation had (for once) been flawless and I was congratulating myself at having very nearly an hour to spare when I tapped the destination for the start of the **Nunimbah to Polly's Ultra Marathon** into the Tom Tom, which at that time had an incredibly annoying Irish man's voice directing me, albeit a slight improvement on the Afrikaans which barked orders at me for a couple of weeks. It was shortly after 4am when I hit the road, heading south towards the border between Queensland and NSW, which I reached just as the sun was poking its head above the stunning mountains of varying shapes and heights. As a man with time on his hands, I had stopped to take in a view soul enriching views and to share banter with the early morning wallabies feeding at the roadside – I did actually wind down the window to exchange pleasantries with the quirky marsupials, which I suspect is not the actions of an altogether stable mind. Anyway, I reached my destination at 6:15am, 45 minutes before the race was due to start but was slightly perturbed to find it appeared to be a private drive to someone's farmhouse, where there were clearly no other vehicles around nor sign of an event. I re-checked the address – I had inputted correctly; what was going on? By the grace of God, despite my remoteness from civilization, there were still two bars of reception on the trusty Telstra iPhone, something I generally curse when clients send weekend wrecking emails but today it told me I had overshot my target by around 50 km's and was, in fact, in the wrong state. This resulted in a fairly insane 35 minutes of tearing the Jazz around windy mountainous roads, although – given the horsepower – it probably just felt fast, like when driving a go kart...Anyway, it had the effect of increasing my heart rate somewhat although these trail type events are somewhat less regimented than city marathons meaning that I actually had around 20 minutes to mooch around the Nunimbah Environmental Education Centre before the race started about 10 minutes late.

There were clearly some ridiculous athletes in the field, evidenced by a small pack disappearing into the undergrowth in no time following the start, and I clung onto the second group of them, until the track steadily started climbing. It gradually tilted further and further up, until they were long gone and my lungs were already bursting, not great news three kilometres into a 48 km event. The ascent seemed never ending, although when it did eventually end, the descent was probably worse still, since it was almost vertical and the ground underfoot was treacherously slippery – due to several months lack of rain which had rendered it parched dust and rocks which gave way on impact. Worse news was to follow when we had to turn straight back around and climb back up the hill of doom before returning to the Education Centre. This was barely even the start of the beginning as by now we had done around 17 km of the 48 to be completed. I appeared to be a fair way back in the field, although some of those ahead were doing the 32 km option so would disappear from the course at that point. On the plus side, the next leg was the most pleasant of the day, taking in undulating forest paths, requiring a number of river crossings.

I foolishly presumed this was it for the remainder of the day and mentally relaxed, only to find that by far the worst section was to come. Stage three entailed three visits to the same drinks station. From there, we were initially required to back track for a kilometre or so before heading for a campsite which was supposedly 2 km's away. After climbing a hill through a thick forest for what seemed like days, I was convinced I had gone wrong and started screaming expletives about race organiser Ian into the sky – sorry Ian. The eventual sight of the orange cone which indicated I could get a stamp on my running bib and turn around was almost spiritual. However, there were two further similar legs, both ending at the same drinks station, and by the end of these three I was tired and angry. It was also incredibly hot and so, when the youth manning the drinks station told me I still had 13 km to go, I would have punched him, had I had the (any) strength. Instead I grimaced and waddled on, briefly getting stuck in an equine traffic jam. The next drinks station appeared fairly quickly and the angel handing out water informed me that there was only around six kilometres to go now. She also informed me that I was second in the race, as some of the elite runners had got lost between checkpoints. I suspected she was wrong on both counts, but it put a sufficient spring in my step to get me home, despite another near vertical ascent through the forest trying to destroy my mood. As I crossed the finish line, it turns out she had been correct on both counts and as I sat enjoying my complementary burger and beer in the sun, waiting for the medal presentation, life suddenly didn't seem so bad, and I almost forgot what all the swearing had been about...

31

SYDNEY 2013

Despite having considered it at length, and determined it needed to be done, the Jazz was neither oiled, watered, nor inflated before we set off on our 1,800 km plus road trip on Friday evening.

I had managed to escape work slightly early, meaning that the southbound traffic on the M1 was lighter than it would otherwise have been on a Friday evening and we made steady progress. That was until the Sat Nav intervened and suggested a turn off which seemed to me incorrect. Having previously overruled the Sat Nav with negative consequences, I decided to obey on this occasion and soon found myself on a windy and terrifying mountain road. Not ideal in the pitch black with a tired driver. After about 60 km of driving literally on the edge of the abyss, we were finally connected with the improved prospect of a straightish highway, which we picked up just before Kypole, a small rural town. From there we pressed on, under a stunning full moon, which threw white light on the occasional lake, which was the only break in the otherwise black blanket which surrounded us except for the odd town. We rejoined the Pacific Highway at the historic mountain town of Grafton and I decided that my aim for the night was to reach at least Coffs Harbour, which was approximately halfway to my destination. With a quick snap of the 'Big Banana' duly taken, I felt fresh enough to chalk off another few kilometres before turning off at a sign for a quiet motel in Macksville. I was slightly perturbed as I crawled down an unlit residential street seemingly heading for nothingness until I finally saw the sign for Bellevue Riverside Motel. It was a classic motel set up, but seemed completely deserted – not entirely surprising at 11.30pm on a Friday night – as I wandered around looking for life. Just as I was about to give up and look elsewhere for accommodation a confused looking old lady appeared behind the mesh of the office door and asked what I wanted. It was a fairly bizarre encounter and I made sure that the door was double locked as I settled into a perfectly decent double room, completely exhausted.

The restorative power of a non-alcohol laced sleep were truly remarkable and I fairly sprung out of bed at 6.30am on Saturday morning, throwing on my running kit for a quick tour of Macksville. It turned out to be a nice enough town, which was just starting to come to life with oyster fishermen and pelicans as I trotted a short way down the river before crossing the bridge towards the town centre. The run did enough to confirm that my body was in acceptable condition ahead of Sunday's marathon and I was soon ready to get on my way – having found an interesting place to visit in the local literature in my room. My initial target was the *'Pub With No Beer'*, apparently Australia's most famous pub, having been immortalised in a song by Slim Dusty. The drive out, narrated by continued repetition of *"turn around when possible"*, which was in no way annoying, was nice enough, taking me through hilly farmland which could easily have been the UK were it not for the odd bouncing marsupial appearing from time to time. The pub itself looked decent – it was naturally not open at 7.30am – and I took a couple of snaps before heading back to the Jazz and retracing my route to Macksville initially. It was now time to clock off some mileage in the right direction and again we progressed well, on sparsely populated roads, before a tourist drive to 'Trial Bay Gaol' caught my eye. The drive out was stunning and, although I decided that $11 was too steep to enter the old jail, it was made worthwhile by the appearance of a number of humpback whales, being shadowed by small boats, a short distance off the coast. This had made my day, and it was not even 9am, and things only improved when I headed to a nearby lighthouse and saw even more whales. Blowhole-in-one!

I felt slightly behind schedule now, but content, and spent the next two hours moderately exceeding the speed limit to try and reduce the projected arrival time being shown by the Sat Nav (which was now back on track). The last detour of the day was out to Forster – which I had been told by an old surfer once was worth a look – which was nice and would have been great had the Doll Museum and Café not been closed *"due to complications with knee surgery"* (the owner, not an exhibit, I assumed). It's nice to get a lot of information with a closed sign. The final stretch to Gosford did nearly involve a disaster, when I looked down to find a relatively large spider on my left hand, screamed and was very close to depositing the Jazz in the forest which ran alongside the highway. My reaction was hopeless and I had no confidence that the evil arachnid had been dealt with, leading to a slightly preoccupied hour or so behind the wheel...

Once in Gosford I soon found Joe and Bel's house, which sat at the top of a steep hill, on the edge of a wildlife reserve. Their life in a lovely property, with recent arrival Harry (who seemed to view me with an appropriate level of suspicion), showed me what life should be at my age and hopefully sowed the seeds for the end of my attempted Peter Pan ways. We shall see. Anyway, we had a pleasant evening of dinner and a few drinks before hitting the sack early – all tired for different reasons.

Alas, my slumber was only to last five hours before the rude iPhone alarm pierced it at 3.15am, being the time for me to get ready for the marathon and make my way on foot to Gosford train station. By complete luck I woke up after about 45 minutes on the train just as everyone else in running kit was getting off, and followed them – sheep style – without needing to double check this was my stop. Having changed trains, we were soon joined by tens of other runners as we heading south towards the start of the marathon at Milson's Point, which sits in the shadow of Harbour Bridge. Aside from the Colosseum in Rome, the view of the Bridge and Opera House was probably the most impressive start to a marathon I had ever been privileged to enjoy. There was the usual pre-race nervous tension, broken by the ramblings of a radio DJ, who introduced the elite athletes to the rest of the field. I was close enough to study these super humans in detail and estimated that the men were probably a third of my weight. I wondered how they might get on if they had to piggy back two mates around the course, and had spent the previous 36 hours eating mostly McDonalds' food...

The run was splendid, although I was struggling quite soon after running over the bridge and by the 12km mark I was positively floundering. It was at this point that we were running through the colourful King's Cross area, where clubbers were still stumbling out of night spots. One of them fixed his attention on me and pointed and shouted, laughing, *"he is spent"*; when I made eye contact, he said – in slightly menacing fashion, *"you, yes, you, you're done"*. He was right. I had been under the weather since the ultra marathon the previous weekend and was struggling to breathe and pouring with sweat as the temperature climbed towards the 20's. I battled on until the halfway point, in Centennial Park, at which point I opted for a short walk to contemplate the next 20km. I also noticed that my left nipple was streaming with blood, vivid red on my white running vest. All in all, not good, but my state of mind was OK and I was trying to pep myself upwards and onwards. By the time we were back in King's Cross, I realised that most of the ascending was behind us and this, coupled with the fact that there were now only 10km left, pushed me along nicely. Before finishing we were looped down to Darling Harbour and a couple of luminous clad workers enquired, *"you look wrecked, why the f*&k don't you just turn around bro?"* as the course doubled back on itself. I winced a smile, but pressed on, passing a bleached blonde beast who had collapsed and was being put into an ambulance, suddenly wondering if the gleaming angels may have an idea…Of course I was going to do this and I suddenly got a third wind when I realised that as long as I kept the 3 hour 15 pacers behind me I would probably break by PB. As it turned out, I did this comfortably, building up a decent pace as I sprinted through the crowd of thousands who had gathered around Circular Quay to watch us finish under the famed curves of the Opera House in **3 hours 11 minutes and 17 seconds.**

After aimlessly milling around the Opera House, and making a slightly strange decision in the circumstances to climb one of the towers of Harbour Bridge, I headed back to Gosford for the perfect afternoon wind down of a few beers and a barbeque at Joe and Bel's friends' house. This meant more babies, but my confidence around little people was now growing and I enjoyed holding Harry and trying to interpret the ramblings of a two year old, which are much like the utterances of a drunken Glaswegian. The afternoon beers meant I had left myself the small matter of a 900 kilometre drive back in one day, but I was positively enthused by this as I said my goodbyes and left Gosford under another cloudless sky. I had absolutely no intention of heading back as the crow flies but took this to slightly ridiculous lengths as I turned down a rocky track – clearly never intended for a Jazz – on seeing a brown sign for *"New South Wales' Tallest Tree – 5km"*. I'm not sure why I had any interest at all in this, or more to the point how it had ever been definitely proven to be the tallest tree in NSW, but I was soon stood looking up at a few hundred feet of wood. I decided I had probably pushed my luck and vowed to remain on sealed roads for the remainder of the day, only to find myself on another gravel track in Myall Lakes National Park, which soon disappeared into a lake. Literally. I needn't have worried as only waited a short time before a private car ferry turned up to take me across the small expanse of water, before the Jazz faced another few kilometres of dirt road. The remainder of the drive back became like a break neck adventure tour of Australia's East Coast – lighthouse, park, run, pictures, car, drive, lookout, park, run, pictures, beach, park, pictures, koala hospital, park, pictures, drive, camels, park, pictures, drive. I think there may be a business plan in there somewhere, for time poor tourists ('B-East Coast Tours'). It was during the koala hospital (ahh, aren't they cute, the little Chlamydia ridden creatures) and camel stop in Port Macquarie that things took a turn for the embarrassing. There are two important, but boring, bits of background required for context. Three, in fact. Firstly, I was wearing tight 'retro' shorts. Secondly, I had packed poorly and run out of clean underwear by Monday. Thirdly, Joe and Bel had very generously given me a microwave that morning. I had heard a slight rip in the shorts on bending to pick up the microwave, but thought nothing of it, even when the boys made an unscheduled appearance from the barracks as I drove due north. I continued on my merry sightseeing adventures for a further five hours before, when walking to see the camels in Port Macquarie, a car packed with hoodlums drove along behind me and seemed very amused by me. I was confused, until I reached down and realised that there was a rip from top to bottom of my shorts, meaning I had been inadvertently mooning (and possibly worse, depending on the breeze) the world all day. I was slightly horrified and spent a few minutes trying to think where I had been – various lookouts and beaches, a supermarket, a couple of service stations. Oops. Oh well, it had all taken place at least 400km's from base so all good.

My final act of the drive home was to park up on a remote spot and turn the lights of the car off and just marvel at the wonder of the unpolluted night sky in the Southern hemisphere. Truly awe inspiring and enough to make one appreciate one's insignificance, and how soon enough the East Coast (and the Universe) will forget a young man's pasty bottom…

32

BEERWAH @ NIGHT 2013

"Beerwah @ Night" brought with it a number of new learning experiences.

Lesson 1: Despite being a proud Olympic sponsor, McDonalds' food is not necessarily a performance enhancer. In fact, I would suggest it is the exact McOpposite. My day had careered somewhat out of control, thanks to having to attend the office, which had meant I was cutting it very fine to make the 4pm start time of the event. This meant that I had time to cook, but not eat, a pasta and instead opted for two double cheeseburgers and small fries from a Drive Thru on the way up. The outcome was that I felt McSick at the start; then had McStomach Cramps; and then thought I was going to McFaint. Somehow I survived, but was at no point was I Loving It.

Lesson 2: Always check, and double check, your equipment before arriving at an event. Given that the event was a 50km run starting at 4pm, at least half of it would be in the dark. As luck (I thought) would have it, I had won a headlamp as a random spot prize at the recent Lamington Eco Challenge Marathon. Having not found any day to day need for such an item, not being a miner, it had stayed in the boot of the Jazz until I arrived (running incredibly late – see above). Imagine my horror when I opened the box to find not a lightweight headlamp, but instead something which looked like it had come from a lighthouse. It was the BIGGEST TORCH EVER. It immediately caused amusement as I arrived at the start line – *"Hey bro, is your torch big enough?"*, etc., and word spread so that at each checkpoint I was greeted with cheers and laughter, *"Oh, you're the guy with the massive torch. We'd been looking forward to seeing you..."* and *"You're going to have arms like Popeye by the end of this, carrying that thing"*. Ha ha ha. My infamy was complete as I finished the first 20km just as people doing the shorter 30km and 20km events were waiting to start. There seemed to be hundreds of them. It was nice to get rapturously cheered and applauded despite a fairly steady run to that point, but their attention soon turned to my torch and the sniggering began. The event organiser asked me to explain myself so he could relay the story over the microphone. To compound matters, the bloody thing gave up emitting light at about 8.45 pm, with still a few kilometres to go. It was pitch black, save for the soft glow of the moon, and I quickly fell twice, the second time slipping into an enormous muddy puddle created by the four wheel drive cars which drive around the area having way more fun than I was by this point...(also, to add a bit of context, there's generally not a lot of amusement in the world of long, long distance running so anything out of the ordinary creates a stir, i.e. in the normal world, a man with a large torch would not be worthy of a second thought, let alone an evening of gags...)

Lesson 3: If the event says that an item is mandatory, it probably is a good idea to take it. In this case, I had ignored the requirement to take a water bottle, assuming that drinks stations would be plentiful. After about 12 kilometres of a fairly hot afternoon, straight off the back of salty McFeast, it would be accurate to say I was thirsty, and starting to wobble around a bit. I was starting to worry about my well being until I saw a fixed light and a luminous clad human. At first I thought it may be an illusion created by my failing brain but thankfully it was a race marshall, bearing gifts of chips, sweets, energy drinks and precious water. I spent several minutes gorging myself before trotting onwards. I had also (again) failed to lube my nipples with predictable results...

Lesson 4: Five and a half hours alone, save for the odd human interaction as I overtook or was overtaken, mostly in the dark is a quite odd experience. To keep my spirits up I opted for the usual random shuffle on my extensive internal jukebox; unsuccessfully attempted to communicate with animals when the sun dropped and the night time chorus began and made many startlingly ambitious plans about the future that I already have no intention of pursuing. I'm not sure if it is good or bad for the soul to live through such experiences and think I may be catching schizophrenia. No I'm not. Well I am. Not. Stop it.

The course itself was set in the beautiful Glasshouse Mountain range, in the shadow of the towering Mount Beerwah. It was generally only mildly undulating, although treacherously slippery underfoot in places after a week of thunderstorms, except for a section called "The Dungeon", which we had to complete twice. As the name suggests, it involved a steep descent into the depths of the forest before a lung and leg blowing almost vertical ascent. The only saving grace was that I got through it the second time just whilst there was enough light to see rocky path. After that, the route was mainly through relatively wide paths cutting through a pine forest. Not a bad place to spend a few hours if you're that way inclined…

Anyway, I have no idea in what time I finished in but was placed fifth out of 21, which was slightly McSurprising, given my choice of fuel.

33

KURRAWA TO DURANBAH ULTRA 2013

In between marathon adventures, I squeezed in the '**Hinterland Half Marathon**', two 10 and a bit kilometre laps of beautiful but brutal and undulating hills. I somehow managed to keep moving and held on for eighth place (out of around 140 runner) and my second fastest half marathon time – **1 hour 30 minutes 30 seconds**.

By now I was akin to an alcoholic who no longer suffers hangovers, having run sufficiently to be in a place where I could run the day after an event without too much discomfort. If anything, I may have slightly overcooked the training in advance of the **Kurrawa to Duranbah 50km Ultra Marathon**, although preparation was otherwise decent and significantly better than my usual efforts. The only slight wrinkle was when I overruled my satnav on arrival down the coast (I have be let down so often that I now assume the machine is lying to me – in fact, I think it has the opposite of artificial intelligence). For once, it turned out that I should have listened to the annoying monotone instructions, although the only damage was a slightly more scrambled dash to the start line, which sat overlooked by the Miami-esque gleaming tower blocks of Australia's holiday capital and was bathed in glorious sunrise orange, than would otherwise have been required. I recognised a number of the faces from previous events, although the field was slightly larger than normal, surprising for an event starting at 5am on a Sunday morning less than three weeks before Christmas.

I kept up with the five or six speedoes leading the race whilst I could, and noticed that all were significantly svelter and more shaven than me. I didn't have too long to consider this as I got a rather urgent, and 'formal', call of nature within the first ten kilometres. By the time I wandered out of the public toilets, the leading pack was long gone. It was a beautiful morning, although already worryingly hot by 6am, and the scenery – primarily hugging the Gold Coast beaches – stunning, if familiar (the course broadly followed large stretches of the Gold Coast Marathon and Gold Coast 100 Supermarathon, two events etched painfully onto my very soul). After about 15km I suffered a second, even more urgent, call of nature and was starting to think that I may not have cooked the pre-run chicken quite as well as I might have done, or that my policy of not washing the wok from previous meals (to add flavour) had backfired. Fortunately, the second movement, which was as significant as it was horrific, was the last of the day and I was able to focus on the job of running down 50 kilometres. Despite these two landslides, I reached the halfway mark in comfortably under two hours. The second half started with an immediate steep climb and I was already well aware that there was insufficient gas in the tank to threaten the four hour mark. The drink and lolly pit stops – placed every 2.5km – were keeping me going well, but the sun was also starting to do its work and the bulk of the second half of the run was a pretty painful, sweaty, chaffing trudge. Due to the number of civilians who were already up enjoying a beach stroll, surf or sit, there were limited opportunities for me to revert to my usual one man skits/jukebox activities to keep boredom and pain at bay, although my mind was still able to wander to some fantastical places which convince me that I would probably be able to write great songs if I opened my world up through the medium of LSD…although this might make drafting robust legal documents (i.e. the day job) a bit trickier.

The whole experience fell way short of being an ordeal so for once I was only mildly relieved when I scampered (my misplaced vanity is such that I speed up whenever there is a camera or a sizeable crowd around) across the finish line at about 9.15am, having finished 12th out of 108 in a time of **4 hours 9 minutes and 21 seconds**. I thought I could have trundled on further if I'd had to, although a stop at a service station on the way home revealed that I had stiffened up pretty quickly and did feel a little bit like I'd been run over by a smallish vehicle…

34

TOOWOOMBA 2013

The 2013 edition of the Toowoomba Marathon unfortunately followed exactly the same route as the 2012 edition (see **Chapter 19** above), making it something of a tough mental exercise to battle through. On the plus side, I was able to locate the start point, again at the University of Southern Queensland, with more ease than the previous year and was lined up on the start line at 5:30am, just as one year previously.

As with 2012, the conditions were perfect – a beautiful clear and pleasantly cool morning – and I set off at an even more reckless pace than I had done a year previously. As a result of a year's worth of improved conditioning, gained over thousands of kilometres, I was moving more swiftly than I had done then and was the on course leader until a few metres after the end of the first of the four 10 and a bit kilometer loops which made up the marathon course.

Loop three was again probably the worst of the event, although my reserves ran deeper and, aside from reverting to walking up the couple of relatively steep inclines which featured on each loop, I generally maintained my pace and eventually finished in third place (out of 35 hardy souls) in a time of **3 hours 14 minutes and 5 seconds** – at fourteen minutes quicker than my time the previous year, a helpful barometer of the benefits of hard roadwork.

35

BRIBIE BEACH BASH (BRIBIE ISLAND) 2013

Preparation for the defence of my Bribie Beach Bash 2012 title was somewhat intense. On Friday evening, together with a number of McCullough Robertson colleague, I had headed up the Sunshine Coast for "The Great Adventure Challenge" – a corporate charity event covering a multitude of disciplines. Luckily one of the required disciplines was not abstaining from alcohol and so it was that I persuaded one of my teammates to join me in working our way through a crate of Asahi beer at the incredibly waterside pad in Noosa which a non-participating colleague's parents had lent us for the night.

Such was my indulgence that I scarcely remember the transfer to the race start line, or the race briefing, but was fortunately not participating in the first event – lake kayaking. By the time our team returned, in last place, having got lost somewhere along the way, I was broadly sober and set off with my sub-team on a cycling leg. We soon realized how misfortune had befallen our kayaking colleagues as we were forced to retrace our tracks more than once as we collected clues around the forested course. It was not going well. Worse was to follow, firstly when my next involvement was as part of a sub-team who got horribly lost on a running leg, resulting in our covering approximately twice the scheduled distance but still not managing to collect all of the required items (failure to do so meant time penalties were added to the team's time at the end of the day). Our team's bad day was deteriorated further our kayaking team encountered such severe headwinds on the return to the waters around Noosa that they had to abandon ship after 30 minutes of hard paddling for zero metre gain. They ended up carrying their two man kayaks through an upmarket restaurant of surprised diners. News of which was something of a highlight of my day. Undeterred by the various setbacks we had suffered, we finished together as a team, smiling through the adversity of the day, albeit slightly lower in the field than we had hoped having spent several weeks training together with early morning and weekend gym sessions (on reflection, our time would have been better spent learning how to map read).

By the time I arrived back in Brisbane late on the Saturday night (having left my colleagues up the coast to commiserate together), an early alarm call for a Sunday morning marathon was a horribly unappealing thought. However, I was defending champion and, as such, felt obliged to "suck it up".

On arrival on Bribie Island, I thought that there were worse places where such a fate could have befallen me, although the fact that the race would again consist of a 21 kilometre southbound run followed by a turn and the same 21 kilometres back did not help raise my spirits. At least the filed had more than trebled, from three in 2012 to 10 in 2013, presumably reducing my chances of a repeat victory by the same ratio. My exercise addled and sleep deprived brain had also led me to the same mistake as a year previously and I was again clad in black, something which would come back to haunt me during the second half of the race on a relatively warm day.

It soon became clear that the 2013 instalment would be a tougher proposition, primarily due to my exertions the previous day. I would also not have the boost of almost certain victory to spur me on as a young gentleman who looked like he knew what he was doing led us out and never looked back. I settled in comfortably to second place as the leader gradually became a dot on the horizon, only to be seen on his return leg, and tried to send my brain to a land far, far away. It was following the turn that life became harder still. As the sun beat down on the black fabric of my running t-shirt, I had a stark choice to make between keeping my t-shirt on and potentially passing out with heatstroke or removing my t-shirt in the certain knowledge that the Australian sun would fry my back. I decided on option 2. And so it was that a few minutes after finishing in second position, in a time of **3 hours 54 minutes and 16 seconds**, I was sat gently sobbing on a bench as the race presentations took place. A truly emotional weekend...

36

LIVERBIRD DOUBLE I
NEW YEAR'S EVE 2013

Having swapped sub-tropical Brisbane weather for sub-prime UK weather for Christmas 2013, I decided to sign up for a tenth marathon of 2013, thus giving me the chance to achieving the 10 marathons in a calendar year which had been denied me in 2010 by a Tuscan ice snap which resulted in the cancellation of the Pisa marathon.

The usual approach to preparation was adopted, as strong ale and red wine flowed in Bacchanalian quantities at a murder mystery evening at Coombe Abbey on the eve of the first marathon of the Liverbird Marathon Double. Eighteen months in Australia had erased from my mind the misery of dark UK winter mornings and it wasn't until 90 minutes after departure, at 8.30am, as I arrived in Liverpool, that the darkness slowly began to give way to the dull grey suggestion of daylight.

By now the sat nav had broken and I was just aiming at the River Mersey in the hope of stumbling across the event. As luck would have it, as I stopped to re-fuel, I noticed the chap filling up the car next door was wearing trainers. Given the driving rain and generally horrific conditions, I decided that he must be either a fellow participant or a murderer, and it turned out I was correct on the former and able to follow him the few hundred metres to the start area. By now the rain was horizontal and the Mersey was in a frothing rage as the wind whipped across the brown water. I had opted for a luminescent orange running t-shirt, which was getting its first outing for a number of years. I assume that it had shrunk in the intervening period, as it was now effectively a neon crop top, pointing towards another "outing" perhaps?

The other runners – all clad in Berghaus jackets, full length trousers and hats – eyed the tanned, bearded, glowing crop topped stranger with understandable suspicion before one commented, *"you're either brave or stupid"*. Stupid. 100%. In truth, I was still a little hungover, so could not really comprehend much of what was going on, but knew that I was not relishing four out and back six plus mile trots along the banks of the Mersey. The first leg was directly into the wind, although by the time I reached the turnaround marker, the wind had dropped and the rain relented and things were not actually looking too bad. My propensity to overheat rapidly when exercising was actually proving to be an advantage in the conditions. By the same point on the second lap, the sun was shyly showing its face and it was threatening to be a relatively pleasant New Year's Eve morning.

Aside from an inexplicable large sculpture of a red bull, there was nothing much to look at on the course and the only real point of note came when I was forced to divert off track on the third lap to undertake 'official' toilet business in a pub. Despite this inconvenience I finished the run in **3 hours 10 minutes 09 seconds** – my quickest ever marathon, a fact that I put down to the stark reality that any lengthy pauses or walks during the marathon would have likely resulted in hypothermia. The marathon on the last day of the year meant that I had run **2,080 miles during 2013**, a feat I thought I was unlikely to ever better…

37

LIVERBIRD DOUBLE II
NEW YEAR'S DAY 2014

I awoke with trepidation on New Year's Day, awaiting feedback from my body on the prospect of back-to-back marathons. Early indications were positive. I was extremely sore, but slightly less so than expected, and did not seem to be injured and so was soon in Mother T's Fiesta, heading up the M6, just as I had 24 hours previously. The news was less good on arrival in the 'Pool, since the weather Gods were as angry as they had been the day before but showed no sign indication of abating their rage this time around. The neon crop top had been replaced with an equally foolish pink cotton creation, drawing similar looks from the now diminished field of fellow competitors, and was soon soaked through and clinging to my skin.

This time the first outward leg was physically painful as the effect of the strong wind and rain was that it felt like being pelted with gravel throughout the three mile duration. On turning around to run back, it felt like a completely different day as the rain was barely perceptible – unfortunately, neither was the wind, which should have been helping. On the second outward leg, the wind increased further, causing the Mersey to regularly drench we fools on the path. I turned round about three quarters of the way into the leg to find a trail of runners sheltering behind my ample frame, using me as a buffer from the elements. I felt like a caravan on a country road and my offer to let someone else bear the brunt was greeted with a sing-song like Scouse reply, *"No thanks – you're doing a great job mate..."* Glad to be of service. The turnaround point revealed that the headwind had taken more than I had realised out of my body and I was soon passed by the quicker moving traffic in the field. It was during the third outbound leg that I first ruminated on the fact that this may be the worst start to a new year I had ever endured, even factoring some epoch defining hangovers. There was no point dwelling on this fact and I scuttled on as best my stiffening limbs would allow and felt almost overcome with emotion on reaching the end of the marathon in a time of **3 hours 21 minutes 40 seconds** for a cumulative time of **6 hours 31 minutes 49 seconds**, and sixth place overall.

It later transpired that a number of runners had been forced to abandon the second day with hypothermia so I again counted my blessings at my poor thermo regulation system.

38

CONVICTS AND WENCHES (VICTORIA POINT) 2014

I returned to Australia from an excellent three weeks of consistently steady drinking in the UK with the eye of the tiger and the annual determination to turn over a new leaf. Alas, the leaf – like the Iron Lady – was not for turning, although things began well enough with a dry first week and weekend back, culminating in an ascent of Mount Warning, to enjoy a primarily cloud obscured sunrise with a handful of unimpressed tourists.

By the second weekend of 2014, I had slid from the path of abstinence and the consumption of a large quantity of vodka partially explains my being one hour late to the start of the Australia Day 'Convicts and Wenches' marathon at Victoria Point. Fortunately, it was a small and relaxed event and so I was allowed to trot off on my own, wearing distasteful Australian garb and carrying the invisible, but significant, burden of a spirit based hangover. The conditions were generally kind, overcast but not humid, but I was soon pouring with 40% proof sweat. I was also running in something of a vacuum, behind those in the marathon who had started on time, but ahead of those in the half marathon who had started a short time after me. This made pacing difficult and the fact that the course was a fairly unmemorable ten kilometre loop through woodland and parkland did not help inspire me to any great pace.

I did however steadily manage to pick off some of the marathon back markers during the second half of the marathon, although I was slowed first by what felt like stitch and secondly that the realisation that the harsh material of my adopted patriotic Aussie flag shorts was slicing into my inner thighs causing streams of blood down my legs. Undeterred, I battled on, enjoying the occasional relief of the aid stations which offered drinks, sweets and banter with individuals in similar condition to me having over indulged for holiday weekend. Unlike me, they did not have to negotiate 42.2 kilometres.

As always, the end was a hugely welcome relief, and my time of **3 hours 35 minutes** was steady but not disastrous given that my personal fallibility had meant that I was forced into solitary race confinement (this is not meant to sound like apartheid, though its short-term effect was arguably the same). Once the reconciliation with my start time was made, it transpired that I had finished fourth, and I would wager that I would have run faster and placed higher given any sort of hare to chase down. Such are the regrets in the life of the weak man.

After an incredibly distressing bath which revealed the full extent of inner thigh chaffing which had gone on, I proceeded on an altogether more satisfactory marathon, this time collecting new pub venues rather than kilometres. All up, I visited 12 establishments, the highlight being piglet racing at 'The Paddo', thereby falling just short of a half marathon to follow up the morning's marathon. Thanks to this, the morning of holiday Monday was probably even more painful than that of Sunday…

39

DUSK 'TIL DAWN (CABOOLTURE) 2014

On 8 February, 2014, I took my body to where it's never been before...

The venue was Caboolture Historical Village, about one hour north of Brisbane, and the event was the 'Dusk to Dawn' run – a 12 hour run starting at 6pm and finishing at 6am. Somewhat depressingly, the format was simply to run as many laps as one could of the 500-metre *'graded decomposed granite 500 metre oval shaped loop with a slight rise and fall'*. The only variation from the repetitive grind was a change of direction every hour. This became more psychologically significant as the event wore on...

I spent most of Saturday prior to the event eating. There was no discernment or prejudice in what I consumed – it was just a question of volume. Cereal was followed by chip butties, followed by fruit, followed by a mountain of pasta and chicken, followed by brownies and more fruit. I had no concern about burning off what must have been a huge number of calories introduced to my system. The final pre-race sustenance was a large coffee, since fatigue was likely to be a factor. Sadly, the iPod had already decided it did not want to be involved – committing electronic hara-kiri hours before the event, rendering me without musical accompaniment.

There were a number of events from which people could choose, from 10km's up to the 12 hour event, so the track was busy as we lined up at 6pm. I had decided the only workable approach was to not consider the full horror of the 12 hours stretched out in front of me and instead to focus on putting one foot in front of the other whilst ever I could. Despite some welcome early drizzle it was a generally humid evening and my first t-shirt was soon soaked through. Most male runners opted to go shirtless, but my muffin top, and fragile ego, would not allow this. Early on in the run, I was ticking along at a steady pace and had developed a routine of taking a drink every 3 kilometres. This served me well for the first couple of hours, although I realized I was steadily slowing down and stopped for a t-shirt change, snack and rub down with freeze gel after three hours, by which time I had run just over 35 kilometres. There was an electronic screen at the start/finish line which flashed up your cumulative distance each time you passed through, although I quickly realized that mileage really wasn't the name of the game. It was survival…Despite that, I was keen to achieve a decent marathon time and managed to get through the first 42.2 km's in just under 3 hours 35 minutes. Unfortunately, having achieved my first (26) milestone, my focus dropped off, particularly when confronted with the stark reality of having another 8 hours 25 minutes of running ahead of me…

I now shifted to hourly breaks, during which time I would spend a couple of minutes eating and catching up on sport/Facebook updates from the UK. These were oases of bliss away from the miserable trudge around the dusty track for which over familiarity had now bred complete contempt. It was impossible to gauge my position in the field, since I did not know what events others were doing or whether they were individual or relay runners and so it was simply a case of trying to stay upright and keep any sort of momentum going. The field thinned noticeably at midnight, when the ordeal ended for the six hour competitors although, thanks to the relay teams, there were more people around than I had expected. I was by now going pretty slowly and taking to walking with most of my increasingly regular drinks stops. My legs were not feeling as bad as I might have expected, but my feet were incredibly sore and I also had a searing pain just below my ribs, which I assume was caused by a six-hour diet which would have contained too much sugar for even an obese, sugar dependent fly.

My darkest moment came around the nine hour mark as, with three hours still to go, the end was still too far away to be tangible and I had started to stagger around as my body realized it should have been in bed hours ago. My mood was (very) briefly lifted when a possum, with a baby (joey) clinging to its back ran across the track, but it was very brief respite. By now, the main challenge was suppressing an overwhelming desire to stop and sleep. The one thing which kept me going was the realization that I could probably beat my previous (and only) best for 100km. I managed to do this with 9 minutes to spare (chalking off the distance in just over 9 hours 45 minutes) and celebrated with my longest break to date, during which I shovelled down bananas, crisps, brownies, sweets and painkillers like an insaniac. My aspirations had been adjusted downwards from outside hopes of reaching 120 kilometres and I had decided that just plodding/walking round for the next two hours would be achievement enough. Turns out that the night really is darkest just before the dawn...

It was around this time that I was informed that I was only a short distance behind the leader (a man I recognized as the winner of the Gold Coast 100). Given my condition at this point, i.e. scarcely human and with extreme chaffage around my inner thighs adding to a growing list of problems, this news was irrelevant. I did not have the where with all, nor desire, to dream of accelerating from my slow plod. However, talking to a human for the first time in over ten hours did lead to a few laps disappearing at a moderately increased speed. In general, my spirits did seem to lift with the rising light (although it was a fairly grey morning) and there was an outside prospect of reaching 120 kilometres. In light of this, I cut my final break down to a very quick snack and freeze rub, gritted my teeth and went as fast as a body which had aged decades in the previous 11 hours would take me. There was also additional support around the track as a number of relay members had awoken from their slumber and we offering encouragement to we weary souls still on the track. One chap in particular latched onto my improved performance and would enthusiastically clap every time I passed him, shouting *"This guy's really stepped it up. Well done buddy!"* I felt slightly embarrassed by this praise since he happened to be located on the slight downward section of the course and I would then proceed to walk as soon as I was around the corner, heading back uphill, and out of his sight.

With 20 minutes left I was all but destroyed, but knew another five laps at full effort would get me to 120 kms. I'm not sure I could do it again, but I managed to dig deeper than ever before and dial-in the necessary laps before having the luxury of a leisurely walk for my last lap. The icing on the cake was that I had placed third, and so had the compensation of an attractive LED light trophy to add to my small collection of prizes. I was within three kilometres of the winner but could not under any circumstances have run further. This was illustrated by spending the hour drive back dry retching, crying and nearly passing out from pain/exhaustion…

40

BEERWAH @ NIGHT 2014

The latest tale would end with some asking why, myself amongst them.

It was a course I knew intimately, painfully in fact. It was an inverted version of the Beerwah@Night event, where I secured infamy by running with an enormous torch. On that occasion I had also lived an anti-athlete build up, lashing it up with some Scandinavian brothers and sisters at Albert & Constance until the early hours before eating only McNotein prior to the event. This time I was much better prepared, having been gifted with a genuine headlamp by the boss, concerned about preserving one of the firm's assets (and avoiding a hefty life insurance payout). Three hours sleep was less than ideal but coffee and the in no way horrific sounding 'Maximus' (for men) energy drink – blue(?) flavour – soon perked me up.

In the negative column was the fact that some overnight rain had rendered the clay surface treacherous. It also turned out that my headlamp emitted an anaemic light which created a glaucomic/tunnel vision effect. This was fine as the course set out on a gently undulating track but as it dived down steeply into the aptly named 'Dungeon' it became a big issue. It was also at this point that the oppressive humidity became apparent and as I slid around before clambering the steep, long path to freedom from the Dungeon I wondered that bed had not been so bad after all. From here the going became easier as I reached a single track road which bisected the pine trees. By the time this stretch had ended the dark was making way to the suggestion of dawn and my spirits lifted accordingly until I realised there will still 30km's to go and I was slipping at every step.

The 20km point meant a return to the start-finish area and the promise of freedom in three hours time. There was also false optimism created by the fact that my arrival coincided with the start of the 20 and 30 km events and meant I was moving forward through the field for the first time. The Dungeon was a completely different proposition in daylight although it felt longer somehow and no more fun although it was quite amusing to be described as a *'crazy Arab'* (bit non-PC) as I galloped past a few older ladies carefully plotting their way down the steep rocky path. My misplaced pride came just before a literal fall moments later as I got carried away and stacked it in what would have been spectacular fashion, had anyone witnessed it. If a twat falls in the forest but no one is around to see it, does he make a sound???

I was trudging a bit by now, the slipping and heavy clay taking their toll on my legs. By the time I reached the 33km checkpoint I was tired but at least the course now branched off to a different section which I had only run in the dark during the last event. A change is as good as a rest, so 'they' say. Wrong 'they' are...

My rare human encounters were with others who were struggling, which made me feel better by comparison. Selfish to the rotten core. By the final checkpoint there were just 10 kilometres to go, and the ladies manning it had put in a fine spread. I loaded up on potatoes, watermelon, sweets, energy drinks and water before setting off on a 4 kilometre loop which was the home to a few 'wild' horses. They looked pretty benign to this observer. My spirits had been lifted by carbs, sugar and the equine encounter and I trotted past a couple of runners and was soon back shoving down more potatoes...

The last six kilometres were similarly painless, save for two more incredibly ungainly falls caused by slips that would have embarrassed Bambi. I positively galloped the final stretch and as awarded with the free barbecue and a third placed finish.

The remainder of the weekend descended into an alcohol fuelled blur. The yin to the yang. The Ovett to the Coe. The Kerrigan to the Harding. Enough, it wasn't that noteworthy although the combination of extreme fatigue and beer did result in a world record eight hours to watch the Great Gatsby as I lurched in and out of comatic slumber.

Why? Why not, I guess?

41

RED ROCK TO COFFS HARBOUR 2014

Waking up on Saturday morning should be a joyous moment but Nicholas had turned this into a not unfamiliar world of dread on account of some decisions, or lack of, made on Friday evening.

As is not uncommon, my intentions for the weekend throughout the week had been above reproach. I was to leave work at a respectable hour on Friday, enjoy a healthy dinner and then start tidying the unit in advance of an inspection the following week. John Lennon once said that life is what happens when you're making other plans and, in this case, my plan was displaced by darkness and then light. The darkness arrived by virtue of a half past midnight finish at the office on Thursday night/Friday morning. The black tie I wore to work on Friday was representative of an angered soul, although I was soon elevated into the light by the offer of free tickets to, and free booze at, the Friday night rugby. And when the Angel of the Lord appeared they had taken the form of a property lawyer. The law truly works in mysterious ways…

The sudden change in my fortunes may me feel like to eponymous hero, Philip Pirrip ("Pip"), from Great Expectations. Like Pip, I am flawed although my weakness manifested itself by ducking out of the office at 3.30pm to Down Under Bar – a grubby backpacker den, with a wet dog smell and sticky floor – for some pre-match stretching (as opposed to disowning my family on achieving greatness). The jug of beer went down like a dream, although I did return to the office to make a couple of calls and finish off the week in semi-professional style before heading out again at 5:01pm. By the time I caught the cab to the Suncorp Stadium with colleague, Dan, and his friend and provider of free tickets, Ross, I was unquestionably on the way. On arrival at the Stadium we wasted no time in sinking a few more at the Members' Bar and the steady flow continued throughout what was a thoroughly enjoyable game, except for the defensive coaches. By the end of the game, like many of the players, I was ruined. From here, we hit fast forward since I cannot provide a single concrete detail of the next few hours of my existence.

We push play again at 6:30am (having almost certainly skipped through the best parts of this made-for-TV movie). I am in my unit, in bed, still wearing my suit trousers (just as well as I had been travelling sans pants during the day). Three huge positives but not enough to disguise the fact that there is a gaping void in my memory. From here, there is a Memento-like exercise to perform. Like Hansel and Gretel I try and follow the trail of items in the unit, hoping for the best. The phone is the first – and potentially most relieving – find, albeit the battery is dead and I dread to see the horrors of the sent items; next up I stumble on the Suncorp Stadium silver membership card – another huge relief; my shirt is on the bathroom floor, apparently having been cast aside with some feeling and next to it lies the wonder of my debit card. The unit key is still MIA but must be around somewhere, as there is no sign of forced entry, and my work pass turns up by the door. A 100% successful mission in terms of retaining possessions (unless memory can be considered in this category). What is inescapable is that I feel appalling. This draws me to the conclusion that liquid stronger than beer may have been involved. In an ideal scenario, I returned straight home following the rugby and there is no foundation to my fears. However, the world is not perfect and I suspect that the family name has been tarnished by yours truly. For now, it is a thought I must bury as instead I have another almost equally hideous prospect to consider. In less than 24 hours (23 in fact, with the time difference) I shall be lining up for a 45 km run approximately 400km's south of my current location. This is simply too much for me at this time and I decide to retreat to bed for the time being, in the hope of a miraculous and speedy recovery. Although sleep came easily enough, its restorative effects were minimal and I was teetering on the brink of not going. This may well have been the catalyst which would have started my decline to an inevitable appearance on the

Biggest Loser within three years. I therefore swallowed some painkillers and trudged to the Jazz for a most unwelcome road trip.

I spent the first part of the drive in some sort of vaguely waking sleep, not entirely conducive to good driving, and so decided that the sensible approach would be to mix up the scenery a bit by heading down some tourist routes, as opposed to following the monotonous drudge of the Pacific Highway the entire way. Kingscliff beach was fairly majestic, offering seemingly miles of sparsely populated white sand reaching down to a beautiful turquoise sea. I would almost have been tempted to dip a toe were my numerous shark facts not always so close to the front of my mind, including the knowledge that one is more likely to be bitten by a shark than to see a wasp, and 99.8% of fatal shark attacks happen in less than three inches of water. Gospel facts. I don't even know the names of the next couple of places I stopped in, but the story was pretty much the same – stunning beaches and luxuriously clear water, filled with presumably suicidal seal shaped surfers. My next destination was slightly inland, as I headed for Ballina to check in on the Big Shrimp, who had been a fairly sorry sight on my last visit as he sat, washed out and tired looking on a closed down restaurant. Just another sign of the times. However, maybe it was evidence of the green shoots of recovery that he had been re-located and resprayed and now sat proudly and brightly outside a Bunnings store. God bless Bunnings!

Anyway, my next detour me through what can only be described as 'Wolf Creek-country', timely given the recent release of the sequel. I was convinced that the demise of the Jazz would have been swiftly followed by the demise of its owner, in some sort of horrifically graphic B-movie fashion. Thankfully, both owner and Jazz survived the drive between wide remote tracts of farm country, which was actually pretty stunning set to the backdrop of a setting sun.

I was finally nearing Coffs Harbour by around 8pm (having lost an hour between the Queensland and New South Wales time zones), after a reconnaissance mission to Red Rock – which was the start point for the run – revealed there was no room at the campsite, and no other accommodation options in the very small town. I actually opted for a motel in a motel rich town north of Coffs Harbour, after swinging by to have a look at the unexpected, and crammed, Sikh temple in an otherwise fairly identikit Australian town.

Despite the embarrassment of motels to choose from, I managed to pick the one with the slightly deranged (possibly drunk) owner who scanned me up and down with a look somewhere between contempt and lust, either of which were likely to end badly for yours truly. I decided not to hang around in my faintly shabby room waiting to find out his intentions and made the every short walk to the next door pub for sustenance. It was far from vibrant, as a male singer performed almost unnoticed to a small, 90% male, audience. I ordered two beers (as they did not serve either jugs or pints) and the house burger, which arrived positively bursting with calorific badness. Just what the doctor (unless a heart specialist) ordered before a long run. With nothing to keep me at the pub, I wandered back to the motel, hoping to survive the night without being turned into a coat, or pet, for the owner...

The 4:30 am alarm confirmed that I had survived, although I felt less than tip top, having worked through a couple of cans of Castlemaine XXXX to ensure some sleep. The bad news was that it was absolutely hammering it down with rain – less than ideal for a beach run thought Mr Glass Half Empty, but at least cooling, thought Mr Glass Half Full. The drive to Red Rock was shorter than I had remembered and I was one of the first to arrive at the start line, although it did mean that I had time to climb the headland and watch the first light of the day arriving. There was soon quite a crowd assembled below me on the beach and I joined them a few minutes before the start time for the race briefing. It was basic, and confirmation that no one had been lost on any of the previous runnings of the event was vaguely reassuring, provided I did not become the first. There is not a whole lot to say about the next 3 hours 42 minutes of my life. The vast majority of it was spent running steadily along the beach, periodically taking in the beautiful run of sunrise on a cloudy morning to my left. We occasionally had to leave the beach to negotiate headlands through housing estates, but the vast majority of the run was on mercifully hard sand.

The undoubted highlight was some kangaroo encounters around two thirds of the way through, and the time I spent trying to take selfies with the animals, who were completely unmoved by my presence, wasted quite a lot of time and cost me a couple of places.

Towards the end of the run the sand became softer, and there were a couple of thigh high creek crossings (sharks operate in this area) to negotiate, but otherwise the generally pleasant experience continued. The finish was also pretty nice, with the run ending under the wooden frame of Coffs Harbour jetty. Thanks to the shock absorbing nature of the surface, I felt in pretty good condition, as I demonstrated when I was told that there were sandwiches and a spread available at the yacht club, which was a few hundred yards down the beach. I positively sprinted there on this proclamation, and was soon crammed full of sandwiches, fruit and homemade cakes. There was also the unexpected surprise of a commemorative flip flop (thong) for having completed the run. The one problem I did have was that I had run 45 kilometres directly south of the Jazz and was therefore in need of a lift back to Red Rock. Event organiser, Steel (actual name – I kid you not), confirmed he would take me but had to wait for everyone to finish before he could do so. I was happy enough with that, although three hours later, when I had eaten enough sandwiches and cake for a week, and read Ultra Runners magazine from cover to cover, twice, I was about ready to go. Upon receiving confirmation that the final two participants on the course had decided to stop for a coffee, me, Steel and Bob jumped into his car and headed back up to Red Rock. It was gentle, miscellaneous chit-chat with the two old timers and a nice end to an excellent event. Unfortunately, I had the small matter of a few hundred kilometre drive to deal with before I could fully relax, but that was a relative breeze compared with previous adventures featuring *Nicky and the Jazz*...

42

NERANG ULTRA 2014

One can move 15,000 miles from home but fail to escape one's biggest nemesis. One's self...

My "Gascoigne throat" and feeble will power were in full effect from the moment someone – me – suggested a cheeky early escape from the office on Friday afternoon to the more comfortable surrounds of the pub. Five hours later and we were still going wrong. Fortunately autopilot finally clicked on the homing chip, just a few hours – and countless drinks – too late.

Saturday was another glorious Australian spring day – all 31 degrees of it – which frankly forced me to the bowls clubs. Two jugs of mid strength, low carb, beer later and I returned to the unit for rest. Not optimal marathon prep.

Anyway, despite being torn between the sense of bed and insensibility of a 100km drive followed by a 50 km run, I hauled my husk out of bed at 4:00am and headed south. The Nerang Velodrome was full of the familiar faces of maniacs who subscribe for this nonsense and by the 6 am start time it was already worrying warm and humid. I had run the race the previous year in beautifully cool conditions, albeit a recent spate of rain had made the forest trails treacherously slippery that time. It was dry under foot this time but the heat soon took a heavy toll and I had drained my Powerade within minutes of starting the run. This resulted in a painfully dry hour or so before the positive oasis of the drinks station at the 12.5 km point. The second section of the first loop of the course started with the brutal 'gut buster' climb into the forest. Despite having been determined to retain my limited refilled bottle for as long as possible, it was all but drained by the summit and it was a long, lonely and thirsty trudge to the halfway point. I was physically done by now but felt a mild lift after clearing about a gallon of water and some banana pieces.

The second half was like some sort of barely living purgatory – the misery increased by the knowledge of what was coming. The only respite was being able to dunk my headband into the three creeks we crossed, but it was limited respite as the humidity intensified. It was too much for some and I passed three stricken competitors – two with cramp and one with heart palpitations. I was slightly concerned about my own condition, but was certainly no longer hungover. The end was such a sweet, sweet sight and I even managed to claim a few places in the field with a spurt of energy on the final descent, which I put down to the remnants of the booze calories. The finishing zone revealed even more carnage as there were numerous bloodied souls who had fallen clearly running too fast on the treacherous rocky trail paths.

Good riddance to another run finished – ninth place in **5 hours 22 minutes**; seventeen minutes slower but one place higher than the previous year. Peace made with this run methinks...

43

WILDHORSE CRITERION 2014

Don't go down to the woods today...for you'll get a terrible surprise...

It was beyond a bracing start to Easter Sunday. On Easter Saturday I had lived the life of a middle aged woman, or their reluctant child, being the description applicable to the vast majority of those waiting in searing heat for the delayed royal visit to Brisbane. Although close, unlike an unfortunate few, I did not feint from heat and excitement as I snapped a few close up pics of the future queen whilst the balding future king, Will.I.Am [balding] (following a recent re-brand), headed for those lining the opposite side of the road. The afternoon served the purpose of keeping this weak willed man from a pub although I did have a couple of drinks on the way home as the beautiful sunny day deserved nothing less. I had also hoped a drink may help me to sleep but, alas, I managed 30 minutes at most before the alarm sounded shortly after midnight (which presumably means that I rose earlier than Jesus on Easter Sunday, although that's where we'll end comparisons) for the one hourish drive north to the Wild Horse Road, just off the Bruce Highway. It was pleasantly cool, and naturally pitch black, but things took a turn for the worse when Welsh race organiser, Alun, announced that – contrary to the published route – the race would start with a lung busting dash up the steep hill to the Wild Horse lookout. I had struggled to walk up this 750 metre slope previously so the prospect of starting an 80km run with it was horrifying. Undeterred, and to my surprise, I bounced up it and was leading by the time we reached the top and touched the map.

Once the steep descent had been dealt with, the run took on more palatable topography as we headed down a gravelly fire track for a few hundred metres before turning sharply left into the depths of the forest where most of the run would be spent. My headlamp was giving off precious little light and it meant that the going was borderline dangerous as I regularly tripped and stumbled over branches and through deep puddles, which appeared from nowhere. The other downside of leading was that I was first to breach the numerous invisible spiders webs which criss crossed the dark forest. After 5.5 kilometres came the first sustenance stop – manned by a dreadlocked couple who looked like they should have been protesting about something somewhere. In a fashion they were, as they stocked 'vegan friendly' muffins, which were completely delicious. Possibly less environmentally sound was their decision to burn a heap of discarded wood to warm them in the cool early morning. I had little need for this as, despite the low temp, I was already sweating...

The second half of the course continued on the same form, through generally flat, although treacherous, forest trail until we hit a firm sandy path. I thought I may actually be able to speed up at this point but was undone when the sand suddenly became deep and soft. This was not a huge problem in my fresh condition but my mind turned to thoughts of the sixth and seventh laps which would cover the same ground. Worse was to follow as a large dark shape covering the width of the track turned out to be one of a series of deep puddles, which could only be avoided by clambering into the undergrowth. It was not really conducive to a decent rhythm and I had by now been joined by another runner. He sized me up for a while before asking about my aspirations. When I responded "survival" he accelerated off. However, I had caught back up with him by the end of the first lap and actually led marginally as we reached the lap one checkpoint, with around 13 km done. My lead did not even last for one metre beyond the turn as Alun – who since the large torch incident at a previous event sees me as a clown – insisted I go to my car and get a water bottle to fill up to give me a chance of avoiding perishing when the heat increased.

The form from here on in was that, although we would cover the same course, the direction would alternate after each lap. A small but appreciated amount of variety. My only human encounters on lap two were with the remaining 13 or so runners and some walkers still completing lap one, appearing like miners from the darkness, and the new agers at the halfway checkpoint (where I hammered down a few more muffins – already on the way to vegan conversion). By the end if the second lap I was still relatively fresh although, like Harvey Dent, more than ready for the dawn, having fallen a few times. Alas, it was another two laps before this joyous – divine? – moment finally arrived and the intervening laps had been broadly indistinguishable from those previous save for the fact that there were a number of other head lamped runners on the course with the 50km runners having started at 4am...

It was like a different course once the sun had shown her welcome face, and the novelty and visibility allowed me to accelerate significantly. The alternating laps meant I knew I was too far back – and losing ground – to win, but fairly comfortable in second place. Unfortunately the renewed hope daylight had brought could not disguise the pain of an ailing body after 50km – each step was an effort and even in the light there were obstacles to jump over, duck, or swerve. All added to the fatigue of less than one hour of sleep in nearly 24 hours. With no one around I adopted tough love, screaming expletive motivational sound bites – worthy of army hazing – at myself. I'm not sure whether it was this or the muffins which resulted in an incredibly welcome and potent second wind which carried me almost all the way home. Unfortunately the second side effect was just as potent but far less welcome as I was suddenly overcome by a dramatic need to empty my bowels. When in life, do as Jesus would; when in the woods, do as Yogi would. The result was a rapid and horrific dispelling a short way into the woods. Thankfully no other runners passed by as this nasty but short and natural occurrence. Without wanting to be too graphic, I may add that bears don't eat curries, nor drink lager, and what I produced can only be described as toxic. My shame was soon displaced by the return of nagging, numbing agony in possibly 90 per cent of my body and a mind which had long since moved to a fantasy land of McDonald's, beer and bed, in any order. Until now, my deteriorating mind had been wondering whether my second wind had been caused by the dreadlocked race support crew having laced their muffins with more than just vegan free produce. Without stereotyping, they looked like a couple who may have access to contraband and I would have welcomed anything from this sphere by this point – EPO, speed, heroin. I had moved myself as far forward as possible in this regard – taking enough coke to down Keith Richards, although mine was from the order of the black wizard as opposed to marching powder...

The beginning of the end of any long distance race always heralds an injection of energy into a delirious and exhausted body. There was no difference on this occasion – especially as the last leg was slightly shorter and the drinks station lady, with whom I had built a short and meaningless relationship rung a cow bell to mark a special moment – and I fairly skipped the first few hundred metres. There was certain determination in me to hold onto the second place I had held got about seven hours. There was no prize money, no acclaim at stake, just personal satisfaction and justification at having got up at midnight for this pain. Forget the stench of doubt (and possibly excrement from the woods' incident) and concentrate on achievement. Aside from the floaty beginnings, the last lap was far from easy going. The temperature had moved into the twenties, mind and body were elsewhere and the only motivation – with no serious challenge expected from third place, who looked equally spent when I passed him in the opposite direction over one kilometre behind me – was breaking eight hours (meaning I had run quicker than 10km per hour). It was a mixture of trudge and trip until I reached the 'new' finishing stretch, turning left instead of right after about 10km for the first time. The rocky track wound its way upwards but, knowing I was in race against the click and it was shorter, I shouted a few more expletives at my pathetic self before gritting my teeth and pounding it home for a finish time of **7 hours 55 minutes**, and second place. My reward was the cheapest chocolate rabbit one can buy from a chain supermarket. In my borderline insanity and exhaustion I felt like smashing the, no doubt paper thin, chocolate on the lady presenter's head, but diplomacy won the day – if not the race – and I thanked her...

44

YULEBA 2014

In a land far, far away from whence he came lived a very, very strange man, prone to doing very, very strange things...

Having spent one third of Easter Sunday, starting at 2am, running around a forest (see above), Nicholas decided to spend one quarter of the Anzac Day national holiday driving deep into the West. The journey was turned into a magical mystery tour by initially heading north, through hippie town Woodford, looking distinctly non-peace loving with a tank parked outside the small RSL to celebrate the servicemen's day, before the road gradually swung west and the farm fields became bigger (seemingly bigger than the entire UK in some cases) and the grain silos, too, became enormous. It is rumoured it's where the Chinese, who are seeking to buy up the entire planet to feed their population, which will hit 10 trillion by 2030 according to a good friend of mine, Mr P. Nocchio, store enormous chickens which live on steroids, red bull and broken dreams...

Anyway, with the Honda Jazz purring along, as she always does, excellent progress was made meaning that by the time I reached the town of Miles, a mere 80 kilometres east of destination Yuleba, I had time to kill. This I did marvellously by visiting the historic village. I was initially slightly disappointed to find out that the 'historic' village had been constructed in 1971 – I have a charity shop jumper which I think is older than that, it certainly smells like it – but my initial scepticism was soon turned around when I strode into what was a decently sized replica town street, which could have been transplanted directly from the set of an Old Western. The very friendly lady behind the counter had warned me that I only had half an hour, and would therefore not be able to see everything, but I assured her that I was very fast and so fancied my chances. She was correct. Every one of the countless buildings was crammed with items and I probably didn't even get through half of it before closing time. Historic Village 1 – Nicholas 0.

Undeterred, I pressed on towards Yuleba, taking a quick detour to watch sun setting behind the tranquillity of Judd's Lagoon, which became less tranquil when I nearly got the Jazz stuck, after ambitiously taking it down a small dirt track, and had to rev aggressively to get her out. On the drive down to the Lagoon I had passed four young chaps looking for a lift and decided to do a good deed on the way back. The only problem being that I generally keep the interior of the Jazz approximately in the condition of a litter bin. Add to that the fact that on long road trips, I live what I imagine to be the existence of a long distance truck driver and a range of fast food wrappers and soft drink cans are added into the mix. At the point I offered the boys I ride, I had been on the road for nearly six hours and was almost too ashamed to let them into conditions which a tramp may have deemed substandard. However, I figured they would forgive me if I saved them a walk and they duly complimented me on my "sick ride", which I took to be well deserved sarcasm and borderline lack of gratitude. After I nearly overshot two turns on the way to drop them off, I think they left the car with an overwhelming sense of relief.

My target was Yuleba Golf Club. Despite a year having passed, I was struck by the familiarity of my surroundings and amazed to find that a number of people remembered me as I entered the club house to collect my race kit. I was greeted with the news that the man who had defeated me the previous year, Gary, was unable to make it and my thoughts flashed with ideas of victory before I was told there were nine runners this year (compared with five in the inaugural event), which immediately lowered my expectations, as did the fact that the course had been changed from a primarily downhill event to an undulating track. As a consolation I was presented with race number "1", something which is unlikely to ever happen again. The key issue now was securing accommodation. Having previously slept both outside and in the back of the Jazz, there was little to choose between them as horrifically unappealing options and so I took a short drive up the road to the Yuleba Hotel Motel (Holiday Inn...). The NO VACANCIES sign was not promising but, to my relief, I was told that there was actually one room available. I celebrated this with a slightly weird pseudo-dance thing, which I instantly regretted, and the guy who I assume was the owner looked like he was deciding whether to repeal his offer of a room. Instead, I think he just decided to up the price, but it was still a pretty reasonable offer for a man with nowhere else to go.

The room was essentially a cargo container which had been converted into a perfectly decent sleeping space, and it was clean and tidy. Good enough for a man used to splitting his time between a crack den unit and dustbin car...Better (and worse) news followed as it turned out that tap beer was a bargain three dollars. I scooped down a couple as I provided a focal point for the five or so staff and drinkers, who could not understand why a man would travel so far to run. I had no answers. By now it was time to wander back to the Golf Club for a pasta dinner, and few more beers under a marquee which had been erected for the event. The event had been a huge success the previous year – raising $70,000 – and logistics had been ramped up a notch with, in addition to the marquee, impressive race banners flying everywhere one looked, live music and free gifts in the race pack. As defending runner up, I was asked to say a few words on the stage in the marquee. Public speaking is not a strength of mine but I was feeling mildly intoxicated by having the number 1 bib, and having had an almost optimal amount of beer, and so think I managed to hold my own. The tale of the previous weekend's 80km jaunt raised a few eyebrows and a couple laughs, which was good. After taking in some live music and a couple more beers I returned to my digs and settled in at the bar to take advantage of the ludicrous beer price. Fortunately, I ran out of cash (only after scrambling under the driver's seat and finding a few extra dollars) by 9:30pm so was unable to take up last orders. Saint Jude must have had a hand in this as I was probably by now on the tightrope between optimal beer intake and EXTREME DANGER. Time for bed whispered the sensible part of my brain which, by now, was very small...

I woke up with a dry mouth but otherwise limited ill effects from slight over consumption the night before, and probably in an altogether better state than following the drive through the night the previous year. I also felt positively energised when I pinned on the number 1 running bib and headed down the road to the start area at the Golf Club. The place was already a hive of activity – with cooked breakfasts on the go (which I could have positively killed for had I not spent all of my money on alcohol), people still registering and other areas being set up for the day. At the appointed hour – 7am – the marathon runners were ushered to the start and there was a nice moment when one of the nine initiated a team huddle (*"Those who are about to die, we salute you"* (well, we were near Roma)). The conditions were perfect, with the sun up, seemingly not a breath of wind, and the air still pleasantly cool as we started. As usual, I had absolutely no game plan and just ended up setting off as quickly as my legs would carry me. The course soon took us outside the town onto a long and primarily straight road. I did not look back until the five kilometre point, when I realised I had quite a large lead and still felt quite good. My mood improved further when three kangaroos bounced across the road a short distance in front of me (I will never tire of seeing a 'roo, I am positive of that) and I felt like I was tracking along at a reasonable tilt. The drinks stations, and welcome encouragement, at the 11.5km and 15 km marks came and went and I still felt good, although the course was generally tougher than the previous year. It was only when I reached the halfway point – stopping to pose for a few photographs – that I realised why the going had felt so easy, as I turned to face the 21 km's return to find that it would all be run into a relatively stiff headwind. This was compounded by the fact that the course initially tracked predominantly uphill on the return leg, and the fact that the sun was now starting to burn a bit more brightly – not great news with minimal shade on offer, although the headwind did keep the temperature generally comfortable…

I passed second and third place – who were running together – after about 1 kilometre of the return and was chastised for having told them the previous night that it was a super-fast, mainly downhill course. I figured I would have some more abuse to look forward to when they found out they would also be running into a headwind for the second half of the event. Despite the deterioration in conditions, I retained optimism and spring until around the 27 km mark, when a sudden wave of physical and mental fatigue struck me (something experienced in most marathons) with the realisation that there was still a way to go and not a huge amount of gas left in the tank. I had slowed down fairly significantly by this point but was determined to keep plodding along, and was saved on reaching the 31.5 km mark, at which point I found myself amongst the half marathon runners. The mere fact of being with fellow humans, after only the most fleeting interactions at drinks stations over the past few hours, injected energy back into my efforts and I felt myself speeding up again. Things got better still at the 37 km mark as I was surrounded by a large number of 10 km runners and by the last three or so kilometres the roads were full of people and I accelerated again and now felt like I was flying along (until a very small boy doing the 3km run burned past me!). I knew the end was now tantalisingly close and managed to summon the strength for a final sprint into a warm welcome at the Golf Club. I had won and it felt good! It felt good for at least 30 seconds and then it felt bad as stopping had revealed a whole range of aches and pains which hadn't seemed to be there when I was moving. After gorging on fruit for a while, I milled around aimlessly before deciding to sit. Sitting felt nice. Until I stood up. Then I wished I had never sat at all as it had made everything ache more. After several repetitions of this, I decided that a massage could save me, and so it proved, except for a brief and painful burst of cramp when I was stretched by my masseur. Post-massage I no longer felt like I was made of wood and tin and could sit or stand without fearing the repercussions. Liberating indeed. It was soon time for the presentations which, listening to the details of the cause and a few others speak about their stories, was a humbling experience. I again was asked to utter a few words – I basically thanked alcohol for providing me with the energy to run, which was probably not entirely on message for an athletics event, but something had got me through in my quickest ever time – **3 hours 9 minutes 1 seconds**. However, the comments that had gone before put my tale into its correctly flimsy perspective…

I was disappointed to have to leave the warmth of the people of Yuleba and the event before the evening's festivities but with the prospect of the office the following day, I decided it was best to face the five-ish hour drive on the Saturday afternoon rather than Sunday morning. What had been a great day did not quite end there, as I spent a couple of hours at Chinchilla Races on the drive back to Brisbane before hitting the town immediately on arrival. I partied hard and felt like I had been a little bit run over by the time I woke up on Sunday morning, but how many times does one win a marathon (probably about as many times as a bridesmaid becomes a bride, unless one's name is Elizabeth Taylor)?!! No regrets…

45

DARKNESS TO LIGHT 2014

"What did you think was going to happen Nicholas?" may end up being the epitaph on my gravestone and certainly sums up the last week or so in the life... With the constant and irrational fear of shark attack weighing heavily on my mind ahead of my second ever corporate sprint triathlon (two hours of Google research did not provide a definitive answer as to whether the relevant water did in fact have the benefit of shark nets), I responded predictably by drinking on the two nights leading up to the event. The first was an impulsive night out after the white knuckle excitement of New Farm Bowls club trivia night. The result was an unpleasant Friday, which I decided could only be curtailed by taking medicine in the form of medium ABV beer, in a jug sized dispenser. More followed, as did more, and I had to tell my tri-team mates that I would leave the door of the unit only to enable them to extract me 'rendition-style' if necessary. Thankfully, this was not necessarily as I awoke from my slumber just before the 5am pick up time, finding I had obliged by leaving the door absolutely wide open, with all of the lights on, as a handy invite to any local drug addicts looking for goods to turn into sweet drugs...

A McDonalds' breakfast on the journey down to the Gold Coast went someway to fixing me, but it was only when I hit the water several hours later – being the third leg man – that I truly sobered up. The water was surprisingly warm, unlike the day, as a cool breeze swept across the expanse of The Spit keeping us all shivering. The swim did not go well – I was asked twice by lifeguards if I was OK – but I fared better than some who stopped part way or, in one case, were hauled back to shore. It was a long 400 metres and my legs were shaky when they hit the thick sand leading to the bike transition zone. I was to borrow teammate Liam's bike for the leg, but had failed to pay much attention to the essential details, save for noting the red water bottle. Around halfway through the 10km ride I reached down for a swig of water and found a dark blue water bottle. Too tired to put two and two together, I took a deep drink and rode onwards. It was a tale of two rides, with a pleasant fast outward half, followed by an infinitely tougher ride back into the wind, which was particularly nasty on the second lap. I was not disappointed to stash the bike (vaguely near where I had collected it) but less pleased to find my legs rendered jellified by the efforts which had gone before. It took around one kilometre of the run before I had a semblance of feeling back in my legs although I did manage a pretty strong second half, including sprint finish, despite the familiar sight of dual bleeding nipples, rubbed raw by the efforts of the day. It felt great to finish, although I was soon informed that I had "borrowed" completely the wrong bike. Happily, it sounded like no harm had been done, and that no angry triathlete was looking for the wally who had taken his bike. Our team had fared decently and, most importantly it was over, I had not been eaten and I was allowed to go out again, this time celebrating, rather than papering over deeply held fears. Saturday night's entertainment consisted of a house party, and the combination of the three days rendered Sunday almost a complete write off as I finally managed to emerge from bed at 5pm. Pathetic...

Having clearly learnt nothing about the edge of endurance, this annihilation was trumped handsomely the following week. After a couple of quiet drinks on Tuesday night, Wednesday was all about clearing the decks at work to allow for a pre-6pm departure. In the event, I only just managed this (via some attempted biblical intervention from a stranger) and it meant that I only had time for a doner kebab 10 minutes before commencing a 110 kilometre run through the night for a domestic violence charity (110 being the number of victims of domestic violence in Australia in 2013).

The field was predictably (very) small – with just five people planning on completing the whole event, which consisted of 100 kilometres through the night, before a 5:30am 10-kilometre run where the hope was that we would be joined by a much larger group.

There were a huge number of marshals, who helped cheer us along, together with soldiers – who were practising drills for the upcoming G20 – and police officers, one of whom escorted me for several kilometres on his segway, which made me feel far more important than I ever will be. Our small group soon thinned out and it revealed that I was relatively normal within the scheme of things. There was a guy at the front I have seen in a number of other events who was basically sprinting in what seemed to be a completely unsustainable fashion (this was correct, as he went home injured after blistering through 52 kilometres in under 4 hours). Behind him, me and another English guy wearing no shoes (literally, not even those hand things – turns out he is the world record holder in this niche pursuit), interchanged positions whilst a short way behind was a maniac wearing a harness and dragging his bulky friend on his roller blades. I assumed they would be swapping throughout the event, but this was not the case. Finally was the event organiser, Rob, who I suspect was not fully prepared for the pain he had unleashed on himself as he struggled with blisters and various other ailments throughout the night. I went pretty well – too well – for the first 50 kilometres or so, chalking it off in under 4 hours 30 minutes.

The inevitable misery and pain came midway through the night and kilometres 55 to 80 were thoroughly unpleasant. With 80 kilometres negotiated, I suddenly became more optimistic and actually managed a pretty decent pace for the last 10 km's, which brought me in at around 4.00am, meaning I had been running for just under 9 hours 30 minutes.

The one and a half hours under a blanket in an army tent was absolute bliss, before me and shoeless Rob were announced to the much larger group of 10 km runners. The roller blade boys and organiser were still out there trying to chalk off the first 100km by this time. Anyway, after a very, very slow start, my body adapted well to the final stretch and I was heading at a pretty decent tilt by the time I reached the final checkpoint with around 1.5 km's left. It was here that I had instructed Liam (of tri fame, above) to bring me a beer. He had duly done so but almost refused to hand it over on seeing my condition. I insisted and eventually got my way, although my right hamstring immediately cramped up as I touched the can, as if the Gods were punishing me. After a stop start few hundred metres the cramp disappeared and I trotted in for a time of around 50 minutes, meaning an aggregate time of under **10 hours 30 minutes** for the 110 kilometres. After a much needed breakfast, I went from here directly to the office for what may charitably be described as an unproductive, and not entirely conscious, day. Sake tasting in the evening followed and my condition on Friday morning was an almost Lazarus-esque improvement...

46

GOLD COAST 80 - 2014

We'll start with a hugely impressive sounding headline, before unravelling its impact:

Nicholas wins the Gold Coast marathon 50 miler by nearly 25 minutes and breaks Australian national record!

Batman teaches us that to overcome fear, we must become fear. Well I don't think I became fear but I did face my fear by returning to the Gold Coast 100 one year after the event hospitalised me. In an act of slight cowardice I did take things down a notch by signing up to the 50-miler (80 km) instead of the full event. Just over seven hours after starting the race, I was very relieved to have made this decision...

The build-up had been suitably poor and booze based. Much of this had been in the call of duty as I deputised for the chairman of the firm at a lecture on happiness at the State Library of Queensland on Monday (I was at my happiest during the free drinks reception). Tuesday was drinks for a worldwide Irish fundraising body at customs house, which features a meeting with the zany father of the latest captain of the Wallabies (Stephen Moore). On Wednesday night I rested. Thursday evening brought a regular seat at the table with the great and the good of local politics and business. Too much wine was imbibed leading to a steady Friday, salvaged by a few beers at lunchtime and après work. As usual Saturday was spent amusing myself between the two nearby bowls clubs, followed by wine. The net result was a predictable sense of dread at the 4am alarm which told me it was time to head down the coast to Burleigh Heads. On the drive down, I speculated that I becoming the James

Hunt of ultra-marathon running – just without the looks, easy charm or women. So, basically, an alcoholic long distance runner...

Otherwise, it was a familiar scene from the previous year, with one key difference. In 2013, my trainers had been a but falling off my feet at the start of the race – thus the hospitalisation – whereas this time around I was wearing sparkling new trainers, fresh from the shop where I was 'up sold' like an absolute novice into my most expensive ever pair of trainers – the Brooks' 'Ghost'. But man they looked cool!

The look of the trainers actually made me feel fast, which may explain like I set off as if I were being pursued by the devil. The course involved three 12.5 km out and back legs followed by the just over 5 km 'true up' at the end. The first turn around point revealed that I was already a couple of kilometres up on the filed in my race and this had been extended to five kilometres a short way after the end of the first 25 kilometre lap. I was clearly travelling too quickly. Undeterred, I pressed on to the 50 kilometre point, which I reached in under 4 hours – my quickest ever time over the distance – and immediately my legs started reporting the over exertion to the pain receptors in my brain.

The only mercy was that I was now on my last full lap, unlike the unfortunates doing the full run (which had included me, one year previously). The temperature was also increasing and there was limited shade on the course, which almost equally followed the attractive coastline and the less attractive – but still pleasant – residential streets of the Gold Coast. There was also a steadily strengthening head wind to deal with on the outward course, although by now I knew that even a shuffled last lap and a bit would see me victorious. This was just enough to suppress the pain and cause me to remember that at a basic level all I needed to do was keep putting one foot in front if the other, albeit a few thousand times more, and it would be over. I also had the luxury of having a sufficient lead to stop for a variety of selfies to help remember the victory...

The leader of the 100km event was positively flying around and I was fully cognisant of the fact that I would be way back in the field had I manned up and entered that event. Little matter, I had picked wisely and took the acclaim of the small crowd as I sprinted home into the park opposite Burleigh Surf Club in a time of **7 hours 3 minutes and 43 seconds** – nearly 25 minutes ahead of the second place finisher. In addition to the glory of a second victory of 2014, I was awarded with a plastic monstrosity of a trophy, which I'm sure will help sooth a week of agony. I was also awarded with a Duff beer (which I did not know was manufactured) by some US marines, awaiting the finish of their friend, who I amused by having to literally roll up a small wall, which my destroyed legs could not climb...

47

WINERY MARATHON 2014

I suspect it would be a very bad thing were I to see myself through others' eyes too often. I caught a glimpse this weekend and did not really know what to make of what I saw...How can a man who has spent most of the waking week (of which there has been plenty) moaning about being tired and overworked justify 20 hours of driving over a weekend to run a marathon?

There is some context to the story, being four weeks or so of the most stressful working weeks of my life and preparing for my personal idea of a firing squad. The latter event was being "selected" for the co-hosting duties at the firm's annual black tie law dinner. *"According to most studies, people's number one fear is public speaking. Number two is death...This means to the average person, if you go to a funeral, you're better off in the casket than doing the eulogy..."* (Jerry Seinfeld). I fall into this category. The heavy workload had been a blessing in that it at least gave me very little time to ponder the encroaching hour. As it turns out, the speech went just fine (including a slightly controversial dogging gag) although my relief manifested itself as a reckless night which rendered my hired dress shirt the material for a washing powder advert as it somehow managed to end an apparently eventful night covered in blood, coffee, beer and whisky (as did its wearer).

Having survived the metaphorical firing squad, I could press ahead with my remaining plans for the weekend. We will never know if I was in a fit state to drive when I finally hit the road at just before noon on Saturday (I have my suspicions that the police's answer would have been a resounding no) but hit the road I did, bound for the picturesque Hunter Valley, just over 800 kilometres south of Brisbane. In partial acknowledgment of my condition and in part because I am a Japanese tourist at heart, the journey down was punctuated with stops at various sites. The highlight of this was when I attempted a cleansing ale at the historic Jennings Hotel on the Queensland/NSW border. The owner had been soaking up the winter sun when I arrived and I thought things were going to turn dark when she announced cards were not accepted so I said I would had to leave it. *"You got me inside just for that?!"* was the slightly narky response, but luckily her second customer of the day arrived just after me so making here five yard walk inside worthwhile...

The excesses of the previous night had meant that I had set off much later than planned and as a result did not arrive into the Hunter Valley until long after it had gone dark. I also misjudged the distances between pseudo-civilization meaning that I arrived in Scone and then Muswellbrook after the pubs had stopped serving meals and the Motel receptions had apparently closed. It was not looking good. Salvation came in the shape of Muswellbrook Motor Inn, on the way out of town, and better news followed as it was only a short walk to Muswellbrook Working Men's Club, which I entered just before non-members curfew at 10pm, to top up on the ample booze probably still in my system. Sleep was not difficult to come by, but ended way too soon, as I had left myself 100km's short of the target destination so faced another miserably early alarm clock at 5am. The only light challenging the darkness at this time was the glittering lights of the mines which never sleep and, like me, look better in the darkness than the light. By the time dawn did begin to break I had left the mines behind and was driving amongst the other "-ines" for which the area is famous – the vines. I could actually have had more time in bed as I arrived at Hunter Valley Gardens by 6am, where it was cold and breezy but already getting fairly busy with competitors for the various events. This was all part of a planned nostalgic 10 week farewell to Australia, as I had run the Winery Marathon in 2012, one month after our arrival in the 'Land of Plenty'. Back then life had been fresh and exciting, the future unknown. Although I will never tire of the sight of a kangaroo merrily going about its business, the subsequent 24 months have somewhat detracted from the sheen of first impressions. Nothing specific. Just life. Just law...

In what was to be an ominous sign of things to come for the entire day, I arrived at the registration desk to find there was no race bib for Nicholas Turner. No biggie, as a replacement was rustled up. The race itself was far harder than I had remembered, even though back in 2012 it was my first significant run after one month recovering from a motorbike crash in Thailand. The course started with a wind through the manicured gardens before opening out into the first vineyard with a mild climb. I was leading at this stage, until an overweight man in a skin-tight red running top – who was to becoming a recurring theme of the morning – came pounding past me, already breathing heavily. The view was beautiful – the mountains under a grey sky, all experienced at chilled temperatures, stirring memories of Europe. Although enjoying the view, I was very conscious that I was not tracking great – my breathing was poor and legs already tight as we hit the first, and most significant, climb on a run that was rarely flat. By the time we reached the summit I had overtaken the Fat Man, but been passed by three other non-fat men, who were already disappearing at pace. At least we now hit a stretch of the course where for nearly seven kilometres, give or take the odd manageable incline, the general theme was descent. It made for a false sense of security, which was soon displaced when the turn at the 11km mark sent us back from whence we had come. Gentle uphills always feel far more pronounced than even steep downhill sections and I was soon struggling again. I reflected that this was probably a result of weeks of accumulated fatigue and exacerbated by the decision to indulge in a large McDonalds' breakfast, but who knows? Whatever it was, I knuckled down to reach the halfway point without stopping running before promptly stopping to walk whilst eating a banana that was the only vaguely healthy thing I had put into my system for probably three days…

A quick look over my shoulder revealed that the Fat Man was still closer than I would have liked and, as another runner passed me, I decided that my only objective for the day was to keep the Fat Man behind me. The second half was truly miserable, my only entertainment coming from flipping the bird to the motivational signs which seemed to be mocking me as I trudged slowly by them. Every time I glanced behind me, there was the red clad Fat Man. Slow but unrelenting. Metronomic. Stay back Fat Man. At the final ascent, approximately three kilometres from the end, I was again reduced to a walk but when I looked back the Fat Man was far enough back that I knew I had defeated him and could take some sort of pathetic comfort from that in what had been an otherwise poor effort. In the end, I finished in **3 hours 17 minutes and 6 seconds**, for sixth place out of 107 finishers. With a near enough ten hour drive to face, there was no time to dwell on this most hollow of victories and the Jazz and I were soon heading north.

Sadly, something – possibly something McNasty – had disagreed with my system and I was soon pulled over for one of a number of stomach emptying stops on the way home. When the stomach cramps and sickness subsided, fatigue was there to fill their place and I had only travelled around 100 km's of the return journey when I had to admit defeat and pull into the Tourist Information Centre car park in Scone for an hour's sleep. It pretty much did the job and I was eating up the road in no time. Sadly I was eating too fast (maybe the cause of my earlier problems as well) and caught the attention of the NSW traffic police who pulled me over and asked why I was travelling 113kmh in a 100 zone? I lied plausibly enough that I had not realised I was and also decided to ham up the British accent a notch. Whether that helped, we will never know, but something caused that kindly patrol officer to let me off with a warning. Frankly, for getting 113kmh out of a Honda Jazz, I think I deserved some merit points. My faked contrition to the officer and promises to take it steady soon expired, replaced by the horrible reality that I was still over five hours from Brisbane and fading fast. Aside from a couple of moments when I seemed to slide into a waking trance, and almost the barriers lining the road at the same time, the remainder of the journey passed incident free (save for a random stop in a tiny town at a café that put anything I visited in Amsterdam to shame for the potency of the cannabis smoke on entry). However, a horror show of a day was nearly complete when I arrived back to Bris just before 11pm to discover that the house key was MIA somewhere in the litter strewn car. I feverishly threw things around, dragged seats forward and backwards and furiously pulled up the carpets, before finally finding the key glinting under the back seat. I'm not honestly sure what I would have done had I not found it, such was my emotionally, physically and spiritually drained condition. I may well have just whispered a few apologies to the stars, crawled onto the road and waited for eternal peace. Again, we will never know...

48

BRISBANE 2014

My training in the week leading up to my third running of the Brisbane Marathon was that of an athlete from a bygone era, when hard drinking was no bar to sporting performance. Wednesday involved steady consumption of cheap wine and was without just cause. Thursday was a remarkable day. It started unremarkably enough with the usual morning constitutional. However, I was stopped in my tracks by a feint plea for help from behind a shelter on the South Bank, an area which hugs the River Bris in Brisbane. I turned to find a young man tip toeing his way over the rocks from out of the river. He was fully clothed, soaking wet and shivering. It transpired he was a 21 year old missing person with voices in his head. I was probably not the best person he could have encountered, as I lack a number of social skills and sometimes have one loud voice in my head – that of evil twin, Rick. I did as well as I could, taking him to sit in the sun and offering him coffee, clean, dry clothes or a walk to the nearby hospital, but all were rebuffed. Fortunately, a better equipped human had stopped and called the police and an ambulance and 20 minutes later my encounter with a broken human was over. I have to admit that the incident had a lasting impact on my fragile emotional fabric, fraying it for the rest if the day and the next few. It was a convenient excuse for the continued assault on booze which continued on Thursday night, Friday afternoon and night (nearly burning house down with another chip based disaster, although on the plus side I created coal) and all day Saturday, which I blame on being held hostage by having to wait at the unit for eBayers, most of whom magically materialised, albeit several hours late, to take my wares. By the time the last buyer had been and gone, 10 cans of beer had too, and it seemed disrespectful not to honour them by heading out into old Brisbane city. By the time I headed home, way too late, the count had nearly been doubled so what followed should not come as a huge surprise...

It was so dark when I awoke that I was fairly sure I had woken up ahead of the 4:30 am alarm and may even have the luxury of another hour of sleep. Absolutely wrong. It was 5:40am and the marathon was starting at 6am, nearly three kilometres away. My mind was scattered and I ended up wearing 'fashion' shorts, rather than running shorts and managing a quick banana before transporting the Jazz as close as possible to the race start line (which was not that close) and then hot stepping it to the start line. I had already seen the race winding its way around the streets so it was no surprise that I had the unique and slightly eerie experience of a solo start. I set off like the Devil was on my heels and was soon passing the race stragglers although my progress was halted as I reached the incline to Story Bridge and was forced to shuffle along the pavement at the side, restricted to the speed of the back markers. It was frustrating, but ultimately my fault, so I had to grin and bear it. After the seemingly interminable trudge of the bridge, the course wound down to the river and opened up, meaning that I was again to move forward fairly rapidly through the filed, although I was wasting a lot of energy running laterally to avoid those out for a leisurely jog, rather than a lung busting PB. After around 12 kilometres I ran past the lunatic who drags his friend around these events on roller blades (previously encountered at the 110km *Darkness to Light* event) and managed a selfie and had another bite of the cherry after 15 km when I passed them again, having been forced to stop for what can only be described as an unpleasant couple of minutes in a 'dunny' (portaloo).

By the halfway point, the day was heating up and the paths were clear as the bulk of runners had been completing the half marathon and had finished their work for the day. My general trajectory was still forward through the field, although encounters with other runners were becoming less frequent. I was generally feeling good, although I had expended an awful lot of energy trying to give myself a chance at a decent time and my legs were quite heavy. It was the usual battle between my mind (evil) and body (good) and my body generally prevailed, save for a couple of short strolls as I took on water and ascended a very gently sloping bridge, which seemed to have been tilted to a much more severe angle since our first encounter. There was a slightly chilling incident in the last two kilometres when a girl in front of me face planted. The group which stopped to help initially reassured her that all was OK until evidently she opened her mouth to reveal that she had knocked out on of her front teeth. Ouch! Undeterred, I pressed on and ramped it up for the last couple of kilometres, in the distant hope of a PB (despite the early travails).

My name was announced as I crossed the finish line, with the total time elapsed showing as around 3 hours 19 minutes. I was not sure quite how late I had started so knew it was going to be incredibly tight. When my chip time finally came in on the results website, it revealed I had missed a PB by an agonising 8 seconds, finishing 24th in **3 hours 9 minutes and 59 seconds**…So basically, an alarm or less involved toilet break away from a best ever time. I was too tired to be annoyed with myself, until Monday although within my anger I realised that my time would have been much worse had I not spent so much time training in bars…

49

LAMINGTON ECO CHALLENGE I – 2014

You know what they say, "a marathon double-header weekend deserves a double-header drinking warm up". This would only be true if "they" was short hand for "no one" or "people who hate you"…

Firstly, I shall deal with the merry aspect of proceedings, which started with a meeting with Sir James Sceats – fellow refugee from the Mother Land – on Thursday evening. We did what men folk from our homeland do when they get together and drank long and hard into the evening (last time James and I imbibed together in Brisbane I ended up waking up under my desk wrapped in Christmas gift wrap at 6am on a Wednesday morning), although the advancing of father time into our respective lives prevented proceedings from extending into the early hours of Friday, which was probably just as well given what was ahead. I had chosen my school night out wisely as I was relatively quiet on Friday at work and only had to survive until the refuge of a boozy lunch to belatedly celebrate the financial year end. The wine flowed well over lunch and meant that my final (and only) act of the afternoon – a basic email – took nearly an hour and an intense level of concentration. It was at this point that I started to make bad (worse?) decisions. I left the office early and headed for a nearby bar, followed by another, before settling at the Bavarian Bier Café, where mid-strength and low-strength beer are harder to find than a genuine German behind the bar.

In exercise parlance, I was by now thoroughly "stretched" (in night parlance, "loose"), which was sub-ideal given that I was required to attend one of the firm's primary client functions of the year – The Queensland Show Week Cocktail Party – that night. Fortunately, it was not a bad event to arrive at en route to the oft-visited destination of Downtown Lashville, and I think that I managed to fit in relatively well with the general air of mirth, before realising that I may be on the verge of falling from the tightrope, thus moving from being entertaining to being a menace. Sadly, rather than deciding to exit civilisation altogether, I returned to the Bavarian. This was Nicholas's last recollection of the evening. The morning brought with it the horrible realisation of another hunger drive, followed by a marathon, together with a strange exchange of texts with a partner from the office:

NT – *"Sorry I missed your calls. Think I might have been arrested..."*

Partner – *"I know, I was there. Told them you were a Pommie Bastard."*

NT – *"Thank you for that."*

I thought nothing more of it, as my attention had now switched to somehow negotiated the Jazz two hours southbound for Part 1 of the defence of my Lamington Eco Challenge double marathon crown. Predictably, I arrived late at the start, somewhat sullying the honour of being given race bib number 1 (for the second time in my life) and requiring help from an elderly gentleman to tie my laces before setting off a small way behind the rest of the field. I tried to ignore the fact that I felt bad, but the fact that I was one of very few to stop at the first drinks station – only 2.5 km in – to throw down several gallons of water probably told its own story...

The course soon came back to me from 2013 and I knew the importance of making progress on the first half, which was all downhill, as things became distinctly nasty after the halfway point. I was steadily progressing through the small field and ran for a short while with a man who told me that he was the *"number one obstacle course runner in Queensland"*, which I didn't know was even a thing. I was glad to have company as we ran through a single track road which bisected the valley floor and were surrounded by spooked cows, who seemed to not know what they were doing, but determined to do it at pace, which is quite scary with animals of that size.

My short time partner eventually scuttled off and I was left alone for the return ascent, which was every bit as brutal as I had remembered, although it did offer the small comfort of shade. After a final lung crippling climb up a grassy hillside, thoughts began to turn to the finish, only for the course to swing into a thick forest that was all but impossible to run through, such were the number of roots and branches covering the floor. I was ready for it to end. The run; the hangover; life itself, when the sweet music of the road, which spelt the final stretch of misery, reached my ears. A few hundred undulating metres of asphalt later and the first day's misery was over – third place in **4 hours 18 minutes 01 seconds**...

I briefly distracted myself from the pain and misery of contemplating it all again in less than 24 hours by visiting some beautiful alpacas at the start of the drive home, before letting the dark clouds build on the sofa, like a death row inmate musing his last thoughts. Luckily, I have a very low concentration span so soon moved from melancholic thoughts to the nearby curry house – replicating last year's mid-race routine, like any good superstitious sportsman – where I enjoyed a slightly over spicy curry and definitely overpriced beer. After a couple more beers, I was ready for a few short hours sleep before hauling ass again for the one hour earlier start time of race number two...

50

LAMINGTON ECO CHALLENGE II – 2014

Overall, the extreme discomfort in my legs was balanced out by the lack of an extraordinary hangover, with the net result being that I felt relatively optimistic for day two. I had also made the start with minutes to spare, the first time I had achieved this most unremarkable feat in three marathons. I responded by setting off like Satan were chasing my bad self in a chariot dragged by the horsemen of the Apocalypse, but this was soon halted by the first steep climb, which reduced me to a slow plod. A slow plod soon turned to a shuffle, and this routine was only broken when the course turned definitively downhill and I ignored the excruciating pain in my quad muscles to let it all go as fast as gravity would carry me.

I was in second place at this point, but soon passed by two others as soon as we hit the flat. The leader was long gone, meaning that so was my crown, but I was determined to hang onto a podium which meant overtaking one of the two men who were still within sight but seemingly edging steadily out of reach. Possibly sensing the prospect of a podium finish, it transpired that one of them had over reached himself and I reeled him in quite quickly after the turn. As he gradually disappeared into the distance behind me, I was able to take some semblance of satisfaction from a podium placing defence, although this was marred by the fact that my calf, quad and hamstring muscles had seemingly turned into wood/steel by the time I reached the finish line in **4 hours 22 minutes and 13 seconds**, for a second third placed finish of the weekend and third place overall…

I decided to metaphorically stop and smell the roses on the return journey as I took time to feed my new found alpaca friends, only for them to literally spit in my face, which itself is probably a metaphor for something. All that remains is to confirm that the epilogue to the text exchange described above, I arrived at work to find said partner enquiring what had become of me on Friday evening. I responded that he was undoubtedly better placed than me to answer that given that I had been "Men in Blacked" at some point in the Bavarian. He explained that he had been calling to see where I had got to, only for a police officer from a part of Brisbane a long way from my home to answer the phone and explain that they had found me, in sub-prime condition, and were going to arrest or send me home. Despite his racial slur, they opted for a taxi home, rather than the boiler suit. Thank you law, all round. Whether or not they believed I had two marathons over the weekend is a moot point (and that, my friends, is an excellent legal-based gag on which to conclude)…

London 2007 – "The Tortoise and the Hare"

Barcelona 2009 – "Salvar Tibet"(?!) (also "Salvar Nickos" after 10 pints the night before…); with Ben, Joe and Richard

Berlin 2010 *– Recovering after a 40ish kilometre walk the night before; Ben, Nicholas and Luke*

Apeldoorn 2012 *– cool runnings…*

Lamington Eco Challenge I – 2013 – *N Turner reporting for action…*

Sunshine Coast 2013 – *the Dark Side…*

Sydney 2013 *– there are worse places to finish a marathon.*

Bribie Beach Bash 2013 *– a failed title defence.*

Liverbird Double 2014 – New Year's Day – make mine a double…

Red Rock to Coffs Harbour 2014 – an early but stunning start to proceedings.

***Gold Coast 80 – 2014** – Championi!*

***Yuleba 2014** – another victory after a 600ish kilometre drive to the race!*

Lamington Eco Challenge 2014 – *another failed title defence but marathon 50 done…*

Sydney 2014 – *the farwell Australia run. Not a bad setting for it…*

Shakespeare Spring 2015 – *budget Bond. Buying full kit an hour before the race.*

North Dorset Village 2015 – *the shake down post run…*

Manchester 2015 – *celebrating breaking three hours at The Theatre of Dreams. Sadly, it turned out the race was a few hundred metres short…*

The Wall 2015 – *With Robin and Liv somewhere on the 69 mile course…*

Chesterfield 2015 – *the fan club! Isobel and Jamie supporting near the end of the marathon.*

Dublin 2015 – *a pint of the black stuff to toast completing another marathon.*

Las Vegas 2015 – *celebrating completing 26 marathons during the year with a few super pals…*

Blackpool 2016 – *two towers, post the finish…*

Nottingham Outlaw 2016 – *toasting the run with the team, Andy (bike), Ennis (swim)*

Petra Desert 2016 – *an awe inspiring setting for the start of the marathon...*

Spartathlon 2016 – *running in Pheiphiddes' steps through beautiful Greece*

Spartathlon 2016 – *the sad end. Note the hundred yard stare of a broken man.*

Amman 2016 – *Mother T and Father T watching me in action for the first time.*

Wrexham 2017 – *pictured with and without Brains...*

Zurich 2017 – *what I thought was the fabulous end to the 100 (in fact, this was number #101)…*

51

RIVER RUN 100 - 2014

On the Friday night before Sunday's 100 latest kilometre challenge, I added a potentially broken hand (random drunken injury) to my mildly cracked ribs from Tough Mudder the previous weekend (which revealed an astounding lack of upper body/core strength). Saturday was spent feeling sorry for myself, especially as a procession of eBayers arrived, starting at 7am, to remove various items from my unit, all being sold in preparation for the return to the UK. Although they had all paid good money for my wares, it somehow felt like having a front row seat as my house was robbed. As a result of the Friday night pre-injury shenanigans, I was also in no way prepared for the eBayers meaning that they had to clamber over piles of junk and watch as I emptied drawers and wardrobes before they were able to take the items. Given what follows, this is ironic considering that a centurion was reputed to be "*strict in exercising and keeping up proper discipline among his soldiers, in obliging them to appear clean and well-dressed and to have their arms constantly rubbed and bright*" (Vegetius. De Re Militari). Mother T would not have been proud...

On the Sunday I sought to dismantle those body parts which were not yet injured. The implement of destruction was a 100km run on the banks of the Brisbane River – scene of a similar demolition job not too long ago. The (slightly random) idea of the River Run 100 was to finish as close to 3pm as possible, meaning one had to work backwards and estimate how long the ordeal would take. Based on previous experience, and building in some small leeway for unforeseen disasters, I decided to start at 5am, giving me ten hours to cover the distance. Two others were starting at this time and a number of other runners were already on the course. After a rare downpour on Saturday, conditions were pretty much perfect and as a result I set off too quickly. There were two alternative loops, of 10km and 5km, on the opposite sides of the river, which provided limited, but crucial, variety for the purposes of retaining a semblance of sanity. It also meant that there was no real way of gauging where one was in relation to other runners. This was of no matter as, when a run is for such a long distance, survival rather than speed is the only objective.

For what it is worth (nothing), I was through the first marathon in about 3 hours 20 minutes, way too fast in the circumstances, and I soon paid the price for my excitement. With 60km gone, any pain in my ribs and hand had been usurped by agony in my legs and feet and I was teetering on the verge of my first ever race withdrawal. I tried to summon resolve from the depths of races past but it was not looking good. There was a sea change when I finally hit the last 15km, meaning just one loop of each lap to go before the misery would end. By this time, it felt like both of my feet were on the verge of breaking (an injury I have picked up before), a muscle around the back of my left knee/calf felt on the verge of tearing and my nipples, inner thighs and the smallest muscle in my body felt as if they had been rubbed with sandpaper for the last eight hours. I was desperately trying to suppress the pain by telling my brain to turn off the pain receptors and take me to a happy place but for once it was demonstrating will power and refusing to weakly submit to mild pressure. Thanks for nothing brainio - where were you on Friday?! Literally...

I received a very small pep up on my last ten kilometre loop, and penultimate loop of all, when a fellow competitor – who turned out to be a decent triathlete, but had long since been reduced to a slow trudge in this event, now with pushchair – described me as a "*machine*". I initially took this as a compliment before realising that a dildo may technically be a machine, which put the praise in some context. My mind was by now too shot to dwell on any one matter, other than excruciating pain, for more than a few seconds and I sadly had to accept that today would not be the day when I discovered the meaning of life out on the lonely road.

The pink inflatable that marked the end of just over nine hours of punishment was a beautiful camp sight at the end of a red brick road of misery as it meant that this heartless, brainless, cowardly fool could return to his rapidly emptying home. The most painful part of the day came now (for reasons elaborated on below) when the race organiser gave me a firm handshake to congratulate me on the run. I positively and involuntarily yelped with the agony. There was the small matter of the world's slowest ever trudge through about two kilometres of Brisbane CBD to negotiate before I could drive home and luxuriate in the all-encompassing pain I had inflicted on myself. Website confirmation that I had finished third (of only 14 competitors) in **9 hours 6 minutes** was meaningless to my battered body and soul…

I had spent less than 10 minutes at my desk on Monday morning before the damage to my right hand was spotted and I was ordered to the doctor by three secretaries/surrogate mothers. The x-ray confirmed a small fracture or two which required a seemingly overly large cast for four weeks. The fact that this was easily the least concerning of my ailments goes some way to explaining the effectiveness of my weekend of self-assault. Like an alcoholic who has not yet made the decision that they want to stop drinking, I made the usual hollow promises to myself and others that this would be the last time that I would reduce myself to such a wreckage, and it will be…until next time…

52

SUNSHINE COAST 2014

In an acknowledgment of my ongoing failings not to walk into weekend temptation, drastic measures were required to give me any hope of a PB at the Sunshine Coast marathon...

The measures taken involved a late drive north to Mooloolaba on Saturday afternoon to collect the race pack, which significantly cut down on time for mischief. My propensity to act like a tourist almost rendered this a disastrous decision as by taking the scenic route and a number of stops on the drive north I very nearly missed the registration cut off time. Given that three other runners were relying on me for their kits, this was not good. However, make it I did.

Stage 2 in the 'Operation Sensible' master plan was to attend a production of Swan Lake by the American Theatre Company at QPAC. I also cut this fine and, as a result, failed to pick up the single page synopsis being handed out in the foyer. This led to a confusing first half of the performance which appeared to feature a 'well pouched' prince giving up on women in favour of a swan he found in the woods. Confusion aside, it was difficult not to be impressed by the performance, particularly the pirouetting on tiptoes. In the interval I managed to procure the summary sheet, which changed my world and improved my enjoyment vastly. I may also take to bowing at the office each time I have completed a difficult task, although won't hold my breath waiting for an ovation for any of my drafting...The knock on effects of spending the day just making everything in the nick of time was a very late dinner/carbo loading session, which I figured may be no bad thing...

For the first time in a while, there were no feelings of dustiness or dread to accompany the 4am alarm and I was organisation personified as I made my way to Mooloolaba and parked up with nearly 20 minutes of pre-race time to spare. Sadly, nothing is ever straightforward and by the time I had made my peace with a portaloo and dropped off the three other race kits to the agreed point, I had to scamper to the start line to avoid another late start. The field was not huge so I set off with the 'elites', although the genuine elite athletes – including world rated Kenyan - were mere dots in the distance within the first three kilometres. The course had been changed slightly from the previous year but, after a couple of mild ups and downs early on, retained a generally flat gradient. It was heating up, but conditions were generally very good and I was tracking at a decent pace, reaching halfway in under 1 hour 30 minutes. Soon after the hallway point, I realised that this pace had possibly been beyond my means and the white swan of optimism and pace was replaced with the black swan fatigue and trepidation at what was to come. Drinks stations became an excuse for a short walk and the cast on my right arm was suddenly feeling like a heavy burden on my once beautiful wing. The balloons of the three hour pace runner soon passed me and hopes of a PB were also steadily evaporating on the first of two 10.5 kilometre loops. The cast did at least prompt a higher level of support than is usual from spectators and fellow runners, with several shouts of "wow – nothing can stop you!" They were nearly wrong, as I was deteriorating rapidly as the heat climbed. The vague hope of a PB roused a decent last loop from my ailing body and I thought I may just crack my previous best of 3:09:50 as I accelerated towards the finish line. Alas, the race clock was ticking towards **3 hours 11 minutes** by the time I made the turn and, just like Siegfried and Odette, I was ready to cast myself into a lake of tears to commiserate…

The predictable post script to a single month including 1 x 100km ultra marathon, 4 x marathons and 1 x Tough Mudder was a battered, scarred body, which is starting to creak at the seams, and an already tired looking cast, which smells like it may be capable of leaving my body independently before its scheduled four week term is up…

53

SYDNEY 2014

…And so we came to an end…After a prolific 27 months of running Down Under, the end finally came with the 17th marathon of the year and my 37th in Australia. I had a singular aim - to finally break my personal Holy Grail of the three hour mark. Sadly, this objective had not been communicated to my friend, Will Power, and nights out on Wednesday and Thursday meant that I was in moderate (at best) shape for the start of the drive south to Sydney which commenced on Friday evening. My first target destination was Gunnedah – purportedly the *"Koala Capital of Australia"* and therefore, by default, the world. Alas, I had again underestimated the vastness of the country and by 10pm had only reached Goondiwindi – a small outback town – where I decided to stop for the night. There were limited signs of life on Goondi's main "strip", save for O'Reilly's Hotel, which for once in Oz, was both a bar and hotel in the English sense of the word. The place was in relatively full Friday swing, primarily thanks to boozed up party of 50-somethings dressed in school uniforms. Elsewhere a small group of 30-somethings seemed to be getting closely acquainted and – given the remoteness and demographics of the town – my suspicion was that the four pairs were shuffled fairly regularly and all familiar with each other. Having confirmed that there was a room available for the night, I decided to settle down and watch the human spectacle unfold over a few beers. Once I had seen enough I retired to my perfectly adequate room where, like Goldilocks, I had the choice of three single beds to choose from, which seemed unnecessary.

After an acceptable night's sleep, I headed out early onto the post-apocalyptic emptiness of Goondiwindi's streets, filled up with petrol and began slowly clicking off the 800 or so kilometres still separating me from Sydney. It was a crisp, sunny morning as I passed through flat farmland whilst the sun slowly peered its head above the horizon. As usual, the roads were generally quiet, the temptation to speed great and progress was generally good. I reached Gunnedah at around 11am and my only koala sighting was on the signs welcoming me to, and then thanking me for visiting, the town. Hats off to the local tourist board who no doubt bolster the economy by luring similarly idealistic and gullible tourists to the town in hope of a 'wild' koala sighting. Undeterred by the shy marsupials' no show I pressed due south east and disaster nearly struck when I made the call to drive past the petrol station on leaving Gunnedah. Although the fuel dial was very close to zero, there were a number of towns marked on the road sign as being within 50 kilometres of Gunnedah and I was sure that one would have a petrol station, if nothing else. My resolve was tested slightly when the orange light, indicating no fuel, lit up almost immediately after passing the road sign. There was a momentary pause before I put my right foot down and hoped all would be OK. My confidence began to ebb when 'towns' one and two turned out to comprise a huge grain silo and two other buildings. 'Towns' three and four were not much more substantial and I was by now just waiting for the Jazz to cough its final cough and leave me stranded in a remote part of Australia. Amazingly the death cough never came and I finally stumbled upon a typically rural gas stop where I was able to give the Jazz a long overdue drink.

I said some sincere but soon forgotten thank yous to whatever guardian angel had overseen my safe passage before pressing on further with my journey. I was soon entering the relatively familiar surrounds of the Hunter Valley, where a spectacular fire ball caused a long queue of traffic. Australians are not always the most patient of nationalities and a couple of drivers decided they had waited long enough and decided to ignore the police cordon and bomb past everyone who was waiting in line. Flaming Gallahs! Anyway, I was in no huge rush so continued to take things steadily as I took in the initial mine pocked scenery of the Hunter, before the industrial landscape gave way to altogether more pleasant rolling vineyard covered land as wine country took over. The afternoon took a turn for the splendid as I wandered around Hunter Valley Gardens, stretching my legs after lunch. I stumbled across a group of people congregated around a small helicopter. Apparently, only one of the group was feeling bold enough for a short flight over Hunter Valley but was not keen on paying 120 dollars for the experience. Enter Nicholas. I agreed to split the costs and was soon donning a head set and taking a seat next to a very fresh faced pilot. When asked by the pilot whether it was my first time, I responded, *"No [I had previously enjoyed a Vegas to Grand Canyon chopper flight] – is it yours?"* Thankfully it was not and he handled the helicopter well despite an at least brisk wind, which blew the small craft around more than I might have liked. Despite the breeze, it was a pretty epic – if short – adventure and a great way to see the miles and miles of vineyards of Hunter Valley. I thanked my new acquaintance for the opportunity and was soon back in the Jazz and on my way southbound to complete my journey.

As with the 2013 iteration of the Sydney Marathon, my initial destination was Joe and Bel's house in Gosford. We enjoyed an excellent catch up over a few glasses of wine and beer before I hit the sack for a relatively early night – prudent, given the fact that I would need to get up at 3am before making my way to Gosford Train Station to catch the train for the 45 minute journey to Sydney. It was quite an emotional experience standing at Milson's Point, under the Harbour Bridge and looking across to the Opera House. Sydney was where my Australian adventure had started in 2012 and it was fitting that I was back in Sydney a week before I would leave the country…

The course was slightly different to the 2013 route, although still fantastic, and a year of additional running in my legs meant that I was covering the ground at a swifter rate than I had done around 12 months previously. Poignantly, the course took me along a number of stretches which I had covered many times during my few months of travelling through and then living in Sydney. Spurred on by some great memories, I managed to maintain a generally strong pace throughout – punctuated by a few short hiccups of walking towards the end – and finished with my best marathon time to date. A time of just over **3 hours 5 minutes**.

Unlike the previous year, there was limited time to soak up the post-race atmosphere nor the sights of Australia's East Coast (primarily as a result of me needing to pack up two years of life in a few days) and, after a quick farewell to Joe and Bel, I blasted the Jazz back up the East Coast to begin final preparations for the return to Blighty...

54

SHAKESPEARE AUTUMN 2014

At the end of the Yellow Brick was a journey home which was at times slightly more petrifying than being transported a long distance via tornado. The end when it came was chaotic, as one would expect for someone dismantling over two years of existence. I also managed to leave Australia without any cash cards, which made survival at times challenging. The month long trip back to the UK, via Hong Kong, Japan and overland through Europe from Istanbul culminated with a stag do in Bath, the sum total of which was a several month reversal in my physical condition. More evidence of how much easier it is to become unfit than fit…

The saddle which I found to clamber back in to in order to begin the hard road back to fitness was the appealing sounding *"Shakespeare Marathon"* in William's home town, Stratford-upon-Avon. With less than two weeks of steady training under generally grey East Midlands' skies, confidence was low, but at least the run would provide a clear measure of my deterioration.

I had enlisted good friend Robin – a multiple marathon runner and recent Ironman (full distance triathlon) – to join me for the run but, sadly, my research into the event had been on the brief side. It transpired that rather than a run around a beautiful historic town which would rekindle my love for my country of birth, we would be bypassing the town and running eight five kilometre laps, plus a shorter loop, of an airfield. Yuk. Robin was very gracious in his thanks for me having put him onto such a prestigious and beautiful marathon.

On the plus side, the conditions were perfect and, as an airfield, the course was almost completely flat. Small mercies. Given the fairly miserable prospect of looping an uninspiring piece of land for several hours, it was slightly surprising to find several hundred people at the event – albeit a number were participating in shorter events than the marathon.

The start line was actually on a tired looking drag racing strip, which formed part of the complex. The race briefing was almost inaudible, although we did manage to hear the warning that there was an outside chance that a plane may need to land, in which case athletes would need to remove themselves from the landing area. I was slightly apprehensive having possibly overcooked my mostly cross country training in the week leading up to the run, but there was no way back now.

The race began with a very short stretch on the drag straight, between tatty wooden stands, before turning onto a pot holed airstrip. There were a few decommissioned grey RAF planes scattered around the grassy areas but, aside from that, very little to distract one from the task at hand, and the fact that the same route would have to be repeated eight times. Urgh. The conditions were perfect though – still, misty and cool. There were a couple of very minor inclines, which felt steeper as the day went on, although naturally – as a lap course – they were balanced out by equivalent downhill stretches. I was running far too fast, but had to slow down a bit when we hit the drag strip as the morning dampness had made it a touch slippery. Despite the minor enforced braking, I completed the first 5k lap in a dangerously fast 19 minutes 29 seconds – a very short way behind the man who won the 5k race. I was however already someway down the field of those participating in the longer events. I gratefully swigged down some water at the refreshments table a couple of hundred metres and pressed on with lap two, trying to forget that I would need to pass this table another six times before finishing...

About half way around lap two a girl latched onto my shoulder, presumably deciding that I was running at a pace which she was comfortable with and – although we did not exchange words – this encouraged me to continue with a pace that was beyond my ideal. I realised that she was winning the ladies' half marathon and felt obliged to continue operating as an unspoken pace maker for the duration of the four laps she would need to complete. As a result, although my speed tailed off slightly it remained swift for the first four laps, which I completed in around 1 hour 22 minutes, which would have been on course for one of my fastest ever half marathons (if only I could have been finishing at this point). In common with the majority of my more recent marathons, the first lap had been mildly painful and made me question whether I had the full distance in me at all, there had then been a period of numbed acceptance where I was convinced I could continue to churn out the full duration at a good speed and by the halfway point I had realised that my optimism was misplaced and it was just a question of gritting my teeth and surviving. It was early on lap six, when I was at a very low ebb, where the lap system paid dividends. I saw Robin a short distance ahead and managed to draw level with him by around the halfway point of the lap. Robin was lapping at a steady pace, which was ideal for my wearied legs. We ran together for a lap and a half, talking the whole way, something which also helped take the edge of the pain now coursing through every sinew of my legs. This had taken me to the refreshments table at the start of my final 5k lap. Robin had two laps to complete so I said I would trot off and aim for a big finish. This was aided by Robin kindly handing me a gel sachet – jet fuel to a tired runner...

My last lap started brightly but gradually slowed to a moderate trudge and eventually a short walk before I was reinvigorated by crossing the start/finish line which meant that I just had the 1,950 metre balance of the marathon to complete. This final stretch also offered some very minor variation on the course I had been looping for the past three hours, which acted as a further encouragement. The final few hundred metres down the drag strip seemed to have lengthened over the day and never felt longer than now as I aimed right for the sweet release of the finish line, which I reached in a time of **3 hours 14 minutes and 32 seconds**. An acceptable result given the six weeks which had preceded the marathon...

55

LIVERBIRD DOUBLE
NEW YEAR'S EVE 2014

It is a strange gentleman indeed that can find no better way to spend nearly half of New Year's Eve than driving to Liverpool, running a marathon and then driving back to Leicestershire. But that is what I did, for the second consecutive year. My twisted mind elevates me to the important central character in a soap opera which it is convinced is being publicly aired (which to an extent it is through the median of social media) and therefore thought there would be a pleasant symmetry in starting and finishing a less than stellar 2014 with marathons. This may indeed be true were there more than 10 occasional viewers (Facebook likers) of this particular story…

As far as the event itself goes, see broadly **Chapters 36** and **37** above. The variations on that tale were a different start point to the drive (Leicestershire instead of Warwickshire), less of a hangover and much better conditions, although there was still a fairly brutal headwind on the outward legs of the out and back marathon. Again the cold weather ensured that I achieved the rare personal feat of running throughout the 26.2 miles, enjoying a number of high fives with fellow runners along the way. I was fairly disappointed that my finishing time was a couple of minutes slower than a year previously although I suspect this can be put down to long runs through the deep Peak District snow on each of the two days preceding the marathon.

The key differential in the 2014 instalment was that I had already determined that I would be cutting loose on New Year's Eve and not returning for the second running of the event on New Year's Day. It was this blissful thought more than anything which helped me through the typically painful final stages of the run which ended a year of 19 marathons/ultra-marathons…

More pressing concerns for now revolved around securing some form of employment which ideally does not involve giving happy endings to middle aged men on darkened canal paths, although the world's oldest profession was certainly on my short list.

56

NEWCASTLE RACECOURSE 2015

A New Year and a new me? Well, not quite. Or, in fact, at all. After a failed attempt to become a laboratory test-chimpanzee and several months of sat in front of the sort of TV output which erodes one's IQ with every banal hour endured, I went back to the past and returned to the job I left in 2012 (and 2008!). I was as surprised as the next man by this. Unless the next man in fact happened to be my mother (and, to be clear, not a man), who is now partially deaf and therefore very prone to surprises. After one week of moderation, my Friday night behaviour reverted immediately to 2006 to 2012 vintage, as I managed to lose some brand new Asics trainers, various items of clothing and wash bag in central Nottingham, before curling up for a hideous sleep on a yoga mat under my desk.

Anyway, at least there was at least a *New*-castle for the first instalment of an attempt to achieve *"A Marathon of Marathons"* (26.2 marathons) in 2015 although, as a result of Friday night, the journey north on Saturday afternoon had to be interspersed with naps at service stations and culminated in a lengthy trek around the Metrocentre to locate replacement trainers. Despite self-imposed trials and tribulations, I arrived at the modest Britannia Hotel, Newcastle Airport, at around 6pm and managed a decent sleep before getting up for the shortish drive to Newcastle Racecourse.

My expectations for the event were fairly low and I was not to be disappointed as I parked up and stepped out of the car into a stiff breeze on a grey morning in the North East. There was a strong threat of rain in the air and the prospect of 16 laps of the ambulance track which runs within the racecourse boundary was somewhat bleak. As is regularly the case with these less appealing events, I was slightly amazed at the large number of runners who crammed into the (as yet) unstarred Pavilion Restaurant to register for either a half or full marathon or 50km (for the real sado's – pronunciation works in more than one way). There were slightly different start points for each of the three events but we all set off at around 9:30am, initially on a slight descent, which meant there would be a matching ascent to deal with at some point (16 times). I led the 50 or so marathon runners out for a glorious two minutes, before being passed by two wirey gents as we weaved our way through the understandably steadier 50km runners. I was passed regularly during the first few laps, after which it became unclear what event anyone was participating in. The psychology of facing 16 laps was difficult, but an element of excitement was added to proceedings by the presence of a golf course in the inner area of the racecourse. The windy day meant that errant shots were not uncommon and several times running technique had to be compromised to avoid an off-line golf ball (something I am normally at the other end of)…

Once beyond half way, at least the lap countdown became comprehendible – an upturn matched by a tentative appearance of the sun – although this coincided with an increase in the strength of the headwind on the final straight of each lap. The arch of my left foot was also starting to cause some discomfort – perhaps not to be unexpected given the baptism of fire the new trainers were being given – and I was yearning for a conclusion to the event. Not unexpectedly, I was lapped by the first three runners in my race – recognising them from having seen them pass me hours previously – but took solace from the fact that I had lapped others on countless occasions, causing me to worry about how much longer those poor souls would be looping the course…

My own trudge finally finished after **3 hours 11 minutes and 38 seconds** (a lap time print off revealing a consistent decline in performance from lap 1 to lap 15, followed by a minor improvement on the final lap) with me in fifth place of what would be 47 finishers. A steady but unspectacular first lap of the latest challenge to erode my knees and soul…

57

GENK (BELGIUM) 2015

The first return to continental Europe for a marathon since 2012 did not disappoint. Due to a sparse range of mid-winter options, the event – the Louis Persoons Memorial (Genk) Marathon – chose itself.

My preparation in the week building up to the marathon was primarily inhibited by my attempt to move to a frugal existence, bordering upon that of a Dickensian miser. I had found an aesthetically acceptable, but service deficient, studio apartment on the northern extreme of the sought after West Bridgford area of Nottingham for a remarkably cheap monthly rent. Sadly, my cursory inspection had failed to identify a complete lack of heating, an issue addressed by sleeping fully clothed, which was soon compounded by a lack of electricity. This led to two nights which would have been helpful conditioning for a Sir Ranulph Fiennes' artic expedition, was I planning such a trip. During the second of these nights, I did have the benefit of a fairly thick beer jacket, which shielded me from the worst of the cold but meant that I awoke early on the Saturday morning of marathon weekend with a 'double headache' (cold + beer). A bracing walk to Nottingham train station did little to shift it but finding myself behind the wheel of Mother T's Ford Fiesta heading south from Chesterfield enforced a measure of recovery.

It was a long painful drive from Chesterfield to Dover – where I was forced to purchase a "Euro driving kit" (consisting of breathalyses – results may have been interesting – spare bulbs, emergency hazard triangle, light dimmers and luminous jacket) – where I was fortunately in plenty of time for my P&O ferry to Calais and therefore able to grab a precious few minutes sleep before departure.

The ferry passengers generally appeared to be of a fairly lowly socio-demographic group allowing my tatty shell to fit in nicely…

Once deposited in Calais there was the odd sign of even more lowly 'citizens' (possibly not officially recognised) by the roadside before the darkness fell and I ploughed on along the quiet motorways into Belgium. By the time I reached the ring road in Brussels, everything was running smoothly and I had visions of a nice meal and some wine before bed. Alas, at this point I discovered that pages three and four of my printed directions (I had no sat-nav and the Blackberry had given up the ghost) had come out blank and so my last instruction was to *"merge onto the E19"*. This would have been helpful were there no more options between here and Genk, but there were countless. What followed was a strategy of stopping in each service station to check current position against the maps helpfully printed on their walls (as above, I am clearly too tight-fisted to have purchased a road map of Belgium). This resulted in a rather long detour, via Liege, and still left me with the problem of finding my "Sports Hotel" in Genk itself. This latter issue was resolved with a multi-stage approach. Firstly I turned off down a road which 'felt promising' and asked a lady where the hotel was. She managed to direct me from there, via three more sets of traffic lights, to a road where *"hopefully you find more signs there. Good luck."* Miraculously she was right as I saw the correct road name, only to turn into a dark forested area on a single lane track. There was the glimmer of disco lights a short way into the forest, which turned out to be coming from the stand of a small sports stadium. So it was that I went to my first and last (probably) junior's disco in a forest in Belgium. After a false start involving a lady blabbering at me in Flemish (presumably along the lines of *"get out of this underage disco before I call the cops"*) it was confirmed that I was in the right place and just needed to follow the single track more deeply into the forest, where I would then find my hotel. Slightly terrifying sounding, but a result. The track eventually ended in a large car park which was adjacent to a sports centre, which in fact turned out to be 'Bloso Sports Hotel' or in English, a sports hall with dormitories and plastic mattresses. It was by now 10:30pm and the front door of the sports hall was locked but I found my way in through a side door and then saw to my delight my name beside a door. The dorms were actually not bad – mine was a spacious affair featuring a mezzanine level and five beds, none of which were occupied, a shower/sink room and a toilet. Sadly, and unsurprisingly, the sports hall and forest offered no late night catering so I was back in the Fiesta until I found a nearby kebab shop for some hearty and healthy pre-race fuel...

It transpires that the benefit of living in a small fridge is that anything remotely larger/warmer seems positively palatial. So it was that I had my best night's sleep in weeks and woke up ready to face the LPM marathon head on. Things got better still when I found that I had the large canteen and continental breakfast all to myself. Unfortunately my tendency when presented with unlimited amounts of food is to unleash the inner Labrador and three cheese and ham sandwiches, one banana, one apple, one yoghurt and countless cups of orange juice and coffee later I felt ready to return to bed rather than the start line of a marathon. It was a generous start time so I had ample time to mooch around the start areas and register before returning to collect my bags from the sports hall. This almost proved fatal as, together with several other runners, I found myself locked in the hall only a few minutes before the start of the run. Happily a cleaner was on hand to release the clowns and disaster was averted. There was a nice touch pre-race when a young boy presented the family of the late Louis Persoons with a bouquet of flowers before me and 200 or so intrepid runners set off on the narrow track through well-developed woodland...

The format of the race was seven six kilometre laps (plus the 195 metre balance which we had dealt with at the kick-off) and, aside from a short sharp hill at the start of the loop, it promised to be a decent track. The one slight wrinkle was that I had not realised the race did not start until 10am (I had thought 9:30am) and was therefore on a very tight schedule if I was to catch my return ferry from Calais at 5:15 pm (meaning being at the port at 4:45pm). In fact, I would miss it if the return from Genk to Calais took as long as the previous evening's drive. This caused some slightly ambitious early pacing, which had me in second place for the first four kilometres or so, after which I managed to calm down and slide down the field accordingly. Conditions were perfect and I clicked up the first three laps with some ease, only for energy levels to trail off dramatically during laps four and five. I was frantically doing the journey-time maths in my head by the end of the fifth lap and managed to summon up reserves of energy for a well-paced last lap which got me round in **3 hours 9 minutes and 19 seconds**, for a ninth place overall finish. Event organiser Micha sought an interview over the microphone but I sadly had to turn him down as I caught my breath before heading directly for the car to set about racing to the port of Calais…I had worn the Australian 'soccer' shirt I had received as a leaving present for the run and did find time to confirm to a Belgian couple that I was Australian and that I had found the day "bloody cold" in the worst Australian accent I for one have ever heard. They looked bemused and have probably crossed a trip Down Under off their bucket list…

I was the last car onto the Calais-Dover ferry, having arrived five minutes before the latest time for embarkation and having to wait as countless trucks (their under carriages no doubt full of immigrants clutching on for a better life) boarded the ferry. After devouring a KFC at Folkestone services, I pressed on relentlessly northbound, finally depositing Mother T's tired car on the road in Chesterfield at around 11:30pm before my battered carcass was heaped into the spare bedroom at my sister's house minutes later. A lot of waffle to describe a non-standard weekend…

58

BROAD MEADOW (STRATFORD-UPON-AVON) 2015

"Wisely and slow; they stumble that run fast..."...so wrote the Bard of Avon – Mr Shakespeare (Romeo and Juliet, *Act II, Scene III*) – and so it was as I stumbled around his hometown, Stratford-upon-Avon on a Saturday morning in spring...

The day started badly when I made the decision that stealing another few minutes sleep would improve my marathon prospects – this was on the back of two largish evenings out (*"For you and I are past our dancing days"* – Romeo & Juliet, *Act I, Scene V*). Unfortunately, the result of this additional slumber (and a cheeky McMuffin meal en route to collect the hire car from the office) was that I needed an error free drive in the hire car to Stratford if I was to make the start of the race on time. This was nearly achieved, until two bad decisions in Stratford left me seeking directions from some passers-by and pulling into the car park of the sports club where the race would start around three minutes before go time. This meant two things – (1) I did not have time to put a pay and display ticket on the car (something which I somehow got away with, unlike fellow tardy runners – *"As good luck would have it"* – The Merry Wives of Windsor, *Act III, Scene V*) and (2) I was still fastening on my running number almost a mile after setting off (*"Though this be madness, yet there is method in 't"* – Hamlet, *Act II, Scene II*).

After meandering around the centre of Stratford, the course took us out in the countryside via the canal, making for a flat first few miles. At this point I wasn't entirely sure why the event organiser had stressed the importance of taking the course plans with us, but this soon became apparent when four of us followed the wrong markings and ended up running about half a mile in the wrong direction (*"Men at some time are masters of their fates: The fault, dear Brutus, is not in our stars, but in ourselves..."* – Julius Caesar, *Act I, Scene II*). This error cost we four a number of positions in the field and, more importantly, vital energy on what was becoming an increasingly dicey course. Within a few miles of the Wrong Direction (good name for an alternative boy band?), it had become so slippery under foot that I could not run without the risk of falling over (which I managed, more than once) so I was reduced to a trudge until the surface became more stable. The reduced pace helped replenish my energy levels, which were boosted further when I tackled a cider (!) at the eight mile drinks station – a truly marvellous bonus (*"Small things make base men proud"* – King Henry the Sixth, *Part II, Act IV, Scene I*).

With the cider working its magic, I made decent progress to the race turn around point in a small village before topping up on cider when returning to the same drinks station after 14 miles. By this point I had been trying to suppress a certain natural calling, desperately hoping that there would be a toilet facility at one of the checkpoints. Alas it was not to be and so when I found myself alone in a wooded section, I did as bears do and it felt glorious and shameful at the same time (*"That it should come to this!"* – Hamlet, *Act I, Scene II*).

Shortly after the Yogi-incident of which we shall speak no more, I caught up with a small bunch of runners, who were re-tracing their steps after a wrong turn. We decided there may be safety in numbers as we tried to navigate the Warwickshire countryside and this approach seemed to work as we found our way back to the canal without further incident. The finish was now tangibly close, or so I thought, but I had forgotten that there was a further three mile or so loop to negotiate once we reached the sports' clubhouse. Although picturesque – running through a park in the town centre before following the River Avon for a short distance – this was undoubtedly the most psychologically challenging aspect of the day, especially as the stretch featured a steep hill at around its halfway point (*"The miserable have no other medicine but only hope"* – Measure for Measure, *Act III, Scene I*).

I did manage to find some final reserves on hitting the park again and a sprint finish over spongy grass to the clubhouse ended a fairly painful day with one of my slowest marathon times to date (**4 hours 8 minutes**, for 11th place out of 44 runners), but at that moment the time was really not important. I was done, at least for a few weeks (*"The common curse of mankind, – folly and ignorance"* – Troilus and Cressida, *Act II, Scene III*)...

59

BELVOIR CHALLENGE - 2015
("Don't Stop Belvoiring")

Due to a strange "reverse-Hyacinthing [Bucket]" (of Keeping Up Appearances fame), the title of this chapter is actually pronounced, "Don't Stop Beavering"...Not sure whether this pronunciation decision is this small enclave of the East Midlands' two fingers up to the French and their language, but I like it (and the "Jump on the Beaver" buses, which also happens to be the name of a film I once saw)...

The story of my preparation for the event could almost be cut and paste from 80% of what has gone before. After a fairly intense week at work (not entirely what the doctor(s) ordered following a stag do featuring mud buggying, medical fancy dress, pole dancing and a startled Chinese man, more details of each available on request), I made entirely The Wrong Decision by heading out for a few late drinks on Friday night. Fast forward a few hours and I woke up in my hovel, still wearing my suit and assuming I had missed the marathon. Sadly not.

As my running kit (and race address) were still at the office, I had to get a taxi there first, instructing the driver to wait outside, before heading for Belvoir. Given that I had not paid for leg one of the journey, I was slightly surprised to find that drives had decided to bugger off, leaving me to book a second taxi for the 30 minute or so drive to Harby, where the marathon would start. I managed to avoid the usual staid exchanges between taxi driver and passenger (*"You busy mate?"* [unlikely at 7am]; generic weather chat; awkward silence) by passing out immediately having given him the postcode of my destination...

The sleep had done some good, but I was still extremely tired when I arrived at the already busy Harby Village Hall for registration. The solution I found to this was in a very dark room at the back of the building, which none of the other runners seemed to have found. Using the glow of my mobile phone I managed to navigate myself to a very comfortable bed. OK, it had a dog bone print, was on the floor and smelt of dog, but it was otherwise absolutely fit for purpose and gave me what felt like the best 20 minutes sleep I have ever had. This was only disturbed when another runner finally discovered the room and came in to get changed, flicking on the light as he did so. He seemed slightly surprised to find a 34-year old man curled up in a dog bed and apologised for waking me up. I explained that this was OK, as I did not live in the room and the bed was not mine, and we parted as firm friends.

It was by now time to face the music, although the sheer volume of participants had caused a fifteen minute delay to proceedings. The race started opposite Harby School, before winding its way out into the countryside where the solid paved road very quickly gave way to a slippery mess of mud. At this point one of my fellow competitors started laughing at the sheer difficulty of the conditions. It would be the last time for four hours that I would hear the sweet music of laughter.

As with the Stratford run two weeks previously, I soon realised that in wearing road trainers I had made The Wrong Decision again. It was like being a Formula One driver with a car fitted with dry tyres trying to drive through a monsoon (comparisons with Formula One perhaps end there, given the pace and the glamour of the respective events – although I was involved in a delicious sandwich at the end of the race, which was ham and cheese as opposed to supermodel and girl band member) and I was soon being passed by those who had made better footwear decisions (or were just better runners, or had maybe prepared without completely reckless abandon). Despite the difficulty of moving at anything beyond walking pace for long stretches, it was a dry morning and a beautiful part of the world and I was generally in decent spirits. Spirits were raised further when I discovered at checkpoint two that, in addition to the usual water and basic race provisions, scones and cream, sandwiches and cake were available. I filled my boots (not literally). Although this resulted in fairly uncomfortable stitch, I was satisfied that it was a Good Decision and stuck with this approach at each of the next three checkpoints...

A slightly more significant problem than stitch arose just before the halfway point, when I was suddenly struck with severe cramp in my right calf. It is pretty rare for me to suffer from cramp and I was concerned that it may end up leading to something slightly worse. However, there was not really any point in dwelling on it so I just tweaked my running style to the tilted lope of a deranged maniac and pressed on. Between the spells of thick mud were short sections of road (including through the grounds of the impressive Belvoir Castle) and it was here that my road trainers were The Right Decision and I was able to pick up my pace slightly. This was somewhat irrelevant, as it was clearly not a day on which a PB would be in the offing, and so I soon slowed to a comfortable meander which allowed me to take in the scenery. This eventually became a very slow plod, followed by a walk, just before the finish line when, in addition to deep, slippery muddy paths, was added the problem of a number of stiles and wire fences to negotiate. By this time, negotiating a three foot high stile felt like clambering over something three times higher on an army assault course and it would be fair to say that I was fairly elated to return to the paved roads of Harby which meant that the finish line (and my sandwich) were only a few hundred metres away. I was bloody, muddy and had turned in one of my slowest ever marathons (**4 hours 13 minutes and 28 seconds**) but there were three friendly faces – Robin (of Shakespeare fame), Ben and Emma – to greet me at the end and the local pub was a very short hobble away. All was well again in the world (insert your own gag about spending the morning in a wet belvoir)...

60

SHAKESPEARE SPRING 2015

Life is easier, but infinitely more boring, when lived in the never, never land that is Hindsight. In the magical kingdom of Hindsight, nothing is ever lost, there are no accidents and the roller coaster that is real life is instead flat and unremarkable. In this parallel universe, Nicholas was not dressed in formal wear at a client's charity ball at the Hilton Metropole at 2am on Saturday morning still sipping a beer, eight hours before the start of a marathon for which he had no kit or means of reaching. He did not creep into a partner's room at the Metropole for four hours sleep curled up in the doorway, still fully black tie'd. He did not have to be shaken awake in reception at the Metropole to be told that his taxi to Stratford had arrived, nor was he Sports Direct, Stratford's, first customer on Saturday morning and first ever customer of the entire Sports Direct chain to arrive at the shop (where one is treated with scarcely disguised loathing by employees) in formal wear. Nope. In Hindsight, Nicholas had a healthy pasta dinner and early night on the Friday before waking early on Saturday, having a solid breakfast, stretching and making his way to the event in good time. One day, I shall move to Hindsight, but not yet. Not just yet. No. For now I will remain in Chaos (a cheap, grubby area on the other side of town awaiting gentrification)…

We'll pick up the tale back at Sports Direct, Stratford at 9am on Saturday morning. To add an additional complication to matters, I had left my debit card in the suit of clothes I had sported in a charity fashion show in Leicester the previous weekend (again, not something which has ever happened in utopian Hindsight), so was restricted to the cash I had managed to withdraw using my passport the previous day. This meant that I had to kit myself out efficiently and asked for *The Cheapest Running Trainers in The Shop*™. This slightly confused the sales assistant as it was somewhat in contrast to my attire, but they duly dug out some £25 Karrimor D30 trainers, to which I added Karrimor shorts and t-shirt and Slazenger socks – a full running kit for just over £40. Things were coming together nicely, although I did feel painfully old and tired...

My next taxi dutifully arrived at the appointed hour – it was driven by a man wearing the sunglasses and jewellery of an initially benevolent dictator who will inevitably become despotic over time – and I was deposited at Shakespeare County Raceway in plenty of time for the 10am start. My appearance in the shabby registration hut in formal wear caused quite a stir and, not for the first time, I felt like the James Hunt of marathon running (in fact, I overheard at least two people say that I looked like a *"Hunt"/"massive Hunt"* (I think I heard them correctly), which was nice). All that was left was to transform from a dishevelled Bruce Wayne into an overweight Superman (my running kit was 'Superman' red and blue). With the changing room cordoned off, I was forced into a toilet cubicle for this exercise (in these austere times, the phone box has made way for a cramped, dirty toilet cubicle). As soon as I pushed the lock across on the toilet door, I realised my error, as it was devoid of a latch to allow me to unlock the door. After the trials and tribulations of the morning, I was not going to be denied a race start by a faulty lock, just 300 yards from the start line. I therefore clambered onto the ledge behind the toilet and poked my head over what I now noticed was a very high cubicle wall. Several people walked by, seemingly oblivious to what I imagine was a slightly strange sight of a man's head above the top of the cubicle before one stopped and asked if I needed any help. With the assistance of a bin, which was dragged under the side of the cubicle, I was able to clamber out and scuttle to the start line, which was at the end of the long straight of what is now a drag racing track.

Conditions were pretty good – generally cool although there was a headwind which was strong enough to be a problem – but I was not great (the rushing around had distracted me from the tiredness and mild hangover). Putting the discomfort aside I set off at a decentish pace around the disused airfield, trying to ignore the fact that I would be running around this fairly unremarkable patch of land eight times over the next few hours.

I think my general fatigue following a dismal night's sleep actually helped and my mind drifted off to contemplate some of life's big issues (why, after so many years of evolution do I still have hair on my shoulders and back, yet no gills or wings?, etc.) rather than my current predicament and the first few laps ticked by nicely. There was the usual dip in condition after about 30 kilometres, although I was helped through some of this by running with a 50-year old runner who was quite interesting. Sadly, our acquaintance had to end when he started experiencing seeming uncontrollable run-flatulence and I wished him the best and ran away (downwind was definitely no place to be).

The Cheapest Running Trainers in The Shop™ started to fail me slightly after about 35 kilometres and I had a severely uncomfortable left foot for a while. However, it was far from fatal and I managed to pick up the pace for the last couple of kilometres to finish in a respectable time of **3 hours 8 minutes 44 seconds**...(in Hindsight, I may have even broken three hours)...

61, 62 & 63

And on the third day, he rose again (just)...

What follows is the tale of one man's modern Easter experience (please note that no offence is intended with any of the vague and inaccurate Biblical references)...

61 - AROUND THE RESERVOIR I - 4 APRIL 2015

For once my preparation for a marathon was very good. On Good Friday, I enjoyed a Last Supper at my parents' house – we ate well but no feet were washed – in fact, my feet have been viewed with suspicion ever since I contracted trench foot on The Most Ill Prepared Coast to Coast Walk Ever (see above). A slight wrinkle came to light on Saturday morning when, after I had denied my alarm three times before dawn (by hitting snooze), it became apparent that I had failed to pack any running shorts. This was resolved when Mother T emerged with some skimpy techni-coloured 'Pegasus' swimming shorts, which I would place at around 10-15 years B.N. (Before Nicholas) and I am fairly confident that Father T has not sported them since the mid-1980s. However, I was just grateful to be shorted as I headed off, bleary eyed, southbound towards Northampton...

Thanks to a quiet Easter Saturday M1 and no navigational issues, despite having forgotten to bring the directions, I pulled into the race venue – The Holiday Inn in Northampton – at 7:30am, 90 minutes before the race start time. I decided that another hour's sleep was in order before registering and taking my place with the 90 or so other runners on a path by the reservoir. Conditions were chilly but otherwise perfect and I set off like a whippet, having been informed there was a gate around 200 metres from the start line which people would have to queue at to get through. Not if you're in first place when you reach the gate. I did soon pay for my Bolt-esque start however, slipping back into a steady rhythm as a couple of altogether more appropriately built young men took up the front running. The course was decent, if unremarkable – it ran straight out on a cycle path alongside a busy road, before looping back through a grassy field populated by three periodically annoyed horses (which was a bit unnerving), and then continuing on a grassy loop of the reservoir for the second half of the 7ish km laps that we would run six times.

About mid-way through lap two a chap pulled alongside me and it appeared we had both settled into a similar pace. I therefore decided to strike up a conversation with him, which lasted until the last few hundred metres of the race. It transpired that he (Paul) was running his 84th marathon and was a significantly better runner than me, so I decided to ask him for tips about how I could break the mythical three hour barrier (which he had done more than 60 times). He took one cursory look at my muffin topped, slightly double chinned profile and suggested that losing at least a stone would do me no harm. Hurtful, but helpful. He then quizzed me on my lifestyle and I realised that some fairly significant adjustments may be required in that area. Paul: *"You don't drink beer do you?"*; Me: *"Not really, nope."* [Actual answer - had about ten pints on Thursday night]; Paul: *"Wine's OK, but try and lay off the beer"*; Me: *"OK"* [Actual answer -Also had some wine on Thursday so that's good]; *"What about chips and food like that – do you eat them"*; Me: *"Not often"* [Actual answer - Three times this week, which is broadly the bottom end of my average intake]. Had I been Pinocchio, I may have won the race in a photo finish at this point, such would have been the length of my nose. I'm not really sure why I was basically lying to a complete stranger, but perhaps it was mild embarrassment. Anyway, aside from the advice (some of which I will hopefully utilise), the conversation had two other benefits – firstly, in order to maintain it I was forced to run at a slightly faster pace than I would normally have run so I ended up finishing third in **3 hours 8 minutes 59 seconds**, despite the off-road course and having to open and close the 42 gates that were on the route; secondly, it took attention from the fact that despite being aptly named for running, the Pegasus (being the winged horse of Greek mythology, who would no doubt have a decent marathon in him) shorts were otherwise completely not fit for purpose and had been slicing my thighs to pieces. When I looked down at the end of the race, the light blue fabric had been rendered blood red by what appeared to be (and apologies for being graphic) the world's first manstrual cycle, but was in fact a minor bloodbath caused by extreme chaffing. Still, at least one of the marathons had been chalked off…

62 - AROUND THE RESERVOIR II - 5 APRIL 2015

The expected wave of pain was mysteriously absent when I awoke on Sunday morning and it was only after getting out of the car after the hour and a half journey south that I felt slightly immobile. However, after a brief walk to the start line, this passed and I set off at a similar pace to day one.

Unlike day one, I did not end up with a run companion and I was instead forced to make my own entertainment. Example as follows (reflecting on the Easter story):

Jesus: *"Hi Luke – I thought I better rise from the dead just to check what you were going to write about this weekend in that Bible you're putting together?"*

Luke: *"Well, I thought I'd call the Friday just gone 'Good Friday' – pretty catchy right?"*

Jesus: *"'Good Friday'? You must be kidding. What was good about it? I had to drag a heavy wooden cross around the streets as people abused me before I was eventually nailed to said cross. It was like the worst Friday EVER. Can we call it 'Bad Friday' or 'Worst Friday'?"*

Luke: *"Erm – we could. It's just that I've already had a load of t-shirts and other marketing materials printed and the budget's a bit tight – Christmas is becoming quite commercialised, which I don't think any of us saw coming, and the Romans keep increasing taxes."*

Jesus: *"So we're sticking with <u>Good</u> Friday? I am not pleased but I'm kind of duty bound to forgive you. Anyway, I'm off to Heaven now. Farewell."*

Luke: *"I'll see you there one day, friend..."*

Jesus: *"I wouldn't be so sure about that...Good Friday indeed..."*

Despite the lack of a companion, I managed to maintain a generally decent pace and finished the run in fourth place in **3 hours 15 minutes and 2 seconds**. The relative consistency of the times across the two days somewhat conceals the psychological impact of not having a partner on day two. I had not appreciated it myself until towards the end of lap five, when I saw a horse which was tethered to the ground looking absolutely depressed. There was a brief connection when our eyes locked and I think I saw something of my own plight in this animal and ended up sitting down and sobbing for a short while on a fence post before carrying on with the run. Most worrying is that I consider this is entirely normal Bank Holiday weekend living...

In common with day one, the finish did reveal some rubbage issues, which had this time resulted in my nipples being all but eroded. I explained to the lady who pointed out the large blood patches where one would traditionally find nipples that it was a deliberate ploy to take my mind off the exquisite pain in various other parts of my body. She seemed happy enough with that response although she did seem to be trying to shield her children's eyes from the spectacle (not the first time that has happened). The net conclusion of two days of extreme skin loss was one of the most painful shower experiences of my life (which is a significant claim for a man who has spent time in a Bolivian jail – true story, although less interesting than it sounds)...

I celebrated having chalked off marathon number two by partially following my new friend Paul's advice and knocking down a bottle of the blood of Christ (Tesco's generic 'Spanish Red' (wine), which contains that delicious superfood group of "sulphites" in abundance) together with half a packet of paracetamol and half a packet of ibuprofen and prayed for the sweet relief of sleep. Pretty sure that's what Paul had in mind...

63 - AROUND THE RESERVOIR III - 6 APRIL 2015

I'm not sure that anybody will be talking about a 34 year old man who managed to raise himself from death-like stupor and his cave of a flat to take on a third marathon in three days in 2,015 years' time, but I will put that down to the fact that a 33-year old man who did similar 2,015 years ago (J.C.) had better script writers...

In an attempt to raise the literary bar for a moment, I could observe how the thick mist which cloaked the land to either side of the M1 on Monday morning, punctuated only by the ghostly silhouettes of the imposing wind turbines which speak of modern man's desire to shape his destiny (our hubris will be our demise), mirrored the clouded body and mind of this book's main protagonist but I won't...Instead I'll provide a very brief summary of the final day...

Although I headed to the start line with a jaded body, there was something uplifting in the knowledge that this was the beginning of the end of the challenge and I managed to persuade my legs to buy into this notion, at least for the first three laps. The next two laps became a case of mind over matter as I urged on a failing body, not aided by this being the nicest day of the three and therefore much more draining on already depleted resources than the previous two days. Reaching the final lap did provide a much needed shot in the arm however and, a slight run in with some gypsy children on a bridge aside, all went well and I finished in **3 hours 17 minutes and 58 seconds**, meaning that I had broken 10 hours in aggregate for the three marathons and actually finished second overall for the three days (of 26 finishers). These last two facts are meaningless in the real world, although I may cling to such memories when Mother T's predictions come true and my over-marathoned body falls to pieces. But that's a story for another day...

64

WORCESTER 2015

A word to the wise, or in fact, just the not simple – six days is perhaps an insufficient period to recover from three marathons in three days. The recovery was not aided by a pretty full on four day week at the office, rounded off with a solo night out on the Friday (*mea culpa* on the latter issue). The net result of all of this was a poor excuse of a man turning up to Sixways Rugby Stadium in Worcester, after the scarcely conceivable horror of a 5am Sunday morning alarm call (a time which should only be a rumour).

Conditions were blustery to say the least as we wandered the few hundred metres from the stadium to the starting pens in a nearby field, before again being trooped along a small laneway for the actual start (which was by now about 20 minutes behind schedule). My spirits were briefly lifted when I realised that the race was being started by two costumed characters – the Free Radio hamster and a Nando's chicken. As it turned out, it was to remain the highlight of my day.

The course immediately set off in the manner it was to follow for its full 26.2 mile length – undulating hills which, together with the stiff wind, made for an uncomfortable combination for a man with very tender nipples, hamstrings which felt like metal rods and general nausea. On the positive side the course followed what was a far from unattractive route through this particular corner of England's green and pleasant land and there were small pockets of spectators in the various small villages we passed through along the way. There had also been a decent number of fellow runners around, as the half marathon had started at the same time and followed the same route until the 11 mile point, at which time the lucky half marathoners branched right, whilst we heroic clowns completed the marathon headed left for another loop of the course. Following this split, it was nearly ten miles before I had any human contact and when it came it was a happy seeming chap (maniac?) overtaking me. He gave me such genuine heartfelt encouragement, including a pat on the back, that I actually became quite emotional – another sign that all of this running may not be great for my mind, or maybe that man-opause has set in…

The pain extended beyond the mental to the physical and by now the feedback from my legs was an unpublishable tirade of abuse about the scale of this misadventure, whilst my poor old nipples were again pouring with blood (although I had had the decency to wear a red t-shirt, which meant that this would have been fairly difficult to discern for the casual observer). The end could not come soon enough although, when it did finally arrive, I was relatively surprised to see a time **of 3 hours 10 minutes and 25 seconds** (for 11th place out of about 220 marathon runners), as one way or another it had felt like a long, long day at the office. My misery was rounded off by my having to have a chat with our Lord on the big porcelain telephone promptly after finishing (i.e. being violently ill into a toilet in the stadium)…

65

MANCHESTER 2015*

For this chapter I took inspiration from publications ranging from The Iliad to Viz magazine...

So it was that the Turneros family were together on the banks of the River Styx in the year 1250 BC, seeking immortality and improvement of the bloodline. As golden child Achilles is dipped into the empowering waters, held by the heel that would ultimately betray him and enter into legend, his simple brother Nippleless watched on idly on the banks of the river whilst playing with Bacchus, who would have a strong influence throughout his formative years. In their wisdom, the Gods looked down favourably on Achilles' weaker brother and provided the divine breeze that caused him tumble into the strengthening waters of the Styx. Sadly, where Achilles' heel had gone before, Nippleless happened to fall into the magical waters wearing nipple clamps – having earlier that day met, and contracted, imperious wing footed athlete Hermes' very popular sister, Herpes, after several hours suckling at the teat of 'princess' Stella Artois on the waters' edge. Whereas Achilles would become a great warrior, Nippleless would become a great coward and very effective evader of fights/minor altercations in city centre nightspots. Little could the family have known that fateful day that the weak nipples and susceptibility to Stella were to transcend the ages...

After centuries of ups and downs for the Turneros family, we fast forward several millennia to find Nippleless's distant ancestor, Nicholas, on the start line of the Manchester marathon. There is an irony in the fact that the start line lay in the shadow of the Theatre of Dreams – home of Nicholas's boyhood team, Manchester United –

as he had arrived there via a week which was towards the nightmare (as opposed to the wet) end of the dream spectrum...

Our tale now takes a turn for the mundane. As always, it is very difficult to describe in an interesting way the 26.2 miles – and three odd hours – of a marathon, itself with its origins from the fabled run of the Greek soldier Pheidippides, a messenger from the Battle of Marathon Athens. Pheidippides promptly dropped dead at the end of his run and, whilst not quite on that scale, of some concern was the fact that Nicholas was coughing up a substance of an almost luminous colouring, which surely has no place in a human body. I also nearly managed to miss the start after a harrowing and lengthy visit to a portaloo (which must have been far more harrowing for the poor soul who followed me) and was making my way steadily to the start line only to hear the announcer say that the race was starting in two minutes. A scurry and what I would like to say elegant leap of the safety barriers followed, although the latter act was undertaken with anything but grace and almost added the crown jewels to currently redundant body parts which running has cost me...

My hop over the barriers had resulted in my being relatively near the front of the huge field, which turned out to very helpful as the road was initially quite narrow and turned back on itself soon after the 9am start. I had been reliably informed that this was a generally fast course and therefore I determined to set off quickly and hope to hang on in there for a tilt at the long sought three hour mark. Save for the cough – which was part of broader man flu and therefore very liable to end in either death or complete recovery within hours/days – my body had shaken off the after effects of the Worcester marathon and the working week and the going was generally smooth throughout the first half.

The half marathon came and went in 1 hour 26 minutes and I sensed the chance of breaking three hours, although I had expended a huge amount of energy in reaching the mid-point. This was briefly resolved when an old lady thrust a bag of jelly babies – truly a food worthy of the Gods – into my grateful hand and I also topped up on lemsip tablets and strepsils as I had started to feel a little dizzy and could also taste the unmistakable metallic tang of the blood of the lining of my lungs with each inhale. Nice...

The route was generally flat and consisted of long straight stretches of dual carriageway through residential areas, which was not entirely inspiring. There were however, numerous spectators at most points, helping to keep things ticking over with sometimes almost indignant encouragement for those who were slowing down/walking. The longer I managed to keep things ticking over, the more I realised that I was going to be close, very close, to breaking three hours. I'm not sure that the fact that I had again forgotten to wear a watch was a help or a hindrance but it meant that I was relying on the clocks of the many churches we passed for time updates. With about three miles to go I was pretty much out on my feet, which nearly became literal when an irate resident – unimpressed with the roadblocks – decided to screech through the cones and nearly take me out with the front of her chariot (a Ford Fiesta). This incident had a strangely galvanising effect on my wearied body, although I was still convinced that the three hour pacer was going to pass me just before the end and spent much of the last two miles looking nervously over my shoulder for him (which would have been a true Greek tragedy). Thankfully that was no to be and I managed to drag my husk of a body to finish in front of Old Trafford in **2 hours 57 minutes and 35 seconds**...Today I had been the player in my own melodrama and this act at least had finished well at the Theatre of Dreams, almost. There were the trademark bloodied nipples (Romulus and Remus should consider themselves lucky that they were able to suckle a she-wolf, as opposed to this particular blood-teated he-wolf) and I was so jacked up on LSP (Lemsip, Strepsils, Paracetamol) that a urine test would have probably made Lance Armstrong's usual results look mundane...

(As a postscript, due to a discrepancy in the measurement system, the Manchester Marathon 2015 was found to have been a few hundred metres short and the results expunged. After initial denial, I have now accepted that my quickest ever marathon must carry an asterisk. Life can be cruel...)

66

STRATFORD BROADMEADOW 2015

All the World's a stage...and all the men and women merely players?

Well, there are all sorts of different "players". Take, as a comparison, Me and Mr. Worldwide (aka Pitbull). Whilst Mr. Pitbull travels to some of the most glamorous locations on the planet, always surrounded by a bevy of stunning honeys, Mr. Turner spends his weekends travelling to English towns, surrounded by mostly wirey, scantily clad middle aged men. I could imagine a review of the play that is my current life along the following lines – *"One would think that the story of a middling aged man seeking to achieve relevance in his otherwise meaningless existence by means of self-destructive running would be engaging and inspiring. But it's not. I found the main character's lack of nipples and emotional depth difficult to relate to and by the end was looking forward to getting home so I could read an intelligent sounding book that I neither understood nor card for, but which would reinforce my assumed superiority over the great unwashed. 2/10..."*

The brief jubilation of breaking the three hour barrier the weekend before had been slightly soured by first suggestion of injury – being a creaking left knee. It was sufficiently settled by Wednesday evening to allow me to risk my first football match in eight months. I felt every bit the "veteran" used by the papers to label professional players of my vintage although some sort of vague muscle memory kicked in and I managed to score a grubby hat-trick. Again, to speculate about third party review of this act, I will call on Gary Neville – *"For me, Turner's finished. Yes, he scores three goals but spends most of the game looking tired and lost – it reminded me of introducing my granddad – Neville Neville Neville – to FIFA Soccer on the PlayStation. An embarrassment."*

By Friday, I still felt like I had been run over and will blame this as a contributing factor to a heavy night out which ended in the very early hours of Saturday. This seemingly hadn't quite satisfied my thirst and I decided to add a few in the sun before catching the northbound train for Chesterfield. It was clear that something was amiss when I woke up and found that I was in Wakefield Kirkgate (another venue rarely used as a backdrop for Pitbull videos) without a phone or debit card. Oops. Several hours of fare dodging and phone borrowing later and I was finally in Chesterfield and confirmed as the least popular member of the Turner family...

It would be fair to say that the combination of the above did not make for an athletic picture of health to be bounding out of bed on Sunday morning, raring to get to Stratford for a marathon which plays second fiddle to some annual fun run in London which takes place on the same weekend. I barely made it in time for the start which meant that I was towards the back of the field and confirmed my decision to take it steady. The course took us out of the attractive town and into similarly attractive countryside although my battered body frankly could not have cared less. The last five miles were particularly tortuous and I was moderately surprised to find that I had broken 3 hours 30 minutes – coming in at **3:26:16**.

It was then that my body went into total meltdown. I cramped up terribly in heavy traffic in Stratford town centre and thought that I was going to have to just drive into a wall to avoid causing a pile up. On the M69 I had to grab an empty ice cream tub to violently throw up the small amount of food I had managed to eat post-race and again nearly crashed. This second warning was enough to persuade me that an hour's sleep in the car park at Leicester Forest East Services was in order. I fear that my final curtain call may not be too far away with any more weekends like that...

67

NORTH DORSET VILLAGE 2015

After the misery of my Stratford experience (mostly self-inflicted), and for various other reasons, I was having something of an existential crisis by midweek when along came two curiously life affirming moments in quick succession. Firstly, on my Thursday 2am post-work run home along canal, I witnessed the following exchange:

Lady hobo [to man hobo and a bit slurry] – *"You don't f**king care about me"*;

Man hobo: *"I don't care about you?! I've just been in jail for two weeks and you didn't visit once – spent the whole time with a needle up your f**king arse..."*

It raises an interesting question as to what would have been the etiquette had I been offered a go with said needle. Being British, I have always been taught that it is bad manners to decline the offer of tea, etc, so I would have needed to decide if this extends to an offer of intravenous Class A drugs by a canal. Anyway, this particular slice of Life in the Real World had a happy ending as lady hobo and man hobo were curled up together under a very feral looking blanket (not unlike the one in my flat) when I ran back to work the next morning, seemingly having made peace with each other. They may not have much, but they do have each other and I look forward to finding a lady hobo companion when my life inevitably takes a turn for the worse.

A short while after having my spirits lifted by this unconventional modern romance, I spotted a pigeon struggling to keep its head above water in the same canal. After a brief internal debate I was down on my hands and knees trying to scoop it out. It took a few attempts before I managed to achieve this and I hope that hadn't just interrupted a key training of the Ian Thorpe of the pigeon world. For once, I left the canal feeling strangely better about the world and my place in it...

I had a meagre three hours sleep before attempting to drive to the South West with a printed AA Route Planner guide as opposed to a sat nav. Despite horrific weather conditions, all went remarkably well until the final few miles when I suddenly doubted said directions and turned around Trusting my gut instinct over the directions provided by one of the UK's most recognised and respected names in motoring went surprisingly badly and meant three journeys down the same fifteen mile stretch of rain drenched road. Until that error things had been going so well that I had been planning breakfast and maybe even a nap before the 8:30am race start. Instead I had to sprint into school hall in Sturminster Newtown, which was serving as Race HQ, have my race numbers pinned on to me by two kind old ladies before running down the hill to just make the start...

The day did not immediately improve as the marathon set-off straight back up the steep hill I had just run down before continuing on a steady incline for the first few miles. My left knee was also fairly uncomfortable and it promised to be a fairly tough day all round. However, as soon as the incessant ascent ended, one was able to enjoy the picturesque rolling green hills and picturesque villages this corner of England has to offer. Slightly sad to see so many purple and gold UKIP hoardings punctuating this landscape, although the only Rivers of Blood ('highbrow' political reference to Enoch Powell here) to reference were again flowing from this man's abused nipples.

The rain had stopped immediately before the start of the race making for excellent conditions and this allowed for good progress until about the sixteen mile point, when general fatigue hit me like a sledge hammer and the who day became very difficult from there to the finish. This was never more so than when a right angle turn to the left about three miles from the finish aimed us directly into a wind which was far from divine ("Divine Wind" is "kamikaze" in

Japanese and this wind was almost soul destroying enough to encourage me to sprint into a slurry silo there and then) and made for a miserable mile or so before a pleasant finishing stretch along a bridleway and, in the circumstances, I was pleased with my **3:16:45** finish time.

It was after the finish that the event truly came into its own. The entry fee had been modest but there was a hog roast, cider and beer and live band for all competitors to enjoy. However, the coup de grace was a free massage from an 'intern chiropractor'. For reasons which I was too tired to investigate, the tent was manned by Swedish girls. This led to the very quick formation of a long queue of middle aged men (including this one). When Helga enquired if her work had helped with my stiffness, I explained that it had certainly moved it – from my hamstrings and calves to the smallest muscle in my body…I would have happily stuck around but this was only part one of a busy couple of days so I parted, reassured that retracing my drive down would be easy and there was no way of getting lost…

An hour later, I had entered more UK counties than a certain failed Austrian painter had entered European countries about 75 years ago, but was finally sure I was on the right track, just by a ludicrously extended route. It reminded me of an amusing episode with an ex-girlfriend in the days before sat navs. I was mandated as navigator only to find the two crucial pages of the road atlas were missing. I confidently gave out left and right instructions with no knowledge of location, only for us to find ourselves back where we had been an hour previously. Atlas and car keys were promptly thrown and we parted ways soon afterwards…Again, this scuppered my plans for some sleep as I had to quickly shower and change for a wedding reception on my return to Nottingham. Such was my fatigue that I had to turn down a spin on the dancefloor at the event (despite having given feedback earlier that week at a meeting with partners at my law firm that my personal answer to *"Does the firm make the best of your skills?"* would be improved if there were more opportunities to showcase my ability as a contemporary dancer when providing legal work…)

68

MILTON KEYNES 2015

Another night of less than five hours sleep had done very little to improve my general condition and a 'clear the air' team talk may have played out as follows:

Brain – *"So, another big day today lads, how are we all doing?"*

Left knee – *"I am creaking and about ready to crack. Could do with a day off."*

Hamstrings/calves – *"We feel like steel rods. Ready to snap."*

Heart – *"I'm not happy that I spend most of my existence operating at about 300 bpm (way beyond operating guidance), based on either cheap instant coffee or too much running. Need a break or we will..."*

Brain – *"Nipples?"* [silence] *"Nipples?"* [silence]

Belly button – *"I think they're gone, boss – haven't seen them in ages..."*

Brain – *"Well, no big loss, male nipples are about as much use as Appendix."*

Appendix – *"That's hurtful..."*

Balls – *"Listen to you lot, moaning away. Whilst ever I'm here (albeit, purely as questionable decorative items only at present), we'll get out there and do this. OK?"*

All – [reluctantly] *"OK..."*

The drive from Nottingham to Milton Keynes was not one even I could mess up and I left the M1 to head eastbound to the jewel in England's heritage towns before 9am, with the race not starting until 10am. Where the ancient Byzantines, Greeks and Romans embellished their towns with magnificent structures and statues, the British town planners of the 1960s had seemingly got slightly fixated with roundabouts (also beautiful in their own way), and nine of the last 12 instructions on my AA Route Planner guide read "*At [name] roundabout, take the [number] exit...*" Just beautiful.

Unfortunately, the relatively pain free drive did not mean that my event preparation would for once be without incident. I had managed to bring my running number from Richmond Marathon (on 17 May) instead of for the MK event, but assumed that this would be easy enough to resolve at the registration desk. Sadly, things did not start well as when I initially explained what I had done and that I had no other proof of entry or phone, etc, the lady slightly unhelpfully told me that there was nothing she could do. I kindly pointed out that she had a long list of names of registered runners literally under her hand and that I had got up at 5am and put a vest on especially to drive to Milton Keynes for a bank holiday day out. However, when she said she could not find my name on the list I panicked that a day out in MK in my running kit but no marathon was exactly what now confronted me (maybe left knee, hamstrings and others would get their cowardly way out). I was about to give up – reasoning that such failure on my behalf was not impossible and not having any money on me to pay for entry on the day even if available – when the angry 'Helper' realised she had reviewed the half marathon list. Phew. Me and The Balls would have or way after all…

The race itself was reputed to be "flat" (Oxford Dictionary – "*Having a **level** surface; without raised areas or indentations*") but in fact started with a series of small climbs followed by equivalent descents. This was quite draining, as was the modestly warm sun, and I was almost completely spent after eight miles, which was a slightly unpleasant thought. By this time, I had also given up on the admittedly deranged notion that counting the number of roundabouts we ran through on the course might add a little something to proceedings (I gave up on "lots" after "not far"). I wasn't the only one struggling and the second half featured leapfrogging between myself and a number of other runners who were having a tough day at the office. My day was improved markedly by the end of the run, which was in itself a highlight – finishing in the MK Stadium after about two thirds of a lap of the football pitch. At **3 hours 21 minutes**, one of my slower runs for a while but poignantly the thirteenth marathon of the year, marking the halfway point in the planned madness...

69

FOXTON 24 - 2015

"If you can't fly then run, if you can't run then walk, if you can't walk then crawl, but whatever you do you have to keep moving forward" (Martin Luther King Jr)

The preparation for what promised to be possibly the most gruelling challenge of my life to date could scarcely have been worse. A working week which started fairly sedately took a dramatic turn for the hectic, sparked by a conference call at 8am on Wednesday morning. From that point, I worked until 12:30am on the Thursday, before getting up at 5am for a 6:30 train to London, where I worked in our London office until 10:30pm before getting the last train back to Nottingham, which arrived at 1:30am. I managed two hours of hugely interrupted sleep on the train (mostly disturbed by my fat head banging on the window as the train jolted) before heading directly to the Nottingham office, where I worked until 5am before running home for one hour's sleep, before running back to work for 7am and working until 8:30pm on Friday night. From there I headed back up to the parents' in Derbyshire and managed a half decent seven hours or so of sleep before getting up to head for the event in Preston...

Just before getting onto the challenge itself, I made a very exciting discovery for men across the world. Some have never found it, some rarely so, but I can confirm that the elusive, some say mythical, **Clit**heroe(™) is actually just off junction 31 of the M6 (no wonder that motorway is always so busy). Onto the event...

The Foxton 24 was the inaugural running of a challenge which involved running as far as possible around the athletics track at the University of Central Lancashire in a period of 24 hours. What one did in those 24 hours was entirely up to each individual entrant but the convivial event organiser, Stanley Jewell, seemed slightly surprised when I confirmed that I had turned up with neither a 'support team' nor a tent. This caused a brief moment of doubt in my mind, but I buried it with all my other doubts in a little place I like to call 'denial' (that particular box is becoming somewhat full). What was of slightly more concern, as I lined up with my 18 fellow competitors, is that I had absolutely no game plan. What I did know is that I was wearing some shiny new illuminous yellow trainers (from Mike Ashley's wacky warehouse), which made me feel FAST. I therefore found myself starting out at a decent marathon pace, whilst the rest of the field was taking it somewhat more sedately and several of them asked me if I knew what I was doing as I repeatedly lapped the entire field (I had absolutely no idea what I was doing was the answer).

Just after the expiry of each hour, Stanley would come out onto the track and update a board with current standings. At the end of hour one, I was three laps up, and this lead continued to extend over the next few hours, which I guessed was a good and bad thing. By mid-afternoon, it was a glorious May day, unless one was involved in a 24 hour running event, in which case it was a worryingly warm May afternoon. Unperturbed, I continued on my merry way, chalking off a marathon in well under four hours and 50 kilometres in 4 hours 30 minutes. By now I was over 10 laps up on the field. The one lady who was now some way behind but running at a similar pace to me had her husband as her support crew. He was sat behind a table laden with energy shots, drinks and various other items and every lap she would shout instructions at him about requirements for the next lap – "*Phil, pepsi shot and gel, next lap*". I was nearby when poor old Phil got it wrong – or wasn't ready – on a couple of occasions and he got whatever item he had wrongfully handed over to her thrown at him, along with a colourful dressing down from his loving wife. I would personally consider it way beyond the call of duty to sit and support surely one of the least spectator friendly events ever conceived of – watching a handful of idiots destroy themselves, very slowly, over the course of a day. Poor Phil...

I clocked up my 100th kilometre after just over ten hours and was still making decent progress – having extended my lead to over 25 laps – prompting the following comments from two different spectators (both clearly maniacs, but which I thoroughly enjoyed and may have turned into t-shirts):

- *"He hasn't got a heart, this man – he has an engine..."*
- *"It's not a person, it's a superhuman thing..."*

Sadly, fast forward a couple of hours and the engine had almost completely broken down and the superhuman had become a subhuman...

Neither boredom nor fatigue had played much of a part up until midnight on the Saturday, helped by the fact that I had obtained some sort of cult status amongst the scouts, who were manning the food/drink station and would applaud wildly each time I finished a lap. At one point a number of them even joined me to run a lap – causing me to feel a bit like a modern day Pied Piper of Hamlin – before their grumpy scout leader ordered them off the track. However, as midnight gave way to the small hours, a number of spectators retreated to their tents, as did a number of runners, and it became a lonely trot around the track with the handful of others who had decided to press on into the night. The main thing which kept me going during this period was that a spectator (he of quote one above), decided that I was to become his personal project and he would shout encouragement and advice to me each time I passed. The one slight problem was that he for some reason thought I was called Nigel, and I failed to correct him the first time that I realised this was the case. It caused some confusion amongst my fellow runners – who knew me as Nick (which is my name) – that a man was shouting *"That's it Nigel – steady pace to the end and you've got this"; "Come on Nigel!"; "Nigel – you've still 11 hours to go, slow down..."* Anyway, it helped pass a few hours...

By 4am, a steady drizzle had set in and I was tired to the point of near collapse. I decided that a short lay down in the medical tent was in order, and gave the young girls marshalling the tent strict instructions that in no circumstances were they to let me sleep for more than 10 minutes. When they nudged me after what felt like seconds, I snoozed them and asked for another wake up call in five minutes. This time, I knew that if I didn't get up, it may well be that I would not be setting foot on the track again, a reality borne out by the fact that I could barely even roll off the bed even after such a short break, such was the stiffness in my legs. I had also noticed a few blisters, which appeared to have come and gone if the now red colouring of my fancy shoes was anything to go by...

The next few hours were amongst the most miserable of my life as I trudged my destroyed body around and around the track through relentless. For a few laps of this I would let the tears flow for 300 metres of each lap, before composing myself at the refreshment station, as I couldn't possibly have my totally misplaced hero status questioned. My 'coach/cheerleader' had retired to his tent shortly before my own brief lie down so it was timely that another saviour arrived around this time. It was a guy who had recently broken the world record for running on a treadmill – he managed 100 miles in 24 hours – and he had come down to help motivate we hardy fools (one of the field having done the same for him during his challenge). Everything in my body was by now suggesting that sitting down was the only sensible thing to do, but the treadmill man's enthusiasm was infectious and he dragged me round a few laps in half decent times, against every instinct in my body. By now my targets for the day had been downgraded multiple times and I had settled on a definitive target – SURVIVAL. Nothing else mattered. Despite this new aim, I did take something from being the first runner in the event to clock up 100 miles. This coincided with the availability of a bacon and egg sandwich, making it THE BEST BACON AND EGG SANDWICH I HAVE (OR WILL) EVER EAT. I took the opportunity to sit down and enjoy the sandwich and it transpired that wearing a non-waterproof top from Primark (thanks to all my sponsors by the way – Primark; JD Wetherspoons; Febreze; Boots Paracetamol Extra) throughout a damp night had resulted in me uncontrollably shivering and apparently *"Looking like you're about to pass out"*. I was soon wrapped in a foil cloak and ushered into a wooden hut where I was ordered to sit by a heater for half an hour, whilst fellow competitors rustled up some dry kit for me to finish the remaining three hours of the race. To be honest, I would have been fairly content to stay sat by that heater, but once I had dried out I headed back out onto the track, where I was scarcely able to muster more than a shuffle for the majority of the time, despite my mentor yelling *"Nigel – you can do better than that. Get bloody running!"* (It later transpired that this gentleman is some sort of Irish record holder for endurance running and I was very grateful for his encouragement).

Thanks to my earlier work, and deterioration throughout all runners (who were now almost exclusively walkers), I knew by now that I was going to win the event and, despite agony in every part of my legs, and strips of blisters on the balls of both feet, I mustered some decent pace for the last few laps, which I felt was only befitting for the winner of a race. I regretted this act of vanity almost immediately and the relief of the air horn, which signalled the end of the race, is impossible to overemphasise as it meant the end of a 24-hour journey I would not wish on anyone…

A short while after the finish, all of the competitors retrenched to a nearby sports hall for the presentation ceremony. My prizes for winning (having completed **178.5km/110.9 miles/455 laps/4.23 marathons/burnt over 16,000 calories**) were a bottle of La Cantera red wine (£8.49 a bottle from Laithwaite's Wines (online)) and a £30 Tesco voucher (£1.25 per hour), which fully justified my efforts and the fact that I could by now barely walk. The sad epilogue to this generally happy tale was the look on my mother's face (on her birthday weekend no less), when I fell out of her car and pretty much had to crawl to get into my family home (reminiscent of the look on her face when I walked sideways down the hill into Robin Hood's Bay at the end of the coast to coast challenge nearly four years earlier)…

70

AMERSFOORT (NETHERLANDS) 2015

If you have ever been on a journey where you have reached several crossroads and taken the wrong option at each one, maybe you can empathise with the below...

The week's journey went wrong, and unbeknown to me very badly wrong, before I even left Nottingham. My first realisation of impending problems came at 5:20pm on Friday evening (by which time I was on a coach heading to Amsterdam), when I realised that I did not have my debit card and was carrying just 130 Euros in cash. I learned long ago – whilst clearly learning nothing – that the art of surviving adversity (and life) is to break issues down into priority order, based on their immediate threat to one's existence. For the time being, I had a valid Eurolines' return ticket to Amsterdam, legitimate currency for target location and I was convinced the rest of the story would fall into place if I applied misplaced optimism to my circumstances.

The journey from Nottingham to London Victoria Coach Station went well enough, although things took a slight turn for the strange following the change from Victoria to Dover, when I acquired a middle aged Ethiopian lady as seat companion, who decided it was a good idea to clutch onto my thigh and utter occasional phrases in broken English. Although this was slightly disconcerting, at this point I was still solvent and remained hopeful of a pleasant weekend adventure...

The ferry crossing was a chance to catch up on some sleep. Anyway, I duly continued the sleep theme on much of the journey from Calais to Amsterdam, where I was deposited outside the Amsterdam Arena at around 10am by coach driver Ron, who had turned out to be a decent tour guide for my waking moments on my journey through Northern Europe. After a short transfer to Central Station, I suddenly became aware of my vaguely precarious financial position and decided that the first order of business was to buy a return train ticket to Amersfoort, the location of Sunday's marathon. Having spent some of my Euros on food on the ferry (and being given change in Sterling), this reduced my available finances by 20%. However, on the basis of immediate problems, finance was less pressing than the fact that I had omitted to write down where I was staying (having thought I had saved it on my phone) and had a very poor, large scale map with only a red blob (marking the location) to guide me. The blob was on an unnamed street on my map and a brief reconnaissance trip confirmed that the actual location of said hostel was completely indiscernible without the hostel name (quelle surprise). I decided that shelter was a problem that could wait and set about enjoying a day in the sunshine in Amsterdam. Fast forward about eight (mostly confusing) hours and I was on the phone to the British Embassy explaining that I was lost and without money or accommodation. Despite being astonishing proper, my contact – who was possibly not receiving the first out of hours call from a destitute Englishman in Amsterdam (and I suspect did not believe my marathon story) – could offer nothing. My next call was the world's local bank (see above), who offered even less, and my final call – should I choose to take it – was Mother T. At this point, I did the decent thing and opted for personal uncertainty over causing familial anxiety (after briefly contemplating the fact that there must be some way for an able bodied man to earn a few Euros in the Red Light District of the 'Dam)…

After this burst of activity, my phone had died, which compounded my sense of hopelessness, until I realised that, if I waited until midnight, I could actually use my train ticket to Amersfoort, and would at least then be in the marathon location. My brain told me that this was a better option than the hope of finding my hostel and so I caught the 12:30am train to Amersfoort, which is around 40 minutes away from Amsterdam. Around four hours later I awoke in a pitch black, deserted train carriage, which turned out to be locked. After around thirty minutes of pacing around like a faintly insane zoo exhibit, a torchlight broke the darkness and I knocked furiously on the window until I was released from my very budget horror film surroundings by a surprised maintenance guy, who explained that I was at a train depot near Amersfoort and wondered why no one had awoken me at the last station. The fact that I was at a depot, rather than a station meant that there was no platform and instead it was a significant jump to the floor, which I managed with no grace, in fact some disgrace. The torch man could not help me any further so instead radioed a security man, who arrived within a few minutes in a white transit van and turned out to be an imposing bald man who towered above me. After a fairly intense interrogation – as with the British Embassy the night before, I may not have been his first confused Englishman – he invited me to climb into his van, which I thought may be my last act on earth, given our interaction up until that point, until I saw the reassuring pouting face of Keira Knightly on a DVD on the floor of the van which suggested maybe this man mountain had the heart of a kitten. Maybe he wouldn't be wearing my skin as a coat within the hour after all. Whatever the case, he deposited me at an exit of the depot and gave me some vague directions to the centre of Amersfoort, where he assumed the marathon may start (if indeed there is one, said his expression)...

With no phone, and therefore no internet, I had no idea where the start actually was and therefore marched blindly for a fairly long time around fairly similar looking residential streets in a town which was far larger than I had expected. It being perhaps 5:30am by now (I had no clue), I wandered to the locked door of a Mercure Hotel from where I expected to be cruelly sent away, but was I instead greeted with warmth of a free coffee and an incredibly helpful concierge who printed race instructions and directions (the start was less than 500 metres away). I thanked him profusely, before confirming the start location. I literally found a space ship in an outdoor beach bar which, although amusing and quirky, was very uncomfortable and so I moved al fresco for a large bench made out of driftwood. I slept beautiful until being kicked awake by a large Dutchman who informed me *"This is not a sleeping place..."* His mood softened slightly when I explained that I had been, but was no longer, a typical English menace and was actually in town for the marathon, but he was opening for Sunday morning business so I decided to move on. By now, it must have been after 7am and the first runners, for the shorter events which started before the marathon, were drifting into the area so I decided to hang around the vicinity of the start line. I also had ulterior motives, as I was so thirsty and hungry – having consumed no food for over 12 hours and no drink (other than the free coffee at the Mercure) for not much less – that I hoped that someone would leave something unattended. The day was already hotting up, and I did not really fancy a marathon after 15 hours nil by mouth, and my prayers were eventually answered after the end of the short children's race just after 9am as a number of the children discarded the water bottles they were given at the end, much to my delight.

It would be in the realms of gross understatement to say I felt entirely unconfident at the start of the marathon but the first few kilometres, initially around the town before heading out into some beautiful (and blissfully flat) Dutch countryside, went by relatively smoothly. I was getting a decent level of encouragement from the occasional groups of people we passed – although thanks to looking I guess passably Dutch – most of it was in Dutch (as with Apeldoorn in 2012), although the sentiment was still appreciated (assuming they were not being abusive). By the halfway point, it was extremely warm and my body was starting to crumble (specifically my right hip and left heel, presumably still as a result of the 24 hour event less than two weeks previously) and I endured a pretty miserable just under two hours for the second loop, not helped by the dawning realisation that my immediate post-race future was uncertain. When the race finished (in a time of just over **3 hours 31 minutes** for me), this was depicted in a metaphorically film noire way as, after limping up a broken escalator, I sat alone on a tired plastic chair in the middle of a large unfinished post-apocalyptic concrete room (of what looked like being a retail space), which had acted as the baggage area for runners, staring at the floor and wondering if I could make it home. My heel and hip were in extreme pain and I was incredibly hungry (although I had enjoyed some banana slices on the course). Eventually a race crew member approached and touched me gently on the shoulder and asked me something in Dutch, before asking (when I replied in a pathetic voice "English only"), *"Are you OK? Are you going to pass out?"* For some reason, this shook me from my stupor and I set about on leg one of the journey home – a slow limp to Amersfoort Station, which was thankfully nearby. After a couple of nano-naps, I awoke at Amsterdam Central Station, from where I had to work out how to get to the Arena on foot. The girl at the Tourist Office seemed to think this was a bad idea, but told me if I followed Amstel River, I should find my way, *"but it is a long way..."*

It was a glorious day and I had managed to snaffle a number of water bottles at the end of the race, meaning I now at least had fluid – if still no food – to help me along the journey. I also had over five hours until my coach, so time was on my side and this meant that I joined some fringe lunatics outside the Intercontinental Hotel, where I spied a brief glimpse of Paul McCartney as he was picked up for his concert at the Arena (could have done with a lift actually Sir Paul, thanks for asking). After this brief interlude, I continued my lonely flip-flopped plod along the banks of the Amstel, which was heaving with Dutch folk loving life on their boats, which strangely lifted my mood, despite my not being a part of that world, or the world of food. My mood was elevated further when the shining glory of the Arena finally appeared in my sights, albeit quite a long way in the distance. This sight had come hot on the heels of my lowest point, when I contemplated eating a crushed sweet from the floor. I convinced myself that I had not yet fallen that far. Not just yet...

Better news came at the Eurolines' office when I was woken up in the waiting room to be told I could catch the 7:30pm instead of 9:30pm coach – *"so you can sleep on coach, not in here"*. I assumed this meant that I would also be back to a world where money can be obtained, either through a kindly colleague or with a passport but this turned out to be wishful thinking as we ended up boarding 2:30am ferry for Calais before being deposited at Victoria Coach Station at 5:30am, where there was no bus to Nottingham until 8:30am. By now, I had eaten nothing but some pieces of banana for about 36 hours and so the cheese roll I was able to buy from Sainsbury's

Victoria when it opened at 7am was understandably THE MOST DELICIOUS FOOD EVER EATEN BY ANYONE EVER. I could have eaten about 20 rolls, but it was enough to carry me through the final leg of my journey, which ended at 12:15pm at Nottingham Broadmarsh Station (nearly 17 hours after leaving Amsterdam), where I promptly trudged up the hill for an afternoon at the office before a truly unwelcome black tie dinner at Colwick Hall (although I consumed the three wonderful courses like Oliver Twist).

I suspect I have not learned enough from the experience, save that if you keep turning in the same direction at crossroads, you eventually end up back where you started…

71

LIVERPOOL ROCK AND ROLL MARATHON 2015

Following the melodramas of the Netherlands, it was with some relief that marathon 16 (/19 depending on your view of life) of 2015 involved a relatively straightforward cross country trip to Liverpool...

Naturally I managed to make things more exciting than they needed to be, turning up in the North West without my running number, which was the only essential item of pre-race kit required. (*Help!*...in the immortal words of the Beatles) I had also given myself slightly less time than ideal to complete the drive, resulting in me turning up in a mildly chaotic city – the half marathon already being in progress meaning that a number of roads were closed – less than half an hour before the start time for the full marathon with no clear idea of where the start line was or how my running number issue was to be resolved. I had also stored up a minor problem for later as I scampered out of the multi-storey car park which seemed to be near to the throngs of half marathoners and therefore presumably near the epicentre of things...

A kindly fellow runner led me to the Expo hall, being the Liverpool Echo Arena, where he assumed my non-bib issue could be resolved but, alas, he was wrong. I was instead sent towards the start line to an information tent. It was now about 10 minutes to the start of the race and mild concern was setting in. (As with Amsterdam, I seek never to let things run above mild concern as, in the words of the great(?) Harold Stephen, *"There is a great difference between worry and concern. A worried person sees a problem, and a concerned person solves a problem..."* *["And an idiot keeps creating problems for himself..."]* (N Turner)).

Unfortunately, by the time I had battled through the crowds across a small bridge and found the Information tent, it turned out the lady running the show shared my approach to anxiety management, when I in fact wanted her to PANIC. There were by now maybe four minutes to the start of the race and it was excruciating to watch as she methodically removed her gloves, one finger at the time (also, not that cold, lady), before slowly typing my surname into the computer, as if she had all the time in the world. Hurry up. I don't want to start that race behind the man in the sumo outfit. Please hurry up. In the nick of time, she handed me a new race number and some safety pins, which I took on the move, already heading towards the start line. In the end my timing was impeccable. I vaulted (OK – fell over, in a most ungainly fashion) the metal barriers between the spectators and the runners, as my race number flapped from the one pin I had managed to fasten, before taking my place maybe 10 metres behind the start line, just in time for the intros from a two time Boston marathon winner from Liverpool and moments later we were on our way…

It was a typical British summer's day – grey, breezy and cool – as we ran from Albert Dock, before briefly swinging towards the Mersey and then heading back into the city. Aware that conditions (including that of my body, still not fully revered from either the 24-hour run or Amersfoort) were likely to deteriorate, I set off at a potentially reckless pace, although this was naturally slowed as we hit a number of minor inclines early on into proceedings. It was the accumulation of them, rather than the severity, which sapped the legs, although I was still tracking at a good pace as we circled Goodison Park, before crossing Stanley Park and running past Anfield (boo!). A short while after leaving Stanley Park, we hit the steepest hill of the day, which was enough to at least semi-permanently reduce my slightly over ambitious pace and I used the hill as an overall brake back to a more sustainable pace.

Sure enough, a short time after halfway, as we faced another small climb into Chinatown, my body started to give way, just as the heat of the day increased (*Here Comes The Sun*, I mused). I fumbled fruitlessly for some painkillers which had been put frustratingly just out of reach thanks to a faulty wedged zip on some Karrimor shorts (thank you Mike Ashley)! By the time we reached Penny Lane – where a lady who may not have been qualified for the job as she shouted encouragement as we had done 18 miles and were now halfway – I had also finally reached my tablets, although they were offering little by way of assistance and I was struggling badly...

In keeping broadly with the Rock 'n Roll them of the race, there had been stages dotted along the course, mostly stocked with bands playing cover numbers (albeit not sure whether Brazilian and Chinese bands are technically either "R" or "R"?), made for an excellent atmosphere, although some of the support was delivered with a faintly aggressive tone; often making it all the more effective...By mile 20, assisted by 'threatcouragement' (*With a Little Help from My Friends*, one might say), my legs had staged something of a recovery although my perennial nipple problem had arisen, with particular severity. I heard a few comments along the lines of "*Look at the state of his nipples – that's why I don't run*" [liar] and "*Jogger's nipple. Ouch!*" In truth, the entire nipple region is now a dead zone where I feel nothing (much like my soul), so I hadn't actually noticed the issue until the kindly spectators pointed it out...

The course had been broadly flat for a reasonable period, and I had been able to slot back into something of a decent rhythm, raising hopes of a good time, until making a short descent onto the banks of the River Mersey to be confronted with a stiff headwind which would clearly be around for the few miles which remained until the finish. I put my head down and pressed steadily on until about two miles from home I was passed by a familiar running vest and gait – it was Ben, who I had beaten into second place in the Foxton 24. After fixing me with the familiar dead eyes of most marathon runners after the 20-mile point there was a small smile of satisfaction as he realised who I was and he trotted off on his way. Given that I was well down the field and clearly not in PB-territory I had been settling for a gentle plod to the line, to save my body for future challenges, but this moment stirred the modicum of spirit which had otherwise been buried deep, deep down, along with hope and concern for nipple welfare. I decided to match Ben's pace as far as possible, to ensure he was in sight for what I expected to be a lengthy home straight along the river. This all worked well, although as I turned and saw the finish line, the path to it lined with a decent crowd, I feared I had given myself too much to do, particularly given the headwind. I put my head down and prayed for the after burners (OK – mild acceleration, from very, very slow to quite slow) which eventually sparked to life (with the magic and awe of an indoor firework), allowing me to edge past Ben with around 20 metres to go and finish in **3 hours 9 minutes and 5 seconds**. We shared what I assume was a joke at the end, when he said, *"you are becoming my nemesis. I am starting to hate you..."* [Ha, ha, the number of people who say that to me, Ben. Ben?! Oh, he's gone, just like the rest...] Would be good to have a nemesis though; would certainly add something to this narrative...(Slow Farah and Insane Bolt? Needs work)

The finish was pure Rock and Roll as each finisher was given a free pint of Tuborg (OK – perhaps more Rolling Stones 2015 (make mine an Evian) than 1965 vintage, but free beer is free beer (unless it's non-alcoholic – take note Manchester Marathon)). I now had to deal with my stored up problem from earlier in the day – I do find that the Nicholas who lives in the moment does store up a number of problems for future iterations of Nicholas's. I had parked the car in a shopping centre, fully aware that I would have to pay the parking fee to exit said car park. Sadly I had omitted to bring any hard currency to the event and was carrying a yet inactivated debit card and mobile phone with almost no charge. This was my last phone call. Come on HSBC – you can do it. We can do it. Let us live your customer promises together. Be the brand we want you to be. (*Money (That's What I Want)*, I said) No, we can't Mr. Turner. I am very, very sorry but your account security is locked due to a request from you (ah, last Saturday's Amsterdam Nicholas, a very dangerous iteration indeed). I was suddenly starting to doubt my own handy list of carefree quotes when a visit to an ATM sorted my immediate problem and I was able to unlock the card. This was also the unlikely scene for some very helpful advice about my nipple condition (my not having yet covered the damage). A lady who appeared to be high on all sorts of flavours of life, I think, approached me and advised in a thick Scouse accent, "*You need to sort out those bleedin' [two meanings I think, or not] and get a friggin' sports bra. You don't have to be a fruit, just pretend it's for your girlie...*" One occasionally receives valuable life advice when least expected – thank you strange lady. And thank you Liverpool…

72

THE WALL
(CARLISLE TO NEWCASTLE) 2015

For the most part, event 17 of 2015 was a unique celebration of the benefits of planning over the chaos which has flavoured most of the challenge to date. The change in my stars was brought about by the involvement of Robin (of *Shakespeare Autumn* fame), Melissa and Liv.

In keeping with (lack of) character, I had done my best to hasten my demise with a night out on Thursday, but had managed to acquire most of the items on my 'mandatory kit list' from Blacks before casting caution to the wind at a Waterloo anniversary dinner. The dinner – at Nottingham's Albert Hall – had been meticulously researched by the host, unlike my return home, via various bars, which was lucky rather than good (like Napoleon's favourite generals).

Notwithstanding my best efforts, I made my 1pm pick up – with (most of) the mandatory kit in tow – and we were heading north broadly on schedule. So far, so mildly unnerving for its lack of disasters. However, for a small island, it takes a while to get anywhere and we did not arrive in Carlisle – home of a McVities' factory which has been said to drive the natives to tracksuits and obesity with its delicious transcendental, saturated fat and chocolate fragrance – until after 7pm. We headed directly for registration where I procured the one gap in my kit list – a back pack (previous one having died in Amsterdam after being overfilled) and with it new identity – that of Salomon Goldsmith, but more of him later. For now, it was the shiniest bit of kit I have ever owned, although the frayed thread – which had reduced the asking price by a third – seemed quite fitting for the bag's new owner…

Our accommodation was a strange family owned B&B, packed full of antique and retro oddments, a thick carpet and a dead lady in the cellar (just joking – ...she was in the attic). Anyway, the fact of four adults spending a night together in a family room seemed to cause some confusion with the owners, but the comfort of decreased chance of being murdered amongst our group. After a very quick trip to the Beehive pub, where the barman spilled a pint on me, I was awarded the bottom bunk, which had limited clearance from the top bunk above. Luckily, the 'mezzanine floor' in my smack den penthouse has made me comfortable with such proximity and I slept with the comfort of a baby – a baby with a well developed snoring problem as it transpires. On the plus side, the morning light confirmed that we were still a group of four breathing humans...

The overcast and cool conditions were perfect for the event – less so for tourists – as we gathered with approximately 600 other maniacs in the grounds of Carlisle Castle for the race briefing.

The initial going was very steady – dictated by single file paths. However, the banter flowed readily and we made decent progress to the first checkpoint. We had opted for a strategy of walking any ascents and otherwise running and maintained a fairly consistent five-ish mile an hour pace for the first four or five hours, during which time we had seen very little of "The Wall" which gave the challenge its name. When we did finally spend a stretch running by said wall, it became slightly difficult to comprehend how such an unimposing structure could possibly have protected Roman England from the Scottish tribes (*"Shite lads, they've built a wee wall. Retreat!!!!"*). Robin and I speculated that Hadrian ("Hadey" to his friends) had probably run into difficulties with the AD122 equivalent of Cumbria County Council's Planning Department and eventually agreed to an unsatisfactory compromise from his initial plans (Grand Designs-style). The slightly disappointing wall aside, the scenery was truly England's green and pleasant land at its best and the misty conditions added an historical air to proceedings (which formed the subject of several skits from yours truly and Robin). It was not until we reached the 'halfway' (sadly not quite) pit stop at Fort Vindaloo (think this is correct) that the sun finally broke through. By now we had covered 32 miles and were greeted by Melissa; some sort of melodic trance from a souped up Red Bull van and more food than one could possibly consume.

In short, it would have been a cracking spot to spend the remainder of the day. Alas after stocking up on food and trance, we were forced to say our goodbyes, only to be immediately faced with what turned out to be the most challenging climb of the day, at the hottest point of the day. There followed probably the quietest period in our trio, as we each dealt with increasing discomfort in our own way, although the banter returned as soon as things flattered out and there followed a lengthy fictional negotiation between Salomon Goldsmith Junior (dealmaker for Wonga) and the Greek Government (played by Robin) about a possible refinancing on very favourable terms (and subject to some minor, tasteful rebranding of some of Greece's historic sites)...

The going was by now getting tough and the tough were getting a bit rough – I'm not sure if a show tunes segway, with occasional duets/trios, helped at this point – as the checkpoints seemed to be stretched farther and farther apart. Shortly before the pit stop at mile 44 in Hexham, Liv announced with delightful British restrain that she was "slightly over this now". Charming to see that understatement cannot be usurped by extreme physical effort. We stocked up on classic athlete friendly foods – quiche, sausage rolls/cheese pasties and shandy – before plodding on into an evening which remained unhelpfully warm. By now, we were somewhere in the midst of a large group who were all adopting the walk/run strategy meaning that we were leapfrogging and seeing many of the same faces periodically. This made for snatched periods of banter, although everyone was fighting their own battles by now so it was all slightly reserved. Any variety was welcomed, including a small community of eclectic static homes on the banks of the Tyne around 15 miles from the end and an unfortunate fellow run who had seemingly slumped into some form of delirium on the road, wrapped in a foil sheet, a short time after that. There was nothing apparently physically wrong with him but the vacuous look in the eyes and inane smile talked of deeper problems. When we asked he smiled madly as he confirmed that he was "*All sorted. Only nine miles. You'll be fine*" – actually we had just under 14 miles to go and clearly all was not well in his world, although a passer-by was attending to him so we pressed on with our own problems.

At the mile 58 checkpoint, Liv decided that her race had been run. On removing her trainers, it appeared that her feet were half bubble wrap blisters so it had been an epic effort to make it through two and a quarter marathons. Dr. Johnston, MD, offered to operate on the blisters with a safety pin but this offer was sensibly (to my mind) rejected and we bid our farewells. It was approaching 10:30pm, yet still vaguely light as Robin and I pressed on into the woodlands which lined the River Tyne. With the finish line now a vaguely comprehendible distance away, we accelerated to an at times reckless pace for the four mile stretch to the final pit stop, where we were greeted with sandwiches, Bovril and eventually Melissa. I was on a sugar high – having gone all the way through the 'Happy World of Haribo' towards the 'Dangerous Dependent World of Type II Diabetes' – and a fellow run asked whether "for the love of God" I would stop dancing. "Hell no". We settled into a swift, but generally more sensible, pace for the last seven miles as I rehearsed my demands to see Emperor Michele Ashmilius to request that he cede the Holy Sports Direct Empire (with the exception of Scunthorpe – his new Rome and the city which bears his name (in part)) due to consistent supply of faulty Karrimor loin cloths (and zips). We were generally moving forwards through the field at this point, although the bright lights of the Quayside seemed to take an eternity to arrive, even after we had descended to the banks of the Tyne. The time was closing in on 1am as we navigated our way down the river, to the generally supportive shouts of late night revellers, and we eventually finished in just under 18 hours after crossing Millennium Bridge. A truly epic feeling after 69 miles re-tracing the steps of the Romans…

The epilogue was a slightly uncomfortable night at Camp Travel Lodge in Newcastle. Following our arrival, the room was soon filled with the smell of three near dead 'humans', whilst my discomfort was such that I spent the majority of the night rolling around trying desperately to reduce the pain to a level where I may find sleep (to little avail). I had also been unsuccessful in sacking the Ashmilius Empire, although in my new guise as Salomon Goldsmith I hold greater hopes of taking Greece by means of big loans and small print...(the modern day Trojan Horse)...

73

CHESTERFIELD 2015

This week's tale starts with an incredible coincidence. For the second consecutive marathon I was given bib number **1144**. By my crude calculations (subject to confirmation from a mathematician or, failing that, Carol Vorderman), the odds of this are around 2,000,000 to one. Safe to say that I would probably rather have won a meaningful amount on the lottery than had the quirk of matching race numbers, but one takes what moments one can in life. Here are some other things which are more likely to happen than getting the same number in consecutive marathons (apparently):

- Becoming a movie star – 1,505,000 to 1
- Being struck by lightning – 576,000 to 1
- Having to visit hospital due to an injury from a pogo stick – 115,300 in 1
- Meeting a suitable life partner in a Wetherspoons before 10 am on any weekday – 1,980,000 to 1*

*(this one may have been made up by yours truly after extensive research)

In a less surprising coincidence, the weekend of a marathon had not for the first time started with me waking up on Saturday morning on a yoga mat in my office instead of in my bed. Leaving my flat keys in the drawer at work had actually been a deliberate ploy by Office Nick, after some champagne had arrived unannounced on Friday afternoon. Sadly, after a few further drinks Fun Time Nick had forgotten all about Office Nick's wisdom and turned up back at said flat with no way of getting into the building. Never one to let a little adversity stand in the way of a good time, Fun Time Nick decided to muse over his next action whilst dancing at The Riverbank before eventually determining that the best course of action was the yoga mat. Office Nick would have despaired...

Aside from the confusion of waking up under a desk, the remainder of weekend marathon preparation was reasonable enough, capped off with an excellent night's sleep at my sister's house, which was only a few hundred metres from the start of the marathon in Queen's Park, Chesterfield. As often seems to be the case, a decent rest seemed to remind my body of what it had been missing for weeks and I had developed a cold overnight. Now, women and children may not understand this but the adult male human does not just develop a cold in the same way as other humans. He develops a life threatening condition of severity unimaginable to anyone who is not Adult Man. With heroics bordering on the super human, I sniffled and coughed my way on the short walk to the race start where the coincidence described above revealed itself when I collected my race number. I am not really one for superstition in any event I thought as I saluted a magpie and kissed my rabbit's foot (not smutty innuendo) on the way to the start line...

The conditions were absolutely perfect for the run. Beams of sunlight slanted diagonally into Queen's Park as we lined up for the start, but conditions were cool and still. Despite my Life Threatening Cold, I adopted my usual approach of setting off Way Too Fast and was gasping by the time we reached the mildly depressing stretch of dual carriageway which had just enough of an upward slope to hurt. Within another three miles or so I was having my first stroll of what would be numerous on a very hilly course. Support was decent and I have not been called "Duck" so often since the critical and technical catastrophe that was my school's budget production of "Swan Lake" – the lesser "Duck Pond" – in which I played a mischievous Mallard named Keith. Times were hard in the 1990s...

I had reached the halfway point comfortably within the top ten runners but paid for my WTF start (and LTC) early into the second half and was soon being passed by a number of runners. It transpired that some of these people were actually participating in the relay, meaning that they were only running five miles or so, which made me feel slightly less annoyed at being passed so readily. Less pleasing was the fact that a number of them were Royal Marines and seeing them up close made me realise what a fairly pathetic specimen of man I am – in fact, the only item which suggested I might be the same species is the recently acquired tattoo…

At mile 23, I was greeted enthusiastically by my cheer squad, sister Rachel, Jamie and their daughters, Poppy (7) and Isobel (3). When I suggested a picture might be nice, Poppy ran away and Isobel sought to do likewise but was too little and we managed to capture her for the picture! Feeling revived by the support, I negotiated the last three miles relatively quickly and nearly managed to break back into the top ten, finishing 11th overall in **3 hours 17 minutes and 55 seconds.** It goes to show you that anyone can become good at anything with enough repetition – reminds me of the time a monkey beat me at basketball in Thailand (but that's another story)…

74

HULL 2015

I probably only visited four of the nine circles of Dante's Hull over the marathon weekend. I also became something of a fan of Hull along the way and recommend an update to the official tourist slogan of Hull, currently *"Lasciate ogne speranza, voi ch'intrate"*, *"Abandon all hope, ye who enter here…"* (**Dante, Divine Comedy**)

Circle One of Hell (Limbo) was visited on Saturday night when, for once, I misplaced my debit card. The very same debit card had been rescued from the pub opposite the office that very Saturday morning, having spent Friday night resident on a shelf at the pub (not for the first time), hopefully playing the role of passive plastic observer as opposed to utilised tab alternative. Having recovered Mr. Debit (and promised him and myself for the hundredth time that I would take better care of him in future – rumour has it that I am the reason that HSBC stopped putting issue numbers on their debit cards – lack of space when one reaches 1,000), I found myself at the bar of a different hostelry in Nottingham – it being my round – and no sign of Mr. Debit. With a train to catch within 20 minutes, Mother T heading to the station to pick me up and no alternative means of finance, I was in the uncomfortable world of Limbo. It was then that a gift from the Gods arrived. As I arrived at the station and weighed the risk and reward of boarding the train with no ticket, I spotted a purple tinged pile of paper fluttering on the road. Surely it couldn't be?! It could! 120 English pounds. Marvellous things truly can happen to moderate people. I quickly scanned the area hoping not to see the unfortunate soul who had lost such a handsome sum (it having been me more than once, I would have repatriated the funds). With no sign of anyone, I trousered the fortunate windfall (thus tiptoeing into the Ninth Circle – Treachery), bought my ticket and boarded the train north…

The Fifth Circle (Anger) was briefly visited on Sunday morning thanks to personal incompetence. Having got up in plenty of time and enjoyed a hearty breakfast, I was feeling positive about the day ahead. For once, I was confident I knew where I was going, so confident that I neglected to double check my AA Route plan instructions. Not for the first time in its career, assumption nearly gave birth to a healthy funk up as by sticking on the M1 all the way to the junction with the M62, I added tens of miles (and minutes, which were rapidly evaporating) to my journey. This was compounded when I missed the junction to the M62 (I blame roadworks, apparently manned by ghosts for that oversight). Despite a beautiful late summer's morning, I was starting to get slightly angry with the driver (me) at this point and so it was some relief that parking near the start line of the marathon proved to be a relative breeze (provided one ignored certain road closed signs and cones)…I was not quite yet ready to take my place on the start line. A further oversight had been revealed on arrival as although I had my running number, I did not have my chip timer. Not headline news in the Real World, but bad news in the strange place which is Marathon World (as it means no official time – a fate worse than chaff…). With a full four minutes to the start time, this issue was resolved, although it also meant replacing my running number so that the two matched, but I was able to slope into the gap between the elite athletes (I looked like a fat baby amongst these hyper toned men and women) and the masses of 'also rans' (most of whom I knew would be passing me soon after the start).

Conditions were absolutely perfect as we set off on our initially merry way around the streets of Hull. The sun was shining but it was a cool and mostly still morning. I exchanged pleasantries with a couple of runners doing their first marathon as the bodies felt good and the mood was optimistic. When I next saw these men, shuffling along at the 20-ish mile mark, we could barely exchange grunts. Such is the destructive nature of a marathon. As for my own race, I made the most of the decent conditions and generally flat course, until a gentle but prolonged ascent to the Humber Bridge put something of a spoke in my previously well-oiled wheels. Sadly, unlike my proverbial wheels, my oft abused nipples were far from well-oiled and this is where we descend into the Seventh Circle of Hell – Violence; being that inflicted on my nipples by the consistent abrasion of my t-shirt. As the blood flowed my legs slowed and by the time I was looping back to re-cross the nearly two kilometre length of the Humber Bridge I took my first stroll of the day. The heat was also just beginning to become an issue – it being no friend of a fat baby – and life was generally becoming a bit of a struggle. As is normally the case, once I had reached the 20-mile marker, the positive sensation of the finish line helped ease the pain.

The end brought with it the usual relief and a certain satisfaction that, after a couple of steady times and significant travails, I had returned to a solid time – **3 hours 12 minutes and 21 seconds** to finish just inside the top 50 (out of just under 800 hardy runners). Somewhere not too far north a man named Mo may have run somewhat faster, but I had clambered though my own tests somewhere distinctly South…

75

WOLVERHAMPTON 2015

Another marathon effort which would make my new chest adornment – Little Chief Bloody Nips – nothing but angered, were he not merely an inked character...

The weekend started very well, with a bar crawl quest for clues for a charity (NSPCC) treasure hunt to be hosted in Nottingham on the upcoming Thursday evening. By bar six the clues were becoming distinctively questionable and by bar nine the sheet with the clues we had commenced the evening by finding so diligently had mysteriously vanished. Between the three bar crawl protagonists, we managed to re-create about three quarters of the questions once back at work, not bad considering we were probably all operating on around 10% brain cells by the end of Friday night (which ended with dancing in a young people's discotheque in which I had no place)...

Saturday was far from a repeat of Friday, although it did involve a cigar and a couple of beers which probably contributed to a very reluctant rise from bed on Sunday morning. Things were made worse by needing to walk the two miles or so to the office to go and collect the car and drive myself halfway across the country for a few hours of misery in the Wolverhampton marathon. Printer issues meant a delay to get my AA route plan for the journey and on arrival at Molineux – the home of Wolverhampton Wanderers FC ("Wolves") – I was told that the event car parks were full. I had around five minutes to the race start, no idea where that was and no race number. All fairly standard as I risked the wrath of an over zealous ASDA parking attendant, lying about my plans for a morning of cut price shopping, knowing full well I had no intention of making a purchase. Nicholas really was "Better Off at ASDA" (to the tune of the two pounds, money saved by avoiding the official event car park)...

A modest walk to the start and a lengthy conversation trying to persuade the race organiser that despite my lack of number, only a lunatic would try and con his way into a marathon in order to save 30 quid or so, meant that as joggled (half jog, half walk) to the start line I found that the race had inevitably left without me. I therefore had to negotiate my way through a 'pack' (a 'nuisance'?) of children waiting to start the kids' run before the slightly underwhelming experience of starting a marathon solo. Rather than soaking up this surreal moment, I decided to set off as if Lucifer were hot on my heels and caught the back markers within a kilometre or so. I decided I quite enjoyed the experience of going through the field and remained at full tilt for the next few kilometres – although 'full tilt' was a slowing concept...

By the 18 mile marker, as the day warmed up, 'full tilt' had become almost 'zero tilt' and I thought I was going to pass out. Thankfully, an area laden with St Johns' Ambulance people (a 'paramedipack'?) was on hand to offer some assistance. As I sat down, I was delighted when a pack of Maoam sweets (making me **Chairman Mao**am?) was put into my hand (although I had asked for **meow meow**, which I gather is quite different). This offered some resuscitation, although one of the ladies suggested that I looked 'dreadful' and should consider a lift back to the start/finish area. There were still over eight miles to go, making this a hugely appealing offer, and potentially life defining moment, but in the end I stuffed my mouthful with Maoam and plodded on. It really was a plod from here on in and my first to second half split would have suggested something dreadful had taken place in the second half of the race. As it was I fought of the final indignity of double hamstring cramp as I tried to push my body for a 'half tilt' finish, only to fail miserably and cut a slowly moving mess of a man as I finished in just a bit under four hours...

A couple of hours later I added Tamworth Services on the M42 to the growing list of service station car parks in which I have slept on the way home from marathons in 2015. Limited shade – two and a half Trip Advisor stars for a car park based nap, which I truly hope you never experience. As the tagline to Dances With Wolves goes, *"Inside everyone is a frontier waiting to be discovered"*. I'm just not sure I like the frontiers I've found so far this year...

76

HALIFAX 2015

My efforts at the Halifax Marathon, my first marathon for a while, were broadly commensurate with Bjorn Borg's attempted return to the pro tennis circuit with a wooden racquet in the early 1990s. Not good.

If I was in any doubt that I was in the North that was soon extinguished by the event host's Yorkshire accent, which was thicker than gravy and almost indecipherable, despite Yorkshire-heritage in my family. I think he said something about the toilets, a whippet and a flat cap, but he could have been saying anything...

I had been forewarned that Halifax would be a challenging course, by both a colleague and one of the event organisers. Undeterred, I bolted off the start line and led for a glorious 200 metres before hitting the first hill. Whilst hill#1 was fairly gentle, hill#2 followed soon after and was far from gentle. So, less than two miles into the event I was walking slowly contemplating sitting down to be returned to the start line. I thought that a by-product of the unspeakable pain of the Indian chief tattoo I had obtained on the Monday – which fluctuated between feeling like being etched with a secondary school compass and having my bone drilled – would be that I could transcend the pain of the marathon, guided by the inked shaman on my chest and recollections of the agony of having him put there. Wrong...

The course eventually levelled off as we reached a high point, offering stunning views down into the valleys of Yorkshire, before plunging down and then steeply back up. The final significant, and most merciless, hill was shortly after the six mile mark and after that it was a relatively steady meander – predominantly downhill – back to the mill at which we had started. Knowing what was coming was both good and bad and at least I knew that after about eight miles the worst of the hills would be behind me. This did not do a huge amount to alleviate the pain and I slowed markedly during the second lap, repeatedly reduced to a slow trudge, but as I returned to the car park of the mill and saw the finish line, at least I could be content at having edged one marathon closer to the end of the challenge (in **3 hours 37 minutes and 1 second** for what it's worth), but by heck it was a tough day at t'office…

77

NOTINGHAM 2015

I few tips for the top (or at least the middle) based on my Nottingham Marathon 2015 experience:

- **Massage** – if you are like me, then the word "massage" may be synonymous with the image of a buxom Swedish male or female in a softly lit room gently manipulating you with a healthy portion of aromatic oils. However, if one adds the prefix "Thai" or "Sports", the whole experience takes on a new dimension. So I discovered (again) when heading to a meeting room at the office on Thursday afternoon for a Sports Massage. I did the sensible manly thing of saying that the pressure was just fine when asked by my masseuse/torturess, all the while nearly biting though my lip. Such was the discomfort that I may well have opted to switch to waterboarding midway through, had that been available as an alternative therapy. That said, the short-term pain did seem to prevent some marginal gain for my otherwise marathon-battered limbs…

- **One gets what one pays for** – after probably suffering 'nipple issues' in 18 of my 21 marathons in 2015 to date, I decided to seek to address the issue. However, deterred by the (perfectly reasonable) price of branded petroleum jelly I opted for a particular high street chemist's own brand of 'Baby Petroleum Jelly'. When added to my other purchases of pain killers and bandages, I got suitably short shrift when trying to make eye contact with the cashier, who presumably assumed something more deviant than a marathon was on the cards with my weekend…Sadly, my shame was to no avail as come Sunday afternoon there were the usual blood pools where once had been nipples…

- **Preparation is Everything** – not entirely unusually, I had signed up to an historical bar crawl of Nottingham the night before the marathon. Whilst reckless, this is becoming fairly standard. It was through luck and lightweight-ism, rather than planning, that I was forced to leave proceedings embarrassingly early but the extra few hours in bed seemed to reap dividends on the day. Despite this, with only a few hundred metres to walk from my flat to the start line, it was an event that even I couldn't miss and the pleasant misty morning helped breed cautious optimism. This was tested early on as the course immediately took us up a number of fairly severe hills. Once negotiated, things settled down onto the flat for the remainder of the first half of the race, which I dealt with in under 1 hour 30 minutes – a might too fast.

I managed to keep things ticking over for the first couple of miles of the second half, which remained flat, until I finally had to succumb to the call of nature and spend a couple of very unpleasant minutes in a portaloo at Colwick Racecourse. Things will have been all the more unpleasant for whichever unfortunate soul followed me. After its flat beginnings, the second half also became a bit challenging and I spent a few minutes walking up Derby Road in Nottingham, cursing the sun and the ascent before managing to get back into something of a rhythm and a finish time of **3 hours 5 minutes and 30 seconds** – my second fastest marathon of all time. **Robin Good?**

78

LEICESTER 2015

Not for the first time in my life, a week of highs and lows (including slamming Mrs. T's car into a pillar in the work car park, with a colleague in the passenger seat, who thankfully opted not to sue) ended with a double-header marathon weekend.

Highs and lows aside, it had been a week of abstinence from alcohol, prompting optimism for the Leicester Marathon. At least this was the case at 3pm on Saturday. Fast forward eight hours and I was eating chips after a few drinks watching the rugby led to a few more, all brought to an early conclusion when I literally had to run away from a female body builder from Grantham who had taken something of a shine to me and could have easily turned me into flour had she chosen to do so...

The undoing of a week's efforts at healthy(ish) living was confirmed on Sunday morning when I opted for a Mc-**Not**rition Breakfast Sandwich™ on my way to the Leicester Marathon. The extra hour in bed – thanks to the changing of the clocks – had convinced me that I had time to spare for the day and I was therefore happy to ditch the car in the first available car park – at The Highcross Shopping Centre. This turned out to be a poor idea as it was nearly two miles from the start line. By the time I reached the starting area, the other runners were ready and the countdown was into the last couple of minutes. I put my belongings into the storage area and (again, not for the first time) jumped the railings just as the race was setting off.

Deeming this as my best chance to break three hour mark in the remaining four marathons of the year (and with a VIP lunch experience at Leicester Tigers starting in less than three hours' time), I set off at a decent/unsustainable lick. For once my nipples would not be a concern, because I had inadvertently taken them off with Veet in the shower the previous day (not a statement I thought I would ever type or would want to have read out in a court transcript, *"My learned friend, whilst your client claims to have pre-removed his nipples with Veet, the prosecution contends that no man would knowingly de-nipple in such fashion...etc"*). I was comfortably under 1 hour 30 minutes for the half marathon and considering that I had a shot at breaking three hours when I suddenly felt a few concerning twinges in my right hamstring. With another marathon the next day, I was not keen to test the elasticity of my notoriously taught hamstrings too far and therefore decided to take my efforts down a notch. By the time the nagging twinges had stopped, there was too little in the tank to accelerate, which meant missing the three hour mark by 215 seconds, finishing in **3 hours 3 minutes and 35 seconds**...

It transpired that my biggest challenge was yet to come as I tried to change into presentable attire for my VIP experience. As a young event marshal watched on, I twice tried and failed to put on my left shoe but severe cramp instead forced me to topple over. I was too proud to ask for his help so ended up wasting several minutes performing a basic human function, meaning a short, unwelcome jog to Welland Road for the rugby. After an excellent afternoon of being (slightly) wined (I was driving) and dined at Leicester Tigers, it was off for my next leg of the journey – to Dublin...

79

DUBLIN 2015

My journey to Dublin and the overnight stay prior to the race as 'eventful', featuring a "fake engagement" in the queue for the Ryanair flight to persuade the airline to let a completely hammered young lady sit beside me on the flight. My pre-night accommodation was also unexpectedly spent at the house of a previous Big Brother contestant (friend of the lashed up lady) and not technically in Dublin, but instead in one of its southern suburbs, Loughlinstown. The outcome of this was that my first obstacle on the Monday morning of the race was persuading a fiery Irish taxi despatch lady that she should send a taxi to a man that could only provide vague directions to his location ("*on a junction of a main road and a smaller street*") and no mobile phone number. Eventually – at the third attempt – my 'charm' paid off and a taxi eventually arrived to take me on what seemed like a much shorter drive than it had the previous evening to central Dublin for the start of the marathon.

I was not quite prepared for the number of participants in the Dublin Marathon and my leisurely pre-race preparation of a coffee and a sandwich turned out to be my demise as I sat in a portaloo as the race announcer – who had been poetic and enthusiastic throughout the morning – proclaimed that 5,000 runners from the first wave (which was supposed to include me) had now passed through the start line. The net result was a fairly eerie start as I wandered down Fitzwilliam Street, completely deserted in front of me, whilst a wall of runners (shepherded by a line of illumines-jacketed volunteers) marched down the street behind me, like a crowd of non-violent protestors slowly hunting down a dissident.

As I finally started the race, it was a grey and drizzly day, but the course was lined with an almost unending line of spectators which made it one of the best atmospheres in which I have ever run a marathon. The combination of the miserable weather and enthusiastic support made stopping unappealing, this despite a reasonable amount of discomfort – particularly in my quads, which felt like they were leaking battery acid into the surrounding area – from efforts less than 24 hours previous. The portaloo delay had also helped by putting me behind 5,000 people, with limited space to pass by them, meaning I was forced to run at a steady pace. In the few spots in which there were no crowds, there were motivational signs to make up for the lack of people, two of my favourite being:

"Hail Mary Mother of Grace, Please Get Me Out of This F**cking Race..."

"Run like you've left on the immersion" ('immersion' not being a word I've heard for many years)

The end (arriving after **3 hours 18 minutes and 43 seconds**) was welcome and the pint of the black stuff which followed promptly afterwards even more so (when in Rome and all that). All in all, it had been excellent craic but a spectacularly draining weekend and I was asleep before the Ryanair flight attendants had delivered their safety demonstration.

80

SACREMENTO, CALIFORNIA, USA (BEAT THE BLERCH) - 2015

"Sometimes the best plan is no plan"
(categorically not 'Art of War' by Sun Tzu)

It was with customary chaos that my trip to the US – which was due to end with a triumphant finish to the 26 Marathon Challenge - began.

The final day at work never really ended and I final threw in the towel at about 2am for three hours stolen sleep on the uncomfortable, elevated bed in the office first aid room before returning to work to the bitter end. With a hospital pass of a handover completed, I was free to sprint down the hill to Nottingham Coach Station to just catch the Gatwick-bound bus for the first leg of my journey. In between emails, I found the sanctuary of some sleep although that came to an abrupt end when the driver announced that due to traffic congestion, we were running nearly 45 minutes late. I was already cutting it fine so this added a very poor action-movie edge to proceedings as we raced (at about an average of 50-mph tops) against the clock to make the flight to New York. In the end, all was fine although things became less fine when I discovered that not only did Norwegian Air need me to pay extra for the one bag I had brought but they would also neither feed nor water me at all on the seven-hour flight without further payment. Scandalous (and a reminder to always read the small print). After some indignant huffing I decided that some wine was in order for two reasons (1) to push aside memories of a fraught couple of days and (2) because I had eight hours to kill before leaving New York baby and was damned if I was sleeping during that time (this turned out to be inaccurate)...

The NYC visit was flying indeed. An interminable queue at JFK further shortened my time in the Big Apple so with the time I had I had for some 'iconic shots' of Times Square and from the top of a misty Empire State Building before taking a taxi to The Meatpacking District where I would like to say I tore things up (and could as there are no witnesses). But no. In fact, I was turned away from one venue (despite showing them how many crisp dollars I had ready to 'invest in fun') before falling asleep in a second venue after the excitement of the days (and my age) caught up with me. Rock and roll (extreme lite version)...

Savannah Marathon

I will blame the itch of unfinished business on the fact that by 11am on Friday I was in Hooters, Orlando Airport, shamelessly showcasing my British accent. This seemed to be going so well that I was quite reluctant to leave and head for my next flight – to Charlotte, from where I would catch a further flight to Savannah. Thanks to a delayed flight and very slow baggage return, another race against the clock was on – this time to register for the Savannah Marathon before the 7pm cut-off. There was less than 30 minutes to do this so I hopped in a cab with a young chap running his first marathon and cab driver who was very keen to extol the virtues of living everyday as if one's last (not necessarily best practice as a cab driver). On arrival at Savannah Convention Centre we were hustled into the registration area just as it was closing down but had made it. Everything was going to turn out just fine. And it did. In the alternative world where I counted numerous lucky breaks and went directly to my delightful sounding Econo Lodge accommodation, everything was just fine, if a little dull. Back in the real world, matters were taking a different turn. In the real world Nicholas was on the free ferry which would take him to search out fun in Savannah. A couple of bars will help deal with jet lag and do no harm was the mantra. When this mantra was replaced by that of Mr.

Cab Driver I'm not sure but I awoke on a sofa – amazingly with all possessions intact – to be told by a new friend, Candice, that *"Yes – you've missed the start of the marathon"*. In fact, I had already missed it quite spectacularly but after faffing around with finding kit and contact lenses, I was running over 90 minutes late. Undeterred – I am after all a problem solver (albeit I create the majority of them), I headed for Bay Street which was where the run had started, although you would not know it now. There were still police officers around – presumably preparing to re-open the closed roads who pointed out where the start had been and marveled as I set off before shouting that I should perhaps stick to the sidewalk. All went well as I ran up a dead straight road, although problems materialised as soon as I started hitting junctions and various plausible marathon alternatives but no signs. Eventually I decided to stop in at a fast food restaurant to ask, *"No mister, we ain't seen no marathon come by here"* was the slightly concerning response. I decided to press on before trying one more shop – a mobile phone shop – which yielded a similar answer but the sales clerk told me that her husband would know. I was passed a mobile phone, at the other end of which a man informed me that I was indeed off course and needed to turn around and return to Martin Luther Kind Junior Avenue and should be OK from there. I was indeed OK and a few billboards of support (if no people) showed I was on the right path. My next problem was at another junction with two very promising looking alternatives. I went left for a short while before heading into the "Information Centre" (they weren't specific about information specialities so I assumed could handle any and all enquiries) where I was again told I was off track. They did offer the consolation of the first water I had consumed in over an hour (the other problem of missing the start so badly is that all of the aid stations had long been dismantled). Not long after returning to the Right Track, I caught the truck which was dismantling the course. This was actually a huge sign of promise as it meant that there should at least be evidence of the marathon to follow from here on in…

Better news followed as I soon stumbled across people with medals who had presumably finished one of the shorter events – everything was going to be fine, although it was hot and I was slightly concerned about how many aid stations I would reach before finishing. Just as I reached the quite probably wrong conclusion that all would be OK, a race volunteer stepped out and asked what I was doing, explaining that the course had been re-routed and shortened as someone had died. Awful news. It happened that I received this news near the finish area so was able to take a few short turns down the beautiful streets of Old Town Savannah and "finish" with a sprint and collect my unearned medal (having maybe run 10 miles in total). All in all, an odd day which led to a return to Southern hospitality and new friends and a boozy day out in lovely Savannah...

With Savannah not counting towards the marathon tally, I needed to act fast if the challenge were still to conclude in Las Vegas. I therefore scoured the internet for marathons taking place in the USA during my visit and ended up sending a pleading email to the organisers of the "Beat the Blerch Marathon", Sacramento, California, which was due to take place the day before the Las Vegas Marathon. There was a fair amount of the USA to cover between Savannah, Georgia and Sacramento, California and I decided to cover it via Greyhound Bus, in a journey of numerous legs and mostly overnight sleeping on buses, as below. It was a journey on which I met a rich tapestry of "real" Americans, including a number of (always wrongly) ex inmates at various penitentiaries and a number of angry ex-servicemen. I can say that without exception they were generous in spirit and seemed to take life's misfortunes, including being on the Greyhound Bus, in their stride and with good humour.

- Savannah, Georgia to Atlanta, Georgia.

- Atlanta, Georgia to Jackson, Mississippi, which I had to exit rapidly after almost getting kidnapped by a strange middle aged man named Robert.

- Jackson, Mississippi (of Bruno Mars' song fame) to Memphis, Tennessee, where I enjoyed a quick pit stop, featuring a lovely visit to Graceland and the fun and games of Beale Street, Memphis' answer to the somewhat more lively Bourbon Street in New Orleans.

- Memphis, Tennessee to Dallas, Texas, where I witnessed a man getting brutally pistol whipped outside a McDonalds at around 4am. The pistol whipper proudly announced, *"Don't mess with us, we kill presidents here son..."* to the pistol whippee (who, in fairness, had been trying to steal a car). The day sort of improved from there with a well-intentioned intervention from a man from Christian Outreach who thought I was a man named Joshua when he found me sleeping on the steps of the Public Information Centre at around 6am; a visit to site of said presidential assassination (as referenced above) and an impressive military parade.
- Dallas, Texas to Los Angeles, California – a lovely 29 hour journey.
- Los Angeles, California to Sacramento, California

In the three and a half days (and circa 2,500 miles) between leaving Memphis, I had not slept in a bed, washed or changed a single item of clothing (most (all) of which hails fittingly from Primark). I felt marathon ready...

Sacramento Marathon

As for Sacramento – well, having arrived in the city after the coach ride described above, the long queue at registration was an unwelcome sight. I was therefore hugely grateful when a chap named Vic offered to drive me downtown. (As an aside – I do seem to be very appealing to middle aged American men, which is not really my targeted audience; may need to consider what vibe I'm giving out)...

Safely deposited downtown, I wandered the pleasant but quiet streets before stumbling across the kitsch but pleasant Old Town. I had been told by Vic that the other side of the river from Old Town – west side – was somewhat sketchy and so, naturally, after a beer at

O'Malley's, that's exactly where I headed in search of accommodation.

Vic was not wrong about the sketchiness and I scuttled along with my fix firmly on the sidewalk after seeing a fairly dangerous looking group of youths outside the bowling alley. Beyond this was a string of motels. A bit like Goldilocks, the first two were no go – only because there was no response to the buzzer – and I would love to say that the third, Crest Motel was Just Right but it was in fact All Wrong. The odour was a heady mix of damp and old cigarette smoke, the décor 1970s gaud and the TV offered only two channels – an obscure news channel and adult movies. Having showered I decided I was safer on the edgy streets than within and headed back to Old Town for dinner and a couple of drinks before an early pre-marathon bedtime.

I awoke to a pleasant but cold morning for the inaugural Sacramento Marathon, which started nearby at the Raley Field baseball stadium. The event had been inspired by a cartoonist who writes of his running efforts in the context of allowing him to live a fulsome life of fast food, cake and beer without conscience – a man after my own heart – and this manifested itself in an eclectic field of runners.

It was not a huge field and, with a week of Greyhound tension to release, I set off out front, leading for the first few miles as we ran along either side of the river. After about five miles, three Real Runners (i.e. lithe men who didn't live on a bus) passed me and I accepted my lot as an also ran with grace. The course soon left the city and followed a pleasant, undulating walking track along the river, which passed through sheep pasture grounds and was altogether pleasant, also offering shade as the Californian sun warmed up. I was fairly coasting it after around 20 miles – still in fourth – and decided on a time check which revealed that if I maintained my current pace I would be pretty close to three hours. The legs were starting to suffer but I gritted my teeth, channelled some of the pain I had endured throughout the year and sucked it up and eventually crossed the line, back in the stadium, in **02:58:50** and retaining fourth position (the equivalent of being an unused bridesmaid at a wedding I guess) out of 215 marathon finishers.

With a flight to Vegas at 1:45pm, there had been a certain imperative to my efforts but I afforded myself a certain amount of reflection and pride in the morning's efforts, given what had proceeded them. Well, we all know what follows pride. Sure enough, the best laid plans of this man-mouse came crashing down when my pre-ordered taxi had not materialised by 12 noon. I was now marginally stressed so told a minor white lie to Sacramento's finest and explained that I had a flight to the UK which I had to make and was in grave danger of missing. He dutifully called dispatch and within ten minutes – was on my way – even taxi drivers don't mess with the cops here – and made my plane with minutes to spare. Too easy. Next stop, Las Vegas baby!!!

81

LAS VEGAS, NEVADA, USA 2015

The fourth placed finish in the Sacramento Marathon and return to airline, as opposed to coach, travel combined to make for a euphoric arrival in the City of Sin – Las Vegas – on Saturday evening.

Better was to come as after a quick shower in the moderate (but improved from previous) surrounds of the Diamond Inn, at the far southern end of The Strip, I headed directly to The Luxor to meet my fellow marathoners, Rebecca, Sarah and Jo. From there we hit a sensible pre-marathon dinner of pasta at New York, New York before moving onto the main event – a Britney Spears' concert at Planet Hollywood. It would be stretching it/a flat lie to say that Britney sung so much as a single note live but she threw plenty into the performance, which covered all her biggest hits and was full value for the admission fee. One can only imagine what her management have to do to keep her out of trouble everyday until show time (my guess is that she lives on tranquillisers in a cage in a car park under Planet Hollywood)...

Three quarters of the group sensibly retired to their hotel rooms at this point but this quarter was far too invigorated by events of the day and so headed on for a short loop involving Hooters, Hard Rock Café, diablo Cantina (in which I was the only non-Hispanic) and Excalibur before crawling into bed at around 4am. In short, 'Oops, he did it again...' There was a certain method in this madness however as there were still over 12 hours until the marathon started which was ample time to restore goodness...('That's my prerogative' anyway)...

Unfortunately, time is a relatively meaningless concept in Vegas and one can procure whatever one wants whenever one chooses. In the next 12 hours I did therefore err and have a relatively harmless cocktail, served (of course) in a zebra's hoof shaped vessel. It was this or more traditional painkillers and I assumed there were no banned substances in the hoof...

The Rock and Roll event itself was on a massive scale – 40,000 runners taking part in various events over the weekend – and the warm up involved a Kid Rock concert, which was pretty damn cool. There was also an electric guitar version of the national anthem and tributes to the French. All very inspiring stuff, but slightly worryingly played out under an increasingly menacing sky over The Strip. We set off southbound very briefly, to take in the famous 'Welcome to Fabulous Las Vegas' sign before swinging back and running all the way down the Strip. This was undoubtedly the coolest experience of my marathons during the year to date and optimism abounded. There were live bands performing periodically, huge crowds shouting 'good job'/'you got this' (neither of which was accurate), over 150 couples getting married during the race and it all seemed like it was going to be a thoroughly life affirming end to my marathon challenge.

This all held throughout Old Town until around mile 10 when the full marathoners branched off right, leaving the strip and the half marathon runners. It was at this point that things changed for the worse. My life script writer was having a ball, as literally immediately upon turning right the crowds vanished, a sharp headwind buffeted me and it began to rain. It was metaphoric perfection and instantly drained all the optimism from my soul. From here the course headed out into soulless industrial wasteland where spectators and bands do not tread. Such was the strength of the wind that the majority of mile markers had blown away leaving one to guesstimate distance covered. Everyone was in their own personal hell and the only interactions I had with other runners was mutual apologising for 'cussing' whenever someone was hit by a particularly strong gust of wind. It was also freezing – not a problem I had envisaged when signing up for the LV marathon...

The lowest point came after around 18 miles when we were returned to a large marquee complex, which I think was Las Vegas Market. For some reason the organisers had opted to stray from the rock and roll theme at this point and instead were playing very deep trance (I think the kids might call it 'grime') against a backdrop of strobe lights. Combined with the wind, the overall impact was hugely oppressive on the senses and my face must have told its own story as I passed through as a concerned race marshal cycled up to enquire of my well-being. It was a thin, shredded thread at which one should not pull and had I started answering beyond the unconvincing, untruthful "yes" that I managed, I fear we would have ended with me on a chez lounge crying and pouring out my life story for a few hours...

By now my legs were almost completely gone – the combination of the previous day's efforts (running and social) and wind having drained any power they had left. I was in a Dark Place and only the thought that I was into the last half dozen miles of the last marathon I would run in 2015 did little to help. Despite only being 7:30pm, it felt like the middle of the night, both actually and spiritually. I was hopeful that a return to the Strip would offer shelter and improved conditions but the impact was minimal and at times the headwind was so strong that it was nearly impossible to move forward at all. As Britney may say, it was all a little "Crazy". The marathon was finishing at The Mirage, which was very fitting, given that when its gleaming sign finally appeared I knew full well that it was probably two miles further away than it looked. I was however determined to finish my final marathon strongly and called on all reserves to at least trot the final couple of miles, although my finish – in just under **3 hours 35 minutes** – was far from glorious. In an attempt to add a dramatic flourish to the conclusion I knelt down and kissed The Strip a short distance after the finish line. Big mistake. I realised I couldn't immediately get out of my kneeling position and my genuflection only ended after I crawled to the railings at the side and hauled my ruined body back onto its feet which I guess in itself was a spectacle for anyone observing...

The wind was still howling and the cold far worse in the absence of movement and I was therefore grateful for the curious distraction of an interview by a Spanish film crew. I'm pretty sure the chap holding the microphone did not understand a word I said as he just stood, smiling and occasionally nodding, all the while carrying a vacuous stare. I suspect my interview has been cut in any event as I can't imagine I was at my most lucid or electrifying after such a gruelling experience. Any appetite for a celebratory night out had evaporated somewhere between miles 10 and 24 and it was decided to call it a night early and live to fight another day...

Monday started with black jack at Hooters at 9:30am and never really stopped being Vegas-fabulous until leaving a swanky, if very eclectic patron and music-wise, nightclub in the Cosmopolitan Hotel about 18 hours later. In fact, aside from three hours sleep, every hour was filled until the flight home (well, via Frankfurt, for some inexplicable reason) at 4:35pm on Tuesday (a highlight being a visit to Heart Attack Grill at which anyone weighing over 25 stone eats free and where one is spanked with a paddle in the middle of the restaurant if failing to finish the meal – I was duly spanked when the last two mouthfuls of my double bypass burger, complete with 10 slices of bacon, proved beyond me). I would love to report more details but, as the rule goes, the rest will have to stay in Vegas...

82

DUBAI 2016

A fairly eclectic weekend of travel and temperatures saw me take in a wintery English morning, followed by a scorching Dubai weekend, a bitterly icy day in Moscow (-25 degrees, complete with a frozen River Moskva), rounded off with a return to the grey winter of the UK. My carrier of choice (a decision based exclusively on price) was Aeroflot. There was a slightly unnerving start to my trip when the lady at the counter at Heathrow Airport informed me that Aeroflot did not fly to Dubai. Her colleague corrected her and I was on my way for a four hour flight to Moscow without in-flight entertainment or any even nod to niceties from the cabin crew. It was the same story for the onward six hour flight to Dubai although the only two pages of the in-flight magazine which were in English did at least entertain me for a short period, as the Russian story had clearly been fed into Google translate (other search engine providers are available) and the translation pasted directly into the magazine without running through an English speaking filter to sense check. The result was an abrupt and very confusing article.

With it being winter in Dubai, the mercury was only touching the mid-20s – which felt positively roasting to my skin which had been starved of vitamin D for several months of the UK winter – but it mattered little as I had to attend the air conditioned office for a few hours before foolishly embarking on a whistle stop tour of Dubai night spots (my colleague Rebecca – of Vegas and Dorset marathons – had kindly collected my running pack) which ended less than two hours before the start of the Dubai Marathon. I decided that sleep was likely to do more harm than good and therefore caught a taxi directly to the start with Rebecca. I did not have time to find the luggage storage so, in hindsight very unhelpfully, placed my rucksack, which contained all of my belongings including mobile phone and passport underneath the start/finish banner. This was to prove to have been a mistake...

The first part of the run was something of a probably still drunken haze and any unrealistic aspirations of a good time evaporated in a portaloo at around the 10 kilometre mark. From that point onwards it was a true battle, particularly so when the sun rose to a point when there was no shade available on the out and back course, which did not even offer glimpses of the sea or major tourist attractions as respite. Further toilet breaks further slowed my pace and a poor day at the office was capped off when a cursory examination of the start/finish area (which I reached in **4 hours 9 minutes and 16 seconds**) revealed that my rucksack had been removed. There followed a long period of enquiry about the whereabouts of my belongings, during which time a number of different officials explained to me how stupid it might be in uncertain modern times to leave an unmarked rucksack at a busy start/finish area of a major international sporting event. Fair point. I was mulling over exactly how Humpty Dumb-ty was going to piece together his latest self-inflicted catastrophe when a man appeared with my bag. I thanked him with all my heart and vowed never to be so stupid again...

83

AROUND THE RESERVOIR 2016

I'm not entirely sure why I found myself back at the Holiday Inn on Easter weekend of 2016. I can only surmise that I am a glutton for punishment...

In any event, rather than relaying the story of running around the grassy surrounds of the reservoir again, see **Chapters 61, 62** and **63** above, the one variation being the finishing time of **3 hours 13 minutes and 31 seconds**...

84

BOSTON 2016

Whether by accident or design, I'm not sure, but the Boston, Lincolnshire, England marathon 2016 coincided with the Boston, Massachusetts, USA marathon 2016. This meant a UK website plastered with warnings that **THIS IS NOT THE BOSTON, USA MARATHON**. Even for me, I think it would be quite a stretch to accidentally book a marathon on the wrong continent, but time will tell…

I had never previously been to the English iteration of Boston but the drive out, almost exclusively through dead flat farming land, promised a nice flat course. I was not to be disappointed.

After starting in the pleasant Market Square, the course headed out into the countryside and we ran primarily along tracks adjacent to farming land. This was fairly welcome as far as demands on the body went, although slightly less pleasing was the unseasonable hot UK sun which eventually slowed me from a promising pace to a broadly par performance, ultimately finishing in just under **3 hours 30 minutes**…

85

BLACKPOOL 2016

Like the Boston Marathon (see above), Blackpool Marathon 2016 shared its date with a somewhat more auspicious event, the London Marathon. My assumption is that the Blackpool run (along with a handful of others around the country) had been initiated to cater for the overspill of those unfortunate souls who had applied and trained for the London Marathon only to not get a place. Whatever the origins, it was a well-attended event and I felt enthused despite the typically North West weather which heralded the start of the race, with rain coming in off the Irish Sea as we started beneath the famous promenade.

The somewhat less star studded composition of the field compared with the marathon taking place da'an South allowed me the brief thrill of leading the marathon as we ran along the coastal road before climbing up to the main road of the promenade and making our way towards and then under the very famous, possibly now rusting, Blackpool Tower. After posing for selfies with some glammed up ponies pulling carts fit for a princess (or a chav) we proceeded along the sea front past the Pleasure Beach, which looked distinctly non-pleasurable on such a grey day. After this we left the more exciting part of town and headed into a housing estate before looping back down along the front. After passing the Tower and the start line, the course progressed moderately uphill, although the length of this stretch was significantly sustained to be uncomfortable. We eventually dropped back down to a path on the sea front back to the start-finish area before repeating the whole thing for a second time in slightly improved conditions.

Given the number of selfies and the occasional coastal headwinds it was with some surprise that I clocked a time of under **3 hours 15**

minutes, after which I gleefully collected my tower shaped medal and tower print t-shirt and made my way to lose some small change in the numerous arcades of this once great seaside town, sparing a thought for those who would have to content themselves with a battle to get from the Mall to wherever they had come from following the London Marathon...

86

MILTON KEYNES 2016

See **Chapter 68** above. I can genuinely remember almost nothing about this marathon (it was purely arranged to move me one marathon closer to 100), save that it went better than the first time around and I finished in the MK Stadium in a time of **3 hours 24 minutes and 41 seconds**...

87

AROUND THE RESERVOIR (AGAIN!) 2016

By the time this event came around, I had abandoned the history of Nottingham and my unremarkable place in it for the bright lights and gleaming skyscrapers of Dubai. This was ultimately a move motivated by money and a desire to exit Britain, which had by now itself decided to exit Europe (the result of which had been an effective overnight sterling pay rise for anyone getting paid in dollars). Within three months of arriving in Dubai, I had however been drawn back to Britain twice (*"the grass is always greener"* – in fact, given the paucity of grass in Dubai, *"the grass is just there"* may be more apt), the second time purely to fulfil a promise I had made before I left the UK.

Earlier in 2016, I had signed up to run the anchor marathon in a full length triathlon on the Sunday (see below) and I was therefore under strict instructions to have a restful Saturday. I took this to mean that it would be OK to sign up for a full marathon, to be undertaken back where I had already spent far too much of my life (see **Chapters 61, 62** and **63** above)…

Fortunately, for my increasingly frail grip on sanity, the course had been slightly altered from previous runnings of the marathon which at least gave me some variety, at least on lap one of the six which made up the full length of the marathon. Less helpfully, there was a stiff headwind for a long straight, which would naturally also need to be run six times, which felt longer with each lap.

As it was, mindful of the marathon the following day, I held back slightly throughout the run and eventually completed the course in **3 hours 42 minutes**, hoping that I had not done too much damage to my body in doing so and praying that my tri-teammates would forgive my preparations…

88

NOTTINGHAM OUTLAW 2016

The morning after the night before (spent at Mecca Bingo)...was actually not too bad. Thanks to the nature of the event, I would be taking on the third leg of a full distance triathlon, which meant that my work would not commence until the afternoon. Without question (in my mind), the most daunting leg of the three was the swim. This would involve a dawn start and swim through the uninviting waters of the National Watersports Centre at Holme Pierrepoint in Nottingham, essentially a long straight of water generally used for rowing events. Whilst this leg took place I could be found sleeping at our swimmer's house and I eventually made my way to the event part way through the cycling leg after a heroic swim by Ennis. Our cycle leg was being completed by Andy, although this was against medical orders, after several weeks of significant discomfort in his back. Ennis and I were somewhat concerned (less so than his wife) when Andy had not arrived in the transition area towards the back-end of his expected arrival time so the relief was palpable when we saw him swing around the corner at the end of the water and completed the handover formalities.

The predominantly grass course the previous day had meant that my joints and muscles were less battered than they might have been and I had a packet of painkillers to hand as I set off on the marathon leg at a slightly ambitious tilt. I knew every inch of the course well, having lived nearby for several years of my time in Nottingham, and managed to maintain a moderate pass throughout the duration of the course, picking up my pace whenever completing laps near the bulk of the spectators. It was the feeling of being the anchor leg of a team which had performed admirably which spurred me on when my legs did start to groan and we fittingly finished as a trio, holding hands as we crossed the finish line in front of the dark water with the marathon time having been **3 hours 24 minutes**…

89

PETRA DESERT (JORDAN) 2016

At first I was afraid, I was petra-fied...No, that's not in fact true. I was in fact blown away by the absolute majestic wonder of Petra and slightly mystified by the limited number of tourists at what was one of the most impressive manmade sights I had ever beheld. This was all on day one of my visit to Petra, by which time I had not even seen "the main event" of the Treasury and The Rose City.

My preparation the evening before had been mildly eclectic. I had determined that a massage might be in order to loosen my limbs, only to climb the stairs of the chosen massage venue and find a young man "choking his chicken" whilst looking at something on his iPhone. To his credit (I think), he quickly regained his composure, put everything away and asked if I wanted a massage, I was almost laughing too much to turn down his kind offer of a massage (which would presumably have offered a quick wash of the hands). With my massage attempts thwarted I decided to repair to the roof of my modest accommodation at The Full Moon Hotel and order a bottle of wine as I took in the beautiful views over Petra. I took the remaining wine to my room and seemingly passed out mid consumption as I awoke half covered in red wine and late for the marathon meet up. I had considered the time of the meet up to be unnecessarily early (6am) but this proved to be incorrect as I had to scamper much of the 2+ kilometres through the stunning rockscape which leads the way to the jaw dropping Treasury (of Indiana Jones' fame). I barely had time for a couple of selfies before I had to make my way the short distance to the start line. To minimise the risk of damage to this true world wonder, we were required to jog slowly behind the race organiser for 500 metres before we were cut loose to run freely. As we cut through the cool air of the desert valley, I led the way for a glorious few hundred metres before being over taken by a Jordanian and a Chinese runner.

We soon climbed steeply into a Bedouin village, the severity of the slope causing me to slow to a stiff march, before winding up and down through spectacular desert and rock outcrops before finally leaving the asphalt road after around three kilometres and heading into the desert "proper". It was life affirming stuff, spoiled slightly by the fact that I desperately needed the toilet and could see limited options for dealing with this and retaining some shred of privacy. My opportunity arrived when we dropped down again to the valley floor and some sparse green vegetation offered both vague cover and also natural toilet paper. I took my chance and immediately felt like a new man, picking up my pace after the brief enforced stoppage. I was still tracking along in third place at this time and briefly became joint second when it turned out that the Chinese runner had taken a wrong turning and been forced to retrace his steps. He soon ran off into the distance when we re-joined the road and there was no sign off the Jordanian runner at this point, so I assumed he was long gone. I was joined at this point by an English man named Tom who explained that he worked as a diplomat in Amman. We shared long distance running stories revealing varying degrees of insanity before the road again started to climb steeply, causing me to slow down to a point where Tom left me again to my own thoughts in this vast desert wonder. The trajectory was primarily downhill at this point, which was good news although I knew that we were eventually going to loop back, which meant nasty uphill stretches would be coming as the heat of the ay increased. I did not have to wait too long for this as a short time after the halfway point, we plunged in shadow down a zig zagging road which culminated in the lowest point of the course to date. After a quick drink at the bottom, it was time to turn around and face the climb back up the zig zags before a steep climb back from whence we had come a short while before. Worse was to come with an absolutely brutal hill featuring cruelly at around the 35 kilometre point in proceedings. Only the hardiest could have run up this slope and I accepted my lot with a slow to a plod, pushing my hands into my quads to seek to offer some small comfort to my ailing body. Around two thirds of the way up I passed the Jordanian who seemed to have picked up an injury along the way. I enquired about his well-being and he said that he was done. It's never nice to see any fellow runners struggling, particularly one who was clearly more talented than most although this had catapulted me undeservedly into third...

Once "the hill" had been tamed, the going became more undulating for the next few kilometres, as we ran a short distance until the ridge of the hillside and were treated to spectacular desert views in every direction. Petra itself finally came into view – meaning that the end was nigh – and a short time afterwards the rocky track started to head steeply downwards. This was good and bad news. Good in that it reaffirmed the fact that the end was coming and bad in so far as my battered quads were now being asked to do much of the work. I decided to focus on the former and let my body relax as far as possible allowing gravity to do the work. Soon the houses of Petra started to pass by and I could even hear the loud speakers of the finish area echoing around the narrow streets. I gritted my teeth for the final spurt and was delighted to find that I had broken four hours (by ten seconds) on a truly brutal course and finished in third position, which meant being awarded with an attractive and hefty wooden trophy. The post run beer/shisha had rarely tasted so sweet...

90

KLADNO (CZECH REPUBLIC) 2016

On reflection, staying in a youth hostel in Prague after a hectic period of work was a mistake. The morning had been a relatively civilised affair, with a few hours taking in picturesque Zurich following an overnight flight from Dubai. However, my desire to blow off steam got the better of me in Prague and my final clear recollection is a selfie in which I had (at least in my mind) brilliantly perched a painting of a green Absinthe Fairy on the wall of an underground bar in Prague atop my right shoulder. Fast forward a few hours and I awoke very confused in the bottom bunk of my hostel dormitory. A quick investigation of my small bed and the surrounding floor area suggested that my mobile phone had not survived the evening revelry and that I would be required to make my way to the hopefully nearby town of Kladno for the marathon without Smartphone assistance. At least the darkness of the morning implied (correctly) that I had awoken early enough to make it to the marathon and this was indeed the state of affairs. Thanks to the Green Fairy and other encounters, I had mixed feelings about this.

I had stayed near the train station and navigating my way to Kladno via train turned out to be remarkably straightforward. Altogether less straightforward was finding the marathon once in Kladno, although I eventually managed this thanks to an initially confused Adidas shell suited taxi driver whose Google guided us to the sports stadium a few kilometres from the city centre from where the marathon would commence.

It was a small but seemingly friendly crowd of marathon runners who lined up on the athletics track in the stadium for the marathon, which would consist of a few loops of the surrounding woodland area. Putting aside the atrocious preparation, I set off running around the pleasant track at a good enough pace and laps one and two went well. My stride was eventually broken by a toilet break, after which I never really recovered but the flat, mostly shaded, course was as gentle as I could have wished and I held in to finish in **3 hours 27 minutes and 30 seconds**, before making my way back to Prague to do it (nearly) all again…

91

WROCLAW (POLAND) 2016

The Wroclaw marathon starts with a truly remarkable journey across Europe, which I would like to think a certain Eastern European taxi driver is still talking about...

Thanks mostly to the after effects of a marathon (and some red wine), I woke up in a confused stupor on the sofa at my hostel in Prague, having missed my coach to Wroclaw by a significant amount of time. I pulled myself together (of a fashion) relatively swiftly, gathered my remaining belongings and staggered out into the early hours of a pitch black Prague morning. Flagging down the first taxi I saw, I explained that I needed to go to Wroclaw. Wroclaw? Replied the confused driver. Yes, I said, and realising that my Eastern European pronunciation may be some way off target, pulled up the location on his Smartphone. It was a mere 400 kilometres away. I'm not sure why the driver was looking at me like I was insane. "*Ah – Vrocloo*" he exclaimed. "Money". Fair enough. I withdrew a couple of hundred Euro and handed them to him, suspecting I may need to hand over more on arrival. With that I passed out in the back of the taxi as we sped across Europe. It was only on arrival into Wroclaw at some time around dawn I was awoken with my newly minted driver asking where I needed to be dropped off. I clearly had no idea and settled for being delivered somewhere which looked vaguely central. I wandered around without too much purpose until eventually spying a few lycra clad folk who I assumed must be marathon-bound and followed them, hoping I was not just following some early morning yoga enthusiasts. Happily I was not and I was soon heading into a large pleasant park which was fairly teeming with marathon activities. I found my way to the registration sports hall where I finished the formalities, having not been able to register online and then found myself a morning beer to seek to take the edge of my aching limbs. The sight of a marathon runner clutching a beer at the start line seemed to cause some, but not undue, amusement but as soon as I had seen off the amber nectar and started on my way into the marathon, I realised I was in for a fairly long miserable day, especially as the sun was soon beating relentlessly down on my dehydrated person.

The thought of a quenching beer to take the edge off my misery proved too much to hold on for and I nipped into a grocery store to allow myself a couple of cans to see me through the final few kilometres, by which time I had long since been reduced to a shuffling mess. The beer seemed sufficiently galvanising to propel me to a moderate pace at the finish line and with it some pictures in which I appear to have been running, which is not necessarily reflective of a full day's effort which resulted in me just breaking the four hour mark...

92

SPARTATHLON
(ATHENS TO SPARTA, GREECE) 2016

It is written that in ancient times, on wings crafted from feathers and wax, Icarus ignored his father's warning and flew too close to the sun causing the wax to melt and Icarus to come to a pretty dreadful end. Several millennia later and Nicholas is being counseled by race veterans about the perils of setting out too quickly in Spartathlon, held by some to be the toughest foot race in the world. Fast forward 10 hours and Nicholas is heading a field of 380 of the world's top ultra-marathon runners, with a personal police escort through Athens. Back in the first person and I can't help but admit this was a fairly intoxicating experience of having my name chanted, high fiving school kids, which I assumed would last for a few minutes at best but which actually lasted for nearly 35 kilometers/two and half hours. It ended with a comfort break at a service station, during which a handful of runners passed me, the wax that was holding me together melted, and Nicarus started to head rapidly to the ground. By now, having 74 marathons and 17 ultra-marathons under my belt, I felt that was running within the bounds of the achievable, even in the context of such a brutal race, but was proved to be misguided. Maybe celebrating my achievements the night *before* the race with a bottle and a half of red wine was also misguided…

The backdrop is an often repeated tale of the consequences of failing to adequately prepare. Not an excuse, but I had been working long hours and weekends so had struggled to put in more than consistent short runs. In a vain attempt to redress this I had run back to back marathons in the UK in July and then in Europe in September (see **Chapters 87 and 88** and **90 and 91** above). This turned out to be the equivalent of reading 'Law for Dummies' and then sitting the New

York bar exam. I was also asked about my 'drop bag' strategy at the race sign up on Thursday afternoon. After Googling this term it appeared I did not have one (to be fair, until I read a previous race report two days before the event I did not even have a head lamp as I had not quite registered that it would be dark for 12 hours of the race). I went back to the hotel and developed a drop bag strategy only to find that I had missed the cut off for delivering drop bags. Thankfully, in a show of the collegiate spirit which makes ultra-running so special, members of the British team introduced me to their support crews who offered to help. The 'strategy' I had developed involved leaving a jacket and head torch at the foot of the mountain, 100 miles in. Genius – until it was pointed out that, unless I was planning to break the course record (I was not), I would have been running in pitch darkness for approximately 10 hours by this point. I called a team meeting (of one) and we decided I would run with the head torch around my neck and have my drop bag (jacket and painkillers) taken to the foot of the mountain. I couldn't help but thinking that I was steadily becoming a knowledgeable ultra-marathon runner…

Friday morning duly arrived and we were escorted to the Acropolis for the 7am start. Goodness knows what the founders of modern civilization would have made of the mass of excited runners crowded at the feet of this historic site. We swung down over paved rocks before heading into the streets of Athens. This is when I saw the opportunity to grab my 15 minutes of fame by hitting the front of the field (and the rest is sad history). By the time I had finished the first marathon of what was due to be 5.8 marathons it was 10:30am and the heat of the day was just starting to rear its head. Aside from some mild cramp in my right leg and a bloodbath down the right hand side of my chest (my right nipple – not for the first time – deciding it had seen enough and would wait for its left side colleague (steadfastly hanging in there) and owner in Tartarus (the deep abyss that is used as a dungeon of torment in the Greek underworld)), physically everything was in check until around the 80 kilometer mark when I realized both feet were in some mild discomfort. The distraction of some company in the form of a few kilometers with some guys from England then a guy from Puerto Rico kept me going until around the

120 kilometer mark, but I then decided it was time to seek some attention for my feet. I had no interest in seeing the condition of my feet in the flesh, which I suspected wasn't great, so settled for them being heavily taped to hopefully block out some of the pain. By now I had fallen into "running" with a South African/honorary Brit called Terrence, although in reality the best either of us could manage was a shuffle. At some point early on in the night (which seemed to last forever) another British athlete passed us and asked what my GPS tracker was showing. I responded that if by GPS he meant 'watch', it was showing me that one gets what one pays for in life (which had several meanings at this point) and all I could see was condensation, rust and – if I strained – the time. On a separate point, and without wanting to be graphic, there was some relatively severe chaffing downstairs and I was reduced to handling my unmentionables with more delicacy than I imagine the North Koreans handle slightly more potent junk. Probably not one for the e-harmony profile under other comments – "*eroded undercarriage*"…

After 100 miles we reached "The Mountain" – a 1,200 meter affair that would be a fairly unpleasant proposition even if confronted on fresh legs in broad daylight for a family picnic, let alone after 160 kilometers and 20 hours of movement. I made the mistake of looking up and seeing headlights weaving their way up seemingly to the stars and was advised by a previous finisher never ever to look up again. It was now that my drop bag was delivered although the gentleman who delivered my jacket suggested that if I took all of the pills in my hand my kidneys may well fail. I have to admit that this did not sound that terrible at this point as I had been looking for a legitimate reason to lay down for hours – I was favouring being slightly run over at this point; renal failure sounded less tempting…On the climb, the stones under foot were slippery, the drops to the side awaiting in the event of a mistake significant and we soon stumbled across an American lady laying on the floor crying because it was all too much. Having helped her out, we pressed on and reached the summit mercifully quickly, only to find the descent to be even worse. Every step was a challenge, with sliding rocks and muscles which felt like they were full of battery acid.

The wise old heads of previous Spartathlon had told me that if you clear the mountain within the cut-off time, you will make it to the end. Sadly, after the mountain we plunged into a valley. It was 5:30am and we had not seen the sun for 10 hours. My t-shirt was proving woefully inadequate and I was shaking uncontrollably with the cold, falling asleep as I ran and mildly hallucinating I think, seeing the wind pass over me in beautiful technicolours (which I have to admit was great and, if commoditised, a multi-million pound industry). Such was the pain in my legs that I could barely even take a step forwards without yelping in pain so when the next check point came, complete with a roaring log fire, I suggested to my companion that he give me ten minutes to recuperate before we carried on. Ten minutes came and went and I knew my race was run – the cut off bus was approaching imminently and I had nothing left to offer. I told the race attendant to give me another 10 minutes, sent Terrence on his way, in the hope he could finish, before shuffling another four kilometers, at which point I dived on a make shift mattress on the floor of a small restaurant and was quickly covered on four blankets, none of which quite warmed me up.

Knowing that my race was run was a strange feeling of depression at failure and elation that the indescribable pain and fatigue had ended. In the condition I was in I knew that there was no way I could finish within the cut off time so I decided I would live to fight another day, a decision which may well haunt me forever – *"we are Spartans and we do not surrender"*. The 'death bus' (for non-finishers), after stops to collect other broken souls hailing from all around the world in various states of disrepair, deposited us – fittingly – opposite a dead, tethered boar in the back of a pick-up truck in Sparta. My final humiliation was shuffling up the finishing straight, which I had hoped to fly down in glory hours later, with my shoes in my hands and my hopes (and feet) in tatters. Sadly a few of the assembled spectators had not grasped that my day was over and for a while it threatened to be a death march accompanied by an undeserved crescendo of cheers until I managed to convey that my race had ended early, before scuttling into the shadows. If the 'death bus' to the finish line in Sparta was bleak, the finish line in Sparta was something else. Several people were put straight into wheelchairs or onto drips and a Taiwanese runner sharing our taxi to the hotel drifted into unconsciousness for 20 minutes until we managed to return him to the medics and thankfully recovery...

In short, the most extraordinary and difficult event in which I have ever participated. The whole event may best be summed up by words from the film 300..."*Madness?...This is Sparta(thlon)...*" Heck, yeah...

93

AMMAN (JORDAN) 2016

It was with some trepidation that I contemplated the Amman Marathon. It would be my first meaningful run since the Greek Tragedy of Spartathlon had unfolded and I just hoped that my body and mind had been sufficiently repaired to prepare me for the challenge. Of significant assistance was the fact that for the first time ever my parents would be in attendance at a marathon, after joining me for a few day tour of the grossly under visited Jordan.

Before race day I had already had a false start, when somehow my instructions to a taxi driver had been lost in translation and I was deposited at the IKEA Amman headquarters instead of the stadium from where I needed to collect my race pack. With that hiccup overcome, I had a decent night's sleep at the very well apportioned Rotana development in central Amman before an early morning taxi to the marathon pre-meeting point – at a sports stadium which was teeming with armed police. There was some confusion as we were allocated buses depending on which distance we were running, before being disembarked, then re-boarded a number of times. We were eventually deposited at the start line – opposite Amman Municipality – barely a few minutes before the planned start time although this was of little matter, given the relative sparsity of the starting field.

It was a pleasantly cool, overcast morning as we headed into the old town streets, which sat deep below steep hillsides, covered by small, mostly white, residences which evoked traditional thoughts of the biblical origins of the Middle East in my mind. The course was to be four loops of the Old Town and my parents offered a much needed boost to my sapping energy when they appeared near the finish area on lap two. Aside from the road closures, life continued seemingly unaffected by the presence of the marathon with the market streets becoming busier with each passing loop. I was lapped by the extremely fast moving leading pair of African runners at some point on lap three – it was a fairly breathtaking spectacle to be passed by such incredible natural athletes...

By the fourth loop, the long stretch back up the dual carriageway which sat below the high perimeter wall of one of the palaces in Amman had become too familiar and I was delighted to be able to turn left into the finish area next to the stunning and well preserved ruins of the Roman amphitheater and finish the run in front of my parents in just under **3 hours 35 minutes**. It appeared that Spartathlon had not completely finished me off as a runner just yet...

94

BEIRUT (LEBANON) 2016

Until moving to the Middle East in 2016, to me Beirut had only ever been somewhere which would occasionally appear on the BBC News as a place where some sort of unrest or other was taking place. As it turned out the reality of 2016 Beirut was quite far removed from my sketchy recollections of Kate Adie, or some other reporter, clad in a bullet proof vest wearing a concerned look as they delivered their piece to camera. Instead I arrived (late, having missed my morning flight and having to re-book on a later flight instead) to find I was staying in a vibrant party district, Gemmayzeh, and wasted no time in making the most of the relative liberalism of Beirut compared to the UAE and enjoyed a few beers along the very European style street, complete with open fronted bars and live music, before returning to my pleasant accommodation for the night.

I felt slightly sketchy on the Saturday morning as I went to collect my running number from a shopping centre across the city. With that done, I procured a driver for the day and proceeded to explore the city and the surrounding area, including the spectacular Jeita Grotto, followed by a ride up the mildly terrifying 1950s looking cable cars up to Our Lady of Harissa, Jounieh (a statute of Mary and small church) which overlooked the city. My driver and I enjoyed a veritable feast of a lunch, with a banquet of various Lebanese delights and fruit, which would have been enough to feed five times as many people. Duly satiated, I returned to the hostel to be told that a friend had checked in and would be joining me for dinner. I was intrigued.

My friend turned out to be Marcel – a heroic warrior of a man who had completed the Spartathlon (see **Chapter 92** above) despite various injuries which made my complaints look inconsequential.

Marcel announced that he drinks only three times a year and certainly never before a marathon but I insisted that all that change and that we prepare in style for the Beirut marathon. A bar crawl along the Gemmayzeh strip followed, on which we were joined by a young Russian chap, who was not running the marathon and therefore was more than happy to indulge in whatever drinks were going. Fast forward a few hours and Marcel had been sick and I only wished I had been as we headed on foot for the relatively short distance to the start of the Beirut Marathon. Whilst I had a decent pool of experience of feeling shaky at the start of various marathons, for some reason this time it was worse and after weaving around a few streets at the start of the run, I realised we were passing my hostel and so decided that a return for a toilet break and stolen few minutes of sleep was in order. This was not a good idea and it was quite a wrench to leave my bed and return to the run, which I knew was not going to go well. This trepidation was well founded...

The route – such as I remember it – was pleasant and the odd armoured vehicle and armed police/soldiers we passed along the way a nod to my childhood perception of the city and the region. By the time I finished, very nearly **five hours** after setting off, I was a broken man, regretting my life choices and just hoping that Marcel had fared better. He had. So much so that he had had time to return to the hostel, wash and head out sight-seeing before my husk of a body had made it back...

95

BANGALORE MIDNIGHT (INDIA) 2016

Whilst I had read something about a currency crisis before heading on my first ever trip to India (the Government had overnight announced that it was demonetising all 1,000, 5,000 and 10,000 Rupee bank notes and removing them from circulation, in an attempt to crack down on the black economy), I had paid it little heed, blithely assuming that it would have little to no impact on tourists. The warning sign was pretty vivid before my departure from Abu Dhabi Airport, which was devoid of Rupees. I therefore arrived at Bangalore Airport with precisely zero local currency and ignored the lengthy queue at the currency exchange counter before the Arrivals Hall, thinking that I would go and change/withdraw some money at a place where the queues were shorter. It became rapidly clear that such a place did not exist in Bangalore. At any ATM which had not already been emptied and a NOT IN USE or OUT OF CURRENCY sign put up, the queues snaked around the block on which such ATM was positioned. The story was the same at each of the banks that me and my driver – who had a vested interest in my local currency search – and I was beginning to lose hope so decided to proceed directly to the marathon sign up point, which was a small barren room up some outside stairs beside a coffee shop. I had not yet paid for my marathon entry, due to difficulties with transferring money online to an Indian account and the lady overseeing proceedings was far from delighted to learn that I came bearing only United Arab Emirate Dirhams. However, as incredible luck would have it, she was heading to Dubai in the next few weeks and therefore agreed to become an unofficial currency exchange, accepting my Dirhams in payment, plus an additional amount which meant that there would be no diplomatic incident with my taxi driver. This has saved me in the short-term but I still had several days to pass and my currency problems were not yet at an end...

My accommodation in Bangalore was pleasant enough, although the velour oak green bed spread and print of a half-naked boy on the wall of my room were slightly curious. My intermediate currency fix was to purchase a cash card from Thomas Cook, which enabled me to complete transactions in shops, etc. However, unsurprisingly, it was not welcomed as payment by taxi drivers, street vendors or the large number of other small enterprises which make up the bulk of the Indian economy. This therefore meant early morning rises to withdraw whatever funds I could from ATMs before they were emptied by the hordes of people in the same predicament. I had fortunately accumulated enough hard cash for the tuk tuk ride out to the marathon, which was taking place outside the city but certainly not enough for the return. Something which I decided to put out of my mind for the duration of the marathon.

The marathon itself started at Midnight (as the name would suggest) and consisted of several laps of a closed off area in the outskirts of Bangalore. There were bands and pockets of support to cheer us along the way in what would otherwise have been a fairly dull event. I inadvertently managed to spice things up on my third lap. I stopped in a portaloo and put my mobile phone on the sink. When I stepped on the pedal below the sink to flush the toilet, the whole plastic sink unit came away from the wall of the portaloo and – to my absolute horror – my phone plunged down the abyss. It would be fair to say that pushing my arm into the dark unknown of a portaloo in the middle of the night in Bangalore was something of a low point. Worse was to come as my best efforts only resulted in fleeting touches of my phone meaning that I had to enlist the assistance of three slightly confused locals to hold the sink and the wall apart as I reached further in and eventually plucked out the – thankfully untarnished and still working – mobile phone from the darkness. Quite a moment.

After Portaloo-Gate the rest of the run was something of an anti-climax and I plodded round, struggling with the heat despite the time of day and eventually finishing in **3 hours 50 minutes**. It was now time to re-focus on the fact that I was several miles away from my hotel and devoid of any Rupees. Several local youths were keen to assist with offers of an Uber pick up but the offer was retracted when they grasped my currency problems. Instead I was forced to trudge across wasteland and back along the dual carriageway I had passed down on my way to the marathon where I had seen a hotel that thankfully accepted my Thomas Cook card as payment before I enjoyed one of the most satisfying night's sleep of my life.

All in all, my first visit to India had been every bit as challenging as I had expected, but for entirely different reasons than those I had envisaged…

96

DUBAI 2017

New Year promises and aspirations of a dry January 2017 had been dashed by a combination of factors, the most compelling of which being a total lack of will power. It was against this backdrop where it seemed foolish to turn down an unexpected invite to free dinner and drinks heralding the celebration of the Dubai Maritime Association (or something along those lines), at the iconic (Disney-esque) Atlantis Hotel on The Palm in Dubai. As I knew no one else going to the event, I was ascribed the "all sorts" table and ended up sitting with two couples, one of whom soon left proceedings. This left me in the company of a middle aged Dutch couple and as the only interested party in a number of unopened bottles of wine. As the after dinner entertainment – a not bad group of singers – set about the work, so did I. Unfortunately, not for the first time (in fact, for a time numbering in the 100s), I over estimated my drinking prowess and found myself "speaking to God" as red wine returned rapidly from whence it had been delivered in one of the public toilets at The Atlantis. Seeing this as a sign from someone, I wisely decided that my evening was done and returned home for a longer than expected pre-marathon sleep, albeit still in the undesirable realms of below five hours.

With the alarm clock, red wine manufacture and my own weakness duly chastised, I hailed a taxi to the start line of the Dubai marathon. Despite the fairly appalling preparations, I was in distinctly better condition than I had been a year earlier at the same event, although (unlike Philip Pirrip) had no great expectations of a strong performance.

My misgivings were seemingly misplaced, at least for the first half of the race as I ticked along at a decent pace, enjoying views of Dubai not available when the invariably jam packed roads are open, including a stunning view of the Downtown skyline – dominated by the silhouette of the Burj Khalifa (the world's tallest building for the time being) – as the sun rose.

The temperature naturally increased as the sun climbed and the fairly dull dead flat out and back course – designed to encourage stellar performances from the world's best marathoners – offered little distraction from the steady deterioration in my body. My pace dipped markedly and I had taken to walking as I took on drinks at the numerous refreshment stations. It was therefore relatively pleasing to finish in just under the **3 hour 30 minute** mark, before a long old walk to find a taxi to take me back to the sanctuary of bed…

97

MUSCAT 2017

In keeping with the self-imposed horror arrangements of numerous of these events, I arrived in Muscat late, less than five hours before the marathon start time. In typically meticulous fashion, I had made no attempt to investigate hotel locations in proximity to the marathon and was not entirely surprised when I was deposited on the opposite side of the city by my taxi. The three hours' sleep I managed before rising for my next taxi was marginal in its benefit and less pleasing still was the lack of a receptionist/any taxis on the main road when I stumbled onto the deserted streets outside my hotel. I was starting to fear the worst when my luck changed and I spotted a taxi at a petrol station on the other side of the dual carriageway. I shouted and sprinted across and my relief was such that I decided not to question what seemed to be a very steep fare to the start of the run in the Al Mouj district of Muscat, a sleek modern development.

The small scale run started in a pedestrianised shopping zone before heading out briefly across somewhat challenging unlit, unpaved dirt roads and then onto the sea front. By now it was approaching 7am and the sight of the sun rising over the Gulf of Oman was a beautiful and humbling start to the race. We headed down the sea front for a number of kilometers before turning 180 degrees and running back the same way. By the time we crossed past the point at which the race had started the sun had steadily climbed its way into the morning sky and it was starting to get distinctly warm. A golf course and industrial estate offered limited respite from the glare of the sun and, but for the distraction of an entertaining saxophone player, I was glad to hit the golf course for a second time, which spelled the near conclusion of my morning exertions in the beautiful Muscat, which finally ended in a time of **3 hours 24 minutes and 49 seconds**.

The day was still young although my tourist experience was curtailed by the fact that (1) I was exhausted and could barely walk and (2) pretty much everything closes in Muscat on a Friday; a fact which – not altogether unhappily – forced me to spend the rest of the day until my evening flight back to Dubai sharing drinks with my driver for the day in various resort bars around the coastline of the impressive city…

98

SHAKESPEARE SPRING 2017

In keeping with the meandering narrative of this running odyssey, the mildly uninspiring surrounds of the Raceway track outside Stratford played host to my 98th marathon only due to aborted marathon attempts in the arguably more exciting locations of Bahrain and Wadi Bih, in Oman.

The circumstances of the two non-runs were somewhat different. Whilst I had made it to Bahrain only to find that the success of some crazy-scientist sounding cloud seeding had resulted in torrential storms which had left most of the island underwater and the marathon therefore cancelled, I had arrived at the UAE-Oman border in the middle of the night (ahead of the 4am start of the 72km event) only to find the border guard asleep and therefore (together with a handful of others) my access to the run blocked at the last. There followed a random run around the deserted streets of Dibba, which culminated in a trip over a street sign which had been blown over and a visit to a police station, courtesy of an overzealous native who did not appreciate my taking selfies in front of what was apparently a government building (I had been oblivious to this fact and drawn in by the flags outside said building)…

Back to the slightly more mundane setting of Long Marston Airfield and I knew full well what to expect – with this being my third running of the event. As can be the case with unguided amateur runners who follow no structure in their race preparations, I felt in fine fettle for no apparent reason and set off at a sub-three hour marathon pace. This afforded me the lead for more than half the race and my own motorbike escort, who guided me around the first few laps of the course to ensure that I knew the route. I was inevitably passed by several runners during the remaining loops of this raceway/landing strip but finished in a credible fifth place in a time of **3 hours 9 minutes**. Any satisfaction this outcome afforded me was soon usurped by the horrible thought that I had to get up the next day and do it all again, albeit a reasonable distance to the south west of the raceway…

99

WREXHAM 2017

As the more observant reader may have gleaned, there was never really a plan in place in terms of the pursuit of the 100, which in itself was only latterly an objective. At various times, the rarely seen romantic iteration, or – more likely – the slightly sozzled version, may have had aspirations of running each of the final few marathons in a different country or at particularly impressive events. Alas, as is often the case in life, pragmatism and economic reality meant that the run in to the one hundred was dictated by available marathons at the relevant times of year rather than any higher order of things. So it was that the day after returning to run around a flat race track in the middle of nowhere, I found myself in Wrexham for the first time, albeit only after taking a number of wrong turns as I headed cross country from Leicestershire…

Wrexham itself – and the marathon it hosted – were something of a pleasant surprise. I had images of a dreary, deserted old coal mining town in my mind (due largely to ignorance) and was pleased to instead find a quaint, compact town centre, from where the marathon departed out into miles of rolling countryside. Despite the previous day's exertions I set out at a solid pace, passing 10 kilometres in less than 45 minutes before a toilet break put an end to any rhythm I had built up, reminded me of the pain and acid lurking in my muscles, and slowed me down to an altogether more sensible and sustainable pace.

This sensible pace was slowed to a gingerly march when the marathon headed steeply uphill in its final few kilometres and it was a huge relief when the finish line arrived (in a time of **3 hours 25 minutes and 25 seconds**), allowing me to resuscitate my ailing limbs with a delicious pint of Brains – something which I otherwise lack in abundance…

100

MARSEILLES 2017

In keeping with the general theme of the tales preceding the glorious 100th marathon, I initially thought that the centenary marathon was in fact my 99th and managed to make general nonsense of the whole event. A miscount which was not corrected until several months after le tragedy unfolded, by which time I had wrongly celebrated the momentous one hundredth several hundred kilometres to the north east of Marseilles, in Zurich.

The trip started in suitably foolish form, with a 4am pint of cider at the Wetherspoons at Stanstead Airport. Stanstead being a low cost airline departure point, I was naturally not alone in my morning drinking and 'Spoons was filling up nicely (if you are a shareholder – as I am proud to say I am – or mortifyingly, if you are a doctor or UK social observer) by the time I had to leave to board my flight to France. Not entirely unsurprisingly, given my morning activities, I slept deeply on the flight and was slightly disappointed to have to alight the aircraft before heading to my underwhelming accommodation – the B&B Hotel in Marseilles. I was sufficiently early to not be allowed to access my room and instead had to deposit my belongings behind reception before heading into central Marseilles to collect my marathon pack and sample a few local wines (very wise). By 9pm I was fading rapidly and decided that a withdrawal was the sensible thing to do, collecting a taxi from near the attractive harbour front, in which I promptly passed out having confirmed the name of my hotel. I was more than slightly confused when the driver woke me up at the B&B Hotel, which bore no resemblance to the hotel in which I was staying, other than the corporate awnings. It transpired that there were two B&B Hotels in Marseille – oh course – and I had been deposited at the "wrong one". Zut alors! Fearing this to be the case (I had gone into the hotel in the vain hope that I had misrecognized it), I had asked my taxi driver to wait outside and now asked him to repair to the second B&B Hotel. It had been expensive error and was compounded by a lengthy detour to find an ATM to pay for this unexpected expense, at which point the driver warned me to be very careful, as it was a dangerous areas. Perfect…

I was somewhat disgruntled when I finally made my way into reception at the correct B&B Hotel and disappointingly took this out on the innocent receptionist who said he did not have the keys to the luggage storage room which meant I could not collect my kit. I barked some utter nonsense about the importance of my kit and how he was ruining my weekend (I was primarily responsible for that) and was feeling slightly mortified by my churlishness when an apologetic knock at the door was followed by the appearance of a sheepish looking receptionist and my luggage. Despite my attempted humblest of apologies, karma was to pay me back almost instantly. My phone was still set to UK time so when I woke a few hours later, feeling slightly sub-par, I consoled myself with the thought that I still had plenty of time to get to the start point of the marathon and with that lolled back to sleep. I woke with a start just under an hour later, when my subconscious mind must have pointed out the time difference and that I was now cutting it extremely fine to dress and find the start of the race. I was therefore relieved to find thousands of fellow runners a short distance from the harbour where I had spent much of the previous day and made little of the fact that they were all wearing different coloured bibs to yours truly. It was only when I dropped off my bag a short distance from the start line that I was informed that this was actually the start point for the half marathon and that I had missed the buses to the start of the marathon. Having travelled so far, I was not going to allow such a minor inconvenience stand in my way and decided I would simply run two laps of the half marathon course. As it transpired, after a short wind around the streets of central Marseilles, we joined the marathon runners, having run only a marginally shorter distance than them at the same point. I therefore decided on an adapted strategy of running with the marathon runners until the end of the race, at which time I would run the necessary "balance" to make up the marathon distance.

Absolutement not a marathon for purists, but the best I could muster in the unfortunate circumstances. It was a beautiful day in Marseilles and the course seemed to take in the best the city had to offer, running through the city centre and attractive parks before hugging the coast line, overlooking the beautiful turquoise sea of the harbour towards the finish point. It was from there that I collected my initially unearned medal for what I didn't realise was the 100th time, before continuing to run along the harbour and back until I had made up the distance, and then some in a time of **3 hours 42 minutes**.

On reflection, the Marseilles' Marathon represents a suitably undignified way to mark what is probably my most significant life achievement to date…

101

ZURICH 2017

The phantom century marathon actually followed a similar formula to what had been the actual 100th marathon (I had not realized my error at the time of travelling to Switzerland and, as such, had taken Union Jack flags to mark my achievement). Again, the weekend commenced with an early flight to the continent preceded with a cheeky "livener" at the airport. On arrival in the attractive Swiss city of Zurich, I wasted no time in collecting my race pack before boarding a train to Geneva to catch up with a friend from Dubai. As the train zipped through the stunning Swiss countryside on a picture perfect day I sipped my way through a few more relaxing beverages. By the time we had enjoyed a few glasses of wine (and a shisha) on the shores on Lake Geneva, sitting in front of stunning surrounding snowcapped mountains I was unquestionably feeling a little "loose" and somehow managed to misplace my marathon pack on the return to Zurich, where the expense of Switzerland was illustrated to me by the uninspiring surrounds of my shower and toilet-less hostel room, which cost a similar amount to the price of a well apportioned hotel room in the UK or less expensive European jurisdiction (or about a year of subsistence in parts of Asia)…

Given this was to be my historic one hundredth marathon, I was slightly perturbed by my lack of a running bib and timing chip and I credit this with helping to clear away the cobwebs which would otherwise surely have been clogging my mind and system. I had managed to cut my arrival at the start line somewhat fine in any event and was only therefore able to visit the registration hut after running 500 metres or so of the race before leaving the course to dart into a car part where the *"INFORMATION"* portakabin was located. The ever efficient Swiss seemed somewhat bemused to meet Nickos and the net result was me running the Zurich marathon sans bib. I decided not to let this detract from the momentous day and instead soaked in the beautiful vista offered by Lake Zurich and an enthusiastic crowd, featuring various musical performances and supporters in colourful national dress.

I managed to maintain a decent pace, even as the temperature gradually increased and finished (what I thought was) the BIG 100 in a respectable time of **3 hours 24 minutes** – even though the record books may record me as a non-starter. I treated myself to a small bottle of cheap sparkling wine in the grounds of Zurich University, which overlooks the city and the lake and for a few precious seconds felt as close to true contentment as I may ever have felt. Sadly, like everything in life, this zen feeling departed as soon as it had arrived and completely evaporated as the organisers of the Zurich Marathon merciless chased the return of the chip I had lost somewhere on the Geneva-Zurich train, before eventually settling for me paying the 60 Swiss Francs fine by bank transfer. Viva Brexit…

EPILOGUE

In a not entirely unexpected turn of events, and much to the dismay of the long suffering Mrs. T, my running life did not cease immediately with the conclusion of what I thought was my 100th marathon (although, as above, it was in fact my 101st). Once something has become engrained into one's existence, with a moderately productive working day reliant on a reasonable morning run, it is difficult to simply stop.

However, the pursuit of marathons has become more intrinsically linked to world exploration and, since completing the century, for the most part my marathons have been a convenient reason to explore previously unexplored lands and I have taken on nine marathons in eight different countries – Lithuania (Kaunas), Jordan (Petra Desert return), Norway (Oslo), Sri Lanka (Colombo), Turkey (Istanbul), UAE (Sharjah and Dubai), Oman (Muscat) and Bahrain (Manama). Lithuania aside (which was part of a fairly raucous five country solo tour of Northern Europe), in each case I have been joined by partner in crime, Gill, who has helped bring a semblance of sanity to proceedings.

Although my running odyssey has no doubt yet to reach its conclusion, completing the first 100 (and change) has encouraged me to reflect on what the journey to date has meant to me. Whilst I have not found the meaning of life out on the road, on a treadmill or battling through a swamp, as a pastime running has given me a lot – fitness, a clear morning mind and a number of experiences I will take with me through life. As with most things in life, it is the people I have encountered who have made the most lasting impressions – I have seen kindness and determination, without the motive of reciprocation, at a level which is capable of simultaneously moving me to a broad smile and tears.

If nothing else (which I suspect is the case), I hope that this book has made you smile and might persuade you to run a little (for the non-runners) or a little more (for the runners). The key for me has to make running an integral part of my life, but at the same time not allow it to impinge on the life I otherwise want to lead. Life is short after all. May as well try and make it remarkable…